EVERYBODY NEEDS A NATHAN

MICHAEL MASON

SONCOAST
PUBLISHING

Soncoast Publishing

PO Box 1504

Hartselle, AL 35640

www.soncoastpublishing.com

CONTENTS

Acknowledgments   vii

Foreword   ix

Introduction   xi

1. Everybody Needs a Nathan   1
   Chapter One Discussion Points   21
2. Who Is Demas and Who Cares?   23
   Chapter 2 Discussion Points   35
3. Change In Your Pocket   37
   Chapter 3 Discussion Points   54
4. David and Cain   55
   Chapter 4 Discussion Points   65
5. Giving The Devil a Place at the Table   67
   Chapter 5 Discussion Points   78
6. The Devil's Playbook   79
   Chapter 6 Discussion Points   95
7. The Domino Effect of Sin   97
   Chapter 7 Discussion Points   110
8. The High Cost Of Sin   111
   Chapter 8 Discussion Points   124
9. Esau's Birthright and a Bowl of Soup   125
   Chapter 9 Discussion Points   134
10. Serving Two Masters   135
    Chapter 10 Discussion Points   149
11. The Flee Factor   151
    Chapter 11 Discussion Points   168
12. Who's at the Door   169
    Chapter 12 Discussion Points   177
13. The Lord Sent Nathan   179
    Chapter 13 Discussion Points   190
14. Pulling Down Strongholds   191
    Chapter 14 Discussion Points   221
15. Except in the Matter of Uriah   223

Chapter 15 Discussion Points   228
16. Everybody Needs a Savior   229

Chapter 16 Discussion Points   238
About the Author   239
Contact Information Michael Mason Ministries   241
Also by Michael Mason   243

*This book is dedicated to the memory of my dad
Lewis Mason and my friend Junior Hill. While
Everybody Needs A Nathan,
it doesn't hurt to have an example like my dad
and an encourager like Brother Junior. I shudder to
think where I would be as a man and as a preacher
without the influence of these two men.*

ACKNOWLEDGMENTS

I want to thank God... I don't deserve His goodness, favor, and blessings. I am grateful for His provision in all things. I pray God will use this book for His glory.

I want to thank Dawn... She is my wife, my best friend, and my partner in ministry. My love for her continues to increase as I watch her live faithfully for Christ. She loves me, prays for me, and believes in me.

I want to thank my Children... I am thankful for all our children: Hunter, Jordan, Alyssa, Garrett, and Grayson. What a pleasure to watch them grow into the men and women God designed them to be. I am also blessed to be Poppa to our seven grandchildren: Harper, Magnolia, Hattie, Levi, Turner, and Lawson. They are a source of pure joy.

I want to thank Carole Hill... She has been faithful to proofread every manuscript I have written. I have been grateful for her help.

I want to thank Decatur Baptist... We are thankful for our home church, Pastor Joe McCaig, and the staff, that prays for us and continues to encourage us.

I want to thank Phil Waldrep... I asked Phil to write the foreword for this book because of his early and ongoing influence on my life. God used him to speak to my life at a youth camp when I was only seventeen. For all of my ministry, he has been a consistent encourager.

I want to thank Martine Bates and Soncoast Publishing...
Mrs. Martine is very busy, but she's never been too busy for me. Her support is a motivation to keep writing.

FOREWORD

Several years ago, a friend asked if I would host John Camp and his wife by taking them to play golf at a nearby course. John was the senior investigative correspondent for CNN. Among his many awards is the Pulitzer Prize. His investigative reports had exposed corruption in major corporations, brought down political leaders, and prompted criminal investigations.

And it was John Camp's reporting in the 1980s that revealed the sexual sins of two famous televangelists – Jim Bakker of PTL and Jimmy Swaggart.

I initially declined, telling my friend I was a terrible golfer and didn't want to embarrass myself. He informed me that John and his wife started playing only recently and had never broken 100, which was why he chose me.

John and his wife were more than gracious. Their friendly conversations put me at ease as we hit our golf balls numerous times. It was a delightful day I will long remember.

A few things, though, surprised me about the Camps. First, they were believers. John shared how he came to Christ after battling alcoholism for years. I discovered I knew his pastor, who later validated his church involvement.

But the biggest surprise came when John, with tears in his eyes, described the pain of exposing the sins of two of America's best-known ministries.

I only had one question: Why? How could two men, sincere in their callings, go astray? How could they preach the gospel with passion while secretly harboring sin? Didn't anyone around them know?

John answered my question clearly and distinctly. "Phil," he said, "It happened because no one could walk into their office and confront them. No one dared to say something was wrong."

He was right. They thought they were getting away with it, but they weren't. What those men needed was a Nathan, someone who wasn't afraid to confront them about their actions, someone to speak the truth at the risk of losing a relationship.

> I need a Nathan.
> You need a Nathan.
> Everybody needs a Nathan.

I am grateful my friend, Michael Mason, addressed this issue in this new book. He creatively shares how many people – once used by God – spiritually fell because they didn't have or didn't listen to the Nathan God sent.

Read this book with an open Bible and an open heart. Ask the Holy Spirit to bring people into your life to speak the truth, even when it hurts.

Above all, invite your Nathan into your sphere of influence. You will be glad you did.

PHIL WALDREP
Phil Waldrep Ministries
Decatur, Alabama

INTRODUCTION

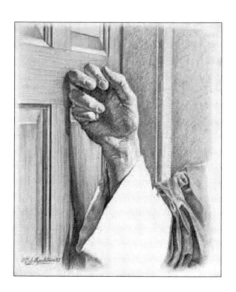

Dr. Adrian Rogers said, "Everybody needs a hero. Jesus is mine."

I trusted the Lord to save me when I was nineteen years old. He has been more than a Savior. He has been my friend, my hope, my strength, my peace, and yes … He has been my hero. The Lord has also brought people into my life to help me, instruct me, guide me, and correct me. I certainly agree with Dr. Rogers that everybody needs a hero. I also believe they need a Nathan. Someone like Nathan the Prophet and how God used him in the life of King David. At some point, everybody needs a Nathan. A Nathan is not someone we might normally consider to be a hero. They may appear to be typical, average, and nothing out of the ordinary. But then God sends them to us in a time of crisis, a time of heartbreak, or a time of personal compromise. They are sent to us by the Lord. They say the words we need to hear. They help us see through the fog. They help us get back on our feet. They point us in the direction we should go. The choice is ours whether we take their advice. But when we heed their words, we gradually find our way back to God, back to hope, and back to life. These Nathans become heroes in their own right. The realization of how God used them in our life may not become clear until many years have passed. Ten or maybe twenty years down the road we look back and see how God used a Nathan. Because they pointed us to truth. Everybody needs a friend like Nathan. Everybody needs a hero named Jesus.

I was asked to speak at a men's conference a few years ago. Initially I had no idea what I would speak about. I knew about King David being a man after God's heart. I thought that would be a good place to start. As I read the story of David, the shepherd boy who became a king, his heart for God, and his victories as a warrior, inevitably I came to 2 Samuel chapters 11 and 12. I had read this story of David and Bathsheba before, but I had never paid attention to Nathan and how God used him in David's life. I sensed the Lord leading me to focus on Nathan. The title for my message came quickly. I preached that day on the subject, *Everybody Needs A Nathan*. I can't tell you how the message may have impacted the men who heard me. But God used that message that day to call me to be a Nathan.

I have needed a Nathan many times in my Christian journey. God has been faithful to send me just who I needed at just the right time. Throughout this book you will read of men who were used of God to direct and redirect my life. I don't believe God needs any help, but I do believe He uses people to get our attention. There are men and women everywhere like David who need a Nathan. Someone sent from God to confront. To care. To be consistent. Someone that will listen to them and love them. Someone they can trust. Everybody needs a Nathan.

In this phase of my life and ministry, I find great joy in being a Nathan to guys that need a friend. Men who have wrecked their life, their marriage, and their family. Their future hopes seem unattainable. Some of these men made some really bad choices. Foolish decisions that have impacted their life in dramatic ways. They've had to start over. Some of these men have been adversely affected by the poor choices others have made. Nonetheless, they find themselves at a turning point not knowing which way to go. They need a friend they can trust. They need to hear the truth. Some of them need to be born again. Some simply need to be restored. They need a Nathan to point them to Jesus. Everybody needs a Nathan.

1

EVERYBODY NEEDS A NATHAN

2 Samuel 12:1 *"…And the Lord sent Nathan to David."*

I magine Nathan knocking on David's door. Nathan has been sent to David. Commissioned by God. Nathan is David's friend, but this is not a friendly visit. Nathan is sent with a word from God. It is disturbing news. This visit could end a long-standing relationship. But Nathan has no choice but to go. God has sent him.

David is King. Bathsheba's husband Uriah is dead. Bathsheba has had a baby. Most folks at the time probably thought David had done the honorable thing by marrying the wife of one of his fallen men. It seems he will be a father to the child of another man. David has married Bathsheba and it appears all is well and good. The ugly sins of adultery and murder have been covered up. But David knows. Bathsheba knows. And somehow, Nathan knows. Nathan is on mission from God to confront David about his sin. 2 Samuel 11:27, *"The thing David had done displeased the Lord…"*

Everybody needs a Nathan. Yet, while most of us at some point will need a Nathan, most of us, at that point, don't really want one. It's not easy on our pride to be on the receiving end of rebuke. After all,

1

David had been a man after God's heart. But in a moment of disregard for everything that mattered he went after Uriah's wife. Imagine with me a fall afternoon at David's house. Bathsheba is relaxing and rocking the baby. David is king and has a kingly attitude. He has conquered nations and armies and it appears he has even conquered the ripple effects of his sin with Bathsheba. But suddenly there's a knock at the door. I imagine David asks Bathsheba, "Who could that be?" Bathsheba answers, "It's Nathan the prophet, I haven't seen him in ages." I picture David anxiously opening the door and there stands Nathan the prophet of God, the man of God, the messenger from God. Nathan gets to the point and asks, "Have you got a minute?" I'm not sure but I can only guess there is suddenly a knot in David's stomach the size of a bowling ball.

The Lord has sent Nathan to David. There's no time for small talk. There's no talk about the weather, his family, or his well-being. David's sin is about to be exposed. The truth about Uriah's death and Bathsheba's pregnancy will soon be revealed. Nathan is about to be used by God to uncover David's secrets. It will be done in love, but it will be in no uncertain terms. Nathan isn't there to comfort David. He's there to confront him.

Everybody needs a Nathan. Nathan and David had a history together. Nathan had influence in David's life. He was a mentor to David. I would suggest David had great respect for Nathan. There is nothing that we find in scripture that would indicate a lack of integrity in Nathan or a compromise of values. He appears to truly be a man of God, about God, for God, and with God. Let's look at a little history of these two men's relationship.

Nathan was a prophet during the reigns of David and Solomon (1 Chronicles 29:29 and 2 Chronicles 9:29). Needless to say, Nathan had been around the block a few times. He was well known and respected. His life as a prophet during the lives of David and Solomon reminds me of the ministry of Billy Graham. Dr. Graham was busy preaching during my dad's life and my life like Nathan was active during David's and Solomon's lives. What a joy to see

2

someone grow old and active in the ministry. What a joy also to see that aging minister continue to grow in wisdom and character. Nathan was a prophet of God. He spoke truth without compromise.

Everybody needs a Nathan. Nathan encouraged David's plans for the building of the temple (2 Samuel 7:2-3). Those plans, however, quickly changed. Nathan had said to David, *"Go, do all that is in your heart, for the Lord is with you."* But that night the Lord came to Nathan and clearly spoke to him about the building of a house for the Lord. David would not be the builder. His son Solomon would have that honor. *"He shall build a house for my name…"* (2 Samuel 7:13). Why wouldn't David be the builder? 1 Chronicles 22:8 plainly tells us, *"The word of the Lord came to me saying, 'You have shed much blood and made great wars; you shall not build a house for my name, because you have shed much blood on the earth in my sight.'"* David had been known for his battling. Solomon would be known, in part, for his building. Again, in 1 Chronicles 22 9-10 we read that Solomon would be the king who would build the house for God's name. According to 2 Samuel 7:17, *"According to all these words and according to all this vision, so Nathan spoke to David."* The details are important not only to be biblically correct, but also to give Nathan the credit he deserves. I admire him for jumping on the bandwagon encouraging David to build. But I also admire him for jumping off just as quickly when he understood God's will. Being willing to go back to David and tell him clearly that he would not be the one to build a house for the Lord speaks to his integrity and heart for God.

Can you imagine the next morning, after hearing from God, Nathan telling David the news that Solomon would be the builder? We could call what Nathan did back-pedaling, changing his mind, and changing course. Or we could call it obedience to God. May God help us, when the Lord changes our course of action to be willing to go where He leads. Nathan could have kept quiet about the information he received that night. He could have encouraged David to go ahead with the building. But being the man he was, he told David all that the Lord told him. That's what a Nathan does. Everybody needs a Nathan.

Everybody needs a Nathan. According to 2 Chronicles 29:25, under King Hezekiah, worship was restored according to the commandment of David, Gad, and Nathan. I find it interesting that Nathan is mentioned here. It would have been convenient to leave the influence of him and Gad out of this story. The Levites were positioned in the house of God with cymbals, stringed instruments, and harps according to the commandment of... Nathan. He was much more than a prophet of God. More than a friend to David. He was an influencer. He lived in such a way that he influenced those around him. Years after Nathan's life had ended, his legacy continued. That's the way legacy works. A life lived poorly also leaves the memory of choices made. Each of us will leave vivid memories with our children and grandchildren. What will they recall about us? Greatest of all, will they remember we lived our life for Christ? Will they remember our love for the Lord?

Nathan's legacy is one of honor, faithfulness, and godliness. David also left a legacy. Sadly, when we mention David's attributes and accomplishments it is often done with an asterisk. Yes, he had been a man after God's heart. But in his life, he also went after so much more that competed with his heart for God, namely war, wealth, and women. God give us a Nathan that will fight through the distractions and stay focused on living and finishing well. God give us men and women whose legacy will be living for Christ and finishing for His glory.

Everybody needs a Nathan. In 1 Chronicles 29:29 and 2 Chronicles 9:29 Nathan wrote the life story of David and Solomon. The book of Nathan is one of those considered lost. I think we should have enough faith in God that if He had wanted it included in the canon of scripture, He could have found it. While some my fret over what Nathan's book might have said, I'd rather focus on what we know he said and what we know he did.

We have sufficient information about David and Solomon to help us understand their heart and character. That aside, imagine Nathan's writings. Not necessarily what he wrote, but that he took the time to write. I think it could be possible that some of the information we have in other books of the Bible, was gleaned from Nathan's writings. No, I can't prove that, but I like to imagine it. I do a lot of writing that I'm almost certain will never be included in any kind of lasting, life-changing, historical account of God and His grace. But, while my writings may never be read by millions, I hope they are read by a few who can find encouragement in the words God gives me. I have that confidence in what Nathan wrote. The fact that Nathan wrote encourages me to keep writing and staying busy even when no one is watching.

Everybody needs a Nathan. He is best known for confronting David about his sin with Bathsheba. The popularity of that story often creates a false narrative about Nathan. Some portray him as critical, mean-spirited, and condescending. I believe nothing could be further from the truth. Nathan went to David because the Lord sent him. And once he arrived, he did what God told him to do with humility and respect for David. As I stated before, we are told, *"The thing that David had done displeased the Lord."* And then we read, *"The Lord sent Nathan to David."* Those words are the last verse of 2 Samuel chapter 11 and the first verse of 2 Samuel chapter 12. After using a parable to make his point Nathan said to David in 12:7, *"You are the man…"* Nathan told the story of a rich man who had taken advantage of a poor man. David was angered by the actions of the rich man in Nathan's story. In essence he said the wealthy man would pay for what he had done. He even said, *"As the Lord lives, the man who has done this shall surely die."* That is when Nathan declared, "You are the man!" David was the man that had taken advantage of Uriah.

Those were tense moments no doubt. If I had been Nathan, I would have made sure I was standing a few feet from David just in case he took a swing at me. But he didn't retaliate. He didn't get angry with Nathan. He didn't deny what he had done. Instead, in 12:13, he confessed, *"I have sinned against the Lord."* On this day in scripture David needed a Nathan. A Nathan who did what God sent him to do, no more and no less. We'll talk more about this event in the pages to come. But for now, I pause with you to reflect on all the folks I know who faithfully obey God without any recognition or fanfare. Folks like Nathan who quietly and sometimes anonymously serve the Lord. I am sure Nathan is more famous than he ever intended to be. I would imagine if it had been left up to him, his name would have been left out of this story. But thankfully we know what he did, what he said, and a little about who he was.

Everybody needs a Nathan. Another Nathan is mentioned in 1 Chronicles 3:5 and in Luke 3:31. This Nathan is one of the sons born to David and Bathsheba in Jerusalem. I can only imagine this child was named after Nathan the prophet. I can't prove that idea, but it's possible. Nathan was a court-prophet, or in other words, an advisor. He was not a prophet like Elijah, Isaiah, or Jeremiah. If my assumption is true, David named his son after an un-heralded prophet. He named him after a prophet whose writing isn't included in the sixty-six books of the Bible. He named him after a small-time, unknown prophet. I'm exaggerating the point on purpose. I know hundreds of guys like Nathan. They're never going to make the headlines. They're never going to be asked to speak at a conference. They preach in small churches. And they're some of the most faithful folks you'll ever meet. These are the guys who serve God in the quiet corners, on the backroads, off the beaten path, and away from the limelight. I admire those guys. They press on when others would have already resigned. That's Nathan. Everybody needs a Nathan they can name their son after. God give us more like him.

When I was 19, I needed a Nathan. And God sent me one that was old enough to be my grandfather. At that time, I was stubborn, prideful, and running. God had been dealing with me about being saved and He was also calling me to preach. I can't fully explain it all, I just remember knowing if I ever gave my life to Christ, I was also going to give my life to the ministry. I was running from God. Running with the wrong folks and looking for opportunities to rebel. I was working at a farm and supply store in a small town near my home. Robert Turney worked there too. He helped me get the job. We went to church together. He was like family to me. His nick-name for me was "Mike-Mike." That's what his grandchildren called me.

I was running from God and living foolishly. While working at the farm supply store, I went to lunch a few times with a lady who was married. Like any other kid my age at that time I didn't care what anybody thought. Robert would see me talking to her and then going to and coming back from lunch with her. One day when I returned, he called out to me, "Michael!" I had never heard him raise his voice like that. He said, "Come here. I need to talk to you." I followed him into the old building where we worked, up to the second floor and into a back room away from everyone else. That's when he became a Nathan to me. He said something like, "You need to get away from that woman. You know what you're doing is wrong. She's married and you need to leave her alone." All the while he was in my face and poking his finger in my chest. After a few minutes of straight talk he paused and said, "I love you, but what you're doing is wrong and I want you to stop it."

I never went to lunch with that lady again. God used Robert Turney to get my attention. The Holy Spirit was convicting me and Robert's finger in my chest had emphasized the point. He loved me enough to talk sternly to me. He cared enough to confront me. Everybody needs a Nathan. I needed a Robert.

For many reasons, David needed a Nathan. He'd been riding a wave of success. He'd won at war, he'd won over the people, and it appeared he had won favor with God. But the man who had been after God's heart went after Uriah's wife. That's when the Lord sent Nathan to David. At the time of this writing, I still need a Nathan, but I have also realized the importance of being a Nathan to others. Several years ago, I began a men's Bible study in the garage of a friend. Over time we have had so many men come through that garage. It's a once a month, third Thursday of every month meeting. We eat a little, laugh a lot, pray, and study the word together. I have witnessed on those Thursday nights what I already thought: most folks are going through some situation, facing some circumstance, and dealing with some kind of heartache. Simply put, most folks need a Nathan. They need someone to care. Someone to pray for them. Someone to shoot straight with them.

Someone to encourage them. I need a Nathan. I also need to be a Nathan.

David's Sin Was Committed

Like many of you, I have read this story of David and Bathsheba a number of times. I have heard it preached and taught about many times as well. And I have referred to, written about, and preached about it numerous times in my own ministry. The danger in hearing the ugly details of this story over and over is that the details become less ugly. We know what's going to happen. Like watching an old movie, we know what to expect. And when it happens, we're not shocked. That's a danger for any of us who read the Bible over and over. The stories lose their shock value so to speak. We know Cain is going to kill Abel. We know Samson is going to lose his hair, his strength, and his sight. We know Peter is going to deny the Lord and Judas is going to betray Him. And so it is with the story of David and Bathsheba. I encourage you today as you are reminded of the devastating details of David's sin that you will allow it to bother you. Imagine David or Bathsheba is your friend or even family. Imagine Uriah is your brother. Imagine admiring David and then being let down by your hero. Imagine Bathsheba being faithful to her husband and then suddenly becoming David's wife.

Unfaithfulness in marriage has ripple effects. David will experience those effects the rest of his life, in his own heart and mind, as well as watching the cavalier attitude being lived out in his children. Choices have consequences. If a man or a woman is reckless in their decision to be less than honorable as a father and husband or a wife and mother, there is a price to be paid. It is most often paid for with sleepless nights and shameful regret. But there is also a price to be paid with children. Sometimes it is the loss of respect for the man or woman who compromised. At other times it's that foolish parent watching their children reenact the choices they made years earlier. Our personal history often repeats itself in the lives of our kids.

David's sin involves Bathsheba, Uriah, pride, and denial. David was drawn away by his own lusts and enticed. He saw her and he sent for her. He was with her and then she was with child. Sin will always take you further that you planned to go. I know of many men and women who have wrecked their lives in some ways like David and Bathsheba did. Did any of them intend to have an affair, embarrass their family, lose their marriage, and disappoint their children? I don't think anyone plans to wreck their life and the life of others. But when a person follows their heart instead of following God, heartache of some kind is inevitable. David never intended to get caught. Some have asked, was this the first time David had sent for a woman who was not his wife? We do not know. But if so, this time was different. Bathsheba is expecting – and David never expected that.

We're all one Bathsheba away from being a David. Nathan said to David, "*You are the man*" (2 Samuel 12:7). I would also say to the ladies reading this, you're one King David away from being a Bathsheba. Most of this chapter is focused on David, but he wasn't alone in this fiasco. I understand she came because she was summoned by the king. And I realize we don't know all that went on behind closed doors. I also understand we know very little of her conversations with David after the fact. But there's no sense of resentment, anger, or refusal to allow the cover-up. Did she know David's plans for Uriah? We don't know. What we do know, however, is that the spirit of King David is still alive and well. Ladies, if someone like David tempts you to be anything less than what God has called you to be, run for your life. It's not worth it! He's not worth it!

Now back to my point… We're all one Bathsheba away from being a David. And sadly, for many it will happen because we believe something like that could never happen to us. We reason with ourselves that we would never do that to our family. Somewhere today a preacher or politician will make the headlines as it is uncovered that he has been unfaithful to his wife. The preacher will most likely step down from the ministry and the politician will suspend his campaign. And at home, his wife and children will begin to ask, "Where do we go from here?" Yes, the headlines are filled with stories of foolish preachers and politicians. But there are many, many more men and woman, not so highly regarded or respected like David was, but they're just as guilty. And their family is just as broken. Adultery never ends well. Somebody always gets hurt. Children always suffer. I beg you today if you are contemplating some act of unfaithfulness – Please stop! Turn to the Lord. Love your wife. Embrace your family. Thank God for your kids.

We're all one secret sin away from public shame. David's sin was "*done in secret*" (2 Samuel 12:1). What was true with David's sin is still true today, whatever is done in secret seldom stays in secret. Several years ago, an advertising campaign used the slogan "What happens in Vegas stays in Vegas" to boost tourism in that part of the country. But, as we all know, what happens in Vegas never stays there. It comes home. And it comes home with baggage. Whether it's gambling, girls, or guys, the guilt seldom stays in Vegas. Truth has a way of following you wherever you go. If you have nothing to hide, enjoy your life. But if you have a Vegas secret there's a good chance someone knows. And there's a better chance that the someone who knows has already told someone else. And that someone has already told someone else. Surprisingly, the guilty party is always shocked that other people know.

I heard Andy Stanley say, "Don't ever do anything that if you were to get caught you would have to stand before your family and apologize." That's a strong reminder that our secret sins seldom stay secret. When I was a pastor, I recall having a man come see me and confess his impropriety. He came seeking help and asked me to "keep this confidential because no one knows." Pastors hear things they don't want to hear. I had heard about his sin several weeks earlier. I told him I already knew. He was amazed that his secret was out.

This is a warning to all of us who might look down on someone because of their sin. It is a warning to any of us who might think we would never do what someone else did. As John Wayne would say,

"Take it easy there, pilgrim." Before you go and judge another so quickly, take a look in the mirror. Take a look at yourself. Judge yourself. If we will take an honest look at our own life and all our shortcomings, and start working on ourselves, we won't have time to be critical of others. Let's clean our own house before we point out the dirt in someone else's.

We're all one confession away from grace. Once David confessed his sin, he experienced grace. In 2 Samuel 12:13 we read, *"you shall not die."* There is grace to be found throughout the Word of God. In this ugly and uncomfortable story of deception, unfaithfulness, disregard, and death there is grace. David deserved whatever punishment God decided to hand out to him. But instead of binding him with guilt, He covered him with grace. That doesn't mean David's sin was overlooked. It doesn't mean David got a free pass. It just means, here in this story, that David would live and not die.

I want to encourage you to look for opportunities to extend grace to those who fail miserably. They may not deserve it, but then again who does? There are always times to notice someone's guilt. But what if we took the time and made the effort to show grace to someone's guilt. I am not suggesting we agree with them. I'm not suggesting we condone what they have done. I'm just suggesting we act like Jesus when he met the woman caught in adultery. He could have pronounced guilt but instead He announced grace. He did tell her to go and stop sinning – but not without an act of undeserved graciousness. God help us do the same.

However… The word *"however"* in 12:14 speaks volumes. I remember when I was about sixteen years old and I drove my dad's truck to the local country grocery store to pick up some things for Mother. While out and about I decided to do a burn-out which is, for those of you who don't know, when you drive around in circles spinning the tires and creating a cloud of smoke from burning rubber. Why did I decide to do that? I have no idea. Did I really need a reason? There is a certain level of natural stupidity that comes with being sixteen. I had a double dose. When I returned home, I thought all was well. No dents in the truck. It still ran like new. No damage that I was aware of. The next day my dad asked me if I knew anything about the back tires on the truck being worn down. He then proceeded to tell me I would never drive his truck again. He told me not to ask. If I had to walk to where I was going, he was sorry but I would never drive his truck again. With sin and stupidity there is always a *"however."* My dad continued to allow me to live at home, however, I never drove his truck again. He allowed me to eat at the family table, however, I never drove his truck again. He still loved me, however, I never drove his truck again. You can't get away from the howevers of sin. You will reap what you've sown even if you're sorry for what you've done, and you promise never to do it again. David confessed his sin, and he was promised he would not die at that time. The child that would be born, however, *"shall surely die."*

As Nathan had said, the baby born to David and Bathsheba died. I would caution anyone who would attempt to make a precedent out of this baby's death. Be careful of suggesting that a person's death, sickness, or trouble is God's judgment on their sin. We can't make that call. God deals with each person as He wills. I do believe, however, we can say what happened to the baby is symbolic of what happens whenever we sin. The end result is sorrow, heartache, and loss of some kind. The Bible says in Romans 6:23, *"the wages of sin is death."* That death is regarding salvation from sin not judgment because of sin. And thankfully, Jesus died that death so that whosoever would believe could be saved from the power and penalty of sin.

Sin always has a however. The greatest however is found in John 10:10, *"The thief does not come except to steal, and to kill, and to destroy. (however) I have come that they may have life, and that they may have it more abundantly."* Amen and Amen! Satan came to destroy life. Jesus, however, came to give life!

David's Sin Was Confronted

As I have already stated, Nathan was sent to David, not to console him but to confront him. Not to tell him everything would be alright but to let him know his actions were all wrong. But he also came, not to hurt him but to help him. Not to shame him but to show him the thing he had done *"displeased the Lord."*

People are not confronted because they are doing things right. They are confronted because they are doing things wrong. Confrontation usually involves correction. Confrontation may bring about a dispute. Confrontations have resulted in fights, firings, and killings to name a few. Friendships have been lost because of confrontation. Families have been divided over it. Two factors kept Nathan's confrontation from ending badly. Number one, Nathan was sent by God. He wasn't angry. He didn't go to pick a fight. He went to do what God told him to do. Number two, David responded with humility. I think his response shows he truly was a man after God's heart. Yes, he had sinned greatly, but he also admitted it. We can all learn two great lessons as we look at this confrontation. First, if you're going to confront someone about their sin make sure God is leading you. Second, if you're being confronted about something you've done wrong, and you know you're guilty – admit it and seek forgiveness. Life is too short to live in the mire of unconfessed sin.

Nathan was Truthful. I appreciate Nathan's use of an illustration to make his point. Over the years I have found that some folks remember my sermon illustrations more than they remember my sermons. I'm not saying I'm proud of that and I'm not suggesting my sermons are weak, but there is that possibility. Nathan used a story about someone else to get David's attention. Why do that? I think he did it to disarm David. The story gave David time to think about the other situation rather than focusing on his own circumstance. David took the bait so to speak. As the king, David would make sure the rich man would surely pay for how he had treated the poor man. His response speaks to the fact that even though David had sinned greatly, he knew what he had done was wrong. David responded to Nathan's parable as a clear-thinking, noble-minded king should. David would take care of the poor man who had been mistreated.

That opened the door for Nathan to say, *"You are the man."* No time for sarcasm, exaggeration, or apologies. Nathan doesn't come across as crass and mean spirited – neither does he cower in the presence of the king. He simply speaks the truth. And David agrees.

Nathan was Timely. It appears Nathan's visit with David happened soon after the birth of the child and was done in private. David was probably still prideful. I think so, not because of any real evidence in scripture, but because of what I know about me and what I have learned from counseling others. If this story is about me instead of David, I think I'd be most proud of the fact that no one knows. I'd be proud of how well I have covered my tracks. In all sin pride is present as it is committed, concealed, and covered up. If I am David, I am prideful about what I have been able to pull off with no one realizing what has happened. I also imagine David was proud that he got what he wanted. I imagine he is proud of his scheming to eliminate Uriah. And proud of the idea that folks don't realize that baby is actually his. He's proud. His sin is covered and quiet. His life can go on as usual with no interruptions.

Whether you're being interrogated by your high school principal, your parents, or the local police, the temptation is to cover it up. Talk your way out of it. Make light of it. David did well at covering his tracks. But God gave Nathan some inside information. This visit was necessary, and it was also important that Nathan went when God told him to. With God, it seems timing is vital. Nathan was right on time.

Nathan was Transparent. Nathan was believable. I remember as a young man, hearing someone describe a man in our community by saying, "He's as good as his word." That man was Lester Whitten. He ran the country store, was a leader in our church, and taught me how to speak pig-latin. If he said it was going to rain, you'd better go get your umbrella. Lester Whitten was trustworthy and transparent. So was Nathan. I believe, in part, it was Nathan's character that initiated David's confession. David responded, *"I have sinned against the Lord."* Nathan was not out to make a name for himself. He was not promoting an agenda. He didn't bring a team of witnesses. He didn't take the time to explain why he was there to see David. He was there because God had sent him. As we've already thought about, Nathan had been in David's life for years. He was a friend. Maybe a father-figure. He was trustworthy.

There was a time when the daily news was reported without commentary. There was a day when preachers preached the Bible without compromise. There was a man named Nathan who went to David's house simply because God sent him.

Nathan's confrontation with David is more about David than it is David's sin. The man who had been after God's heart had now sinned against God. He sinned against the God who knew him, ordained his position, and blessed him in his victories. That's big news. And that's sad news. It's big because of who he was, how he sinned, and who he sinned against. It's sad because of Uriah, the baby, and the echo effect of his sin for years to come. So, what do we do with David? He's had the hand of God on him. He's been a mighty man of God. We certainly can't ignore what he did as if it never happened. And we can't deny the shame and consequences of it. With that in mind, we might make a big deal of his sin. We could do that. There are many lessons to be learned from what he did and how it changed David and all those connected to him. But I'd like to suggest if we are going to make a big deal of his sin then we should also make a big deal of God's grace.

It amazes me today how quickly we disqualify someone from serving God for much lesser offenses than David's. The biggest news out of this painful story is not how a great king fell, but how great a God forgave. It's not so much about his terrible sin but the amazing grace that forgave it. There are many good men and women sitting on back rows of local churches that have been labeled disqualified because of foolish choices in their past. David wouldn't have a chance in most churches today. Neither would Jacob. Neither would

Paul. David is an adulterer and a murderer. He's been forgiven and restored. But nonetheless, there are too many like David today who will never get the opportunity to serve and make a difference for Christ. The memory of their sin looms much larger than the miracle of their forgiveness. God help us.

May we be **Motivated by Concern...** Most of us are familiar with the story of the Good Samaritan in the Gospel of Luke 10:25-37. Jesus told the story of a man who had gone down to Jericho and fell among thieves. He was robbed, stripped of his clothing, beaten, and left for dead. A priest and a Levite, religious people, walked by never paying him any attention. Then a Samaritan came by, stopped, and did everything necessary to get the man well and back on his feet. Why? It appears he was genuinely motivated by concern for another human being. It doesn't matter why the man was going down to Jericho. It really doesn't matter if he was Jew or Gentile. All that matters in Luke 10 is that one man is hurting, and another man is helping. The point I want to make is this: We will never stop to help the man who has been left on the side of the road until we have been that man, that woman. If we can't put ourselves in their shoes, even a little, we will never fully appreciate what it means to get in that predicament and what it means to get out.

We are **Mandated by Conviction...** Galatians 6:1 *"Brethren...you who are spiritual...consider yourselves!"* We will talk more about this verse in the next chapter. But for now, I think most of us who are saved would agree, our response to men like David and women like Bathsheba is based on our response to the Holy Spirit. Honestly folks, what are we going to do with prodigals when they finally leave the far country and come home? Do we stand in the way, or do we point them in the direction of the Father? I would never suggest that we allow sin to be flaunted. I would never agree to putting someone onstage who is unrepentant. But restoration has to begin some-where. The Good Samaritan began on the side of the road.

I have a friend who is a physician. When he was younger, he made some foolish decisions that almost cost him his practice and his life. He became addicted to the very drugs he was prescribing to some of his patients. To make a long story short, he entered rehab for an extended period. He was eventually completely rehabbed and restored. He came back to Christ, and he was also able to restore his practice as a doctor. One Sunday, he decided it was time to get back in church. He went that morning to the church he had attended as a young man believing that it would be a safe place to attend and that he would be welcome. Many of the people were very loving and kind. But not all. One gentleman approached him and said, "You have some nerve coming in here after all you've done." My friend was taken aback by his comments but had enough courage to ask this man, "Where are people like me supposed to go?" Great question! Where are men like him, sinners like Rahab, people like Mary Magdalene, men like David, and women like Bathsheba supposed to go? Are there churches especially designed for sinners who have sinned really bad? God help us to help the prodigals who are coming home. If they're headed to the far country, sometimes we must let them go and pray they'll come back. But if they're like my friend, broken and repentant, who are we to stand in their way?

There is a line of inconvenience we must cross if we are going to reach those who have been overcome in some fault. The inconvenience of our time. The inconvenience of an awkward conversation between two people where one person might not fully appreciate where the other one has been. The inconvenience of building a relationship outside our circle of friends. The inconvenience of committing for the long haul. Compassion and conviction demand that I do something. This is part of *"being conformed to the image of Christ"* (Romans 8:29).

David's Sin Was Confessed

David had sinned against the Lord. He had also sinned against Bathsheba and Uriah, but mostly against God. In 2 Samuel 12:13 David said, *"I have sinned against the Lord."* There can be no cleansing from sin without confession of sin. Confession of sin is telling God what He already knows. It is admitting what He already sees. It is being honest with God. Confession doesn't change God's mind about me – it changes my mind about God. Repentance and confession are good friends. They go hand in hand. Repentance is a change of mind about my sin, myself, and my relationship with God. David confessed and repented. But it didn't come about easily. There's an old song that says, "Everybody wants to go to Heaven, but nobody wants to die." And I would add everybody wants to be right with God, but nobody wants to confess their sin.

Back to Nathan's parable: Why steal another man's sheep when your flocks are abundant? Why take another man's wife? Why take another man's life? David's ego got the best of him. God was using Nathan to bring him back to reality and back to Himself. Everybody needs a Nathan to remind us of who we are and what matters. But men like Nathan are few and hard to find. Men with a courageous spirit and a compassionate heart. We need men, whether they sit behind a desk or behind the wheel of a tractor, who will stand for God without compromise. Where are they? Are they dying out never to be replaced? May God raise up a new generation of men and women who take their walk with God seriously. Those who not only believe what is right but also live according to the same standard.

Nathan said, *"You are the man…"* For six verses, 2 Samuel 12: 7-12, Nathan exposes David for the sinner he is. David doesn't even put up a fight. He doesn't give any excuses. He doesn't blame anyone else. He admits and confesses.

Everyone else sees David as a king – But David knows he is a coward.

David has been living with his cowardly act for some time. Tony Evans says, "Sin is like a woodpecker. It keeps pecking at your life." And when that woodpecker is finished you have a hole in your life. After all this time, David has a hole in his heart. It's almost as if he was eager and ready to confess. It's almost as if he'd been waiting for this moment.

Everyone else sees him as a warrior – But David knows he is weak.

The memory of what he did must have haunted him. The affair. Arranging the opportunity for Uriah to be killed. Marrying Bathsheba knowing the baby she was carrying was that of Uriah. The secrets grew heavy. He's looking over his shoulder. His actions didn't prove he was strong. It only revealed his weaknesses. His confession is like a cleansing.

Everyone sees self-control – But David knows he is out of control.

Sadly, David's self-control was only a veneer. That thin layer of confidence had served him well. But now, it's as if Nathan sees through it all. This isn't new. It's as old as the Garden of Eden. And as current as the daily news. Politicians, preachers, and professional athletes often find their name in the headlines. We read in utter disbelief of what they have done. If there had been cable news in David's day, he would have gotten plenty of attention for all the wrong reasons.

Before we make too much of David's sin and too little of our own, let us be reminded of 2 Corinthians 13:5 that says *"Examine yourselves to see whether you are in the faith. Test yourselves. Do you not know yourselves, that Jesus Christ is in you – unless indeed you are disqualified."* To examine yourself is like looking in the mirror and being honest about what you see. Most of us who looked in the mirror this morning lied to ourselves. Maybe we told ourselves we didn't look that old…hadn't gained that much weight…hadn't lost that much hair, etc. David may have lied to himself too. Maybe he had been telling himself what he'd done wasn't all that bad. Maybe he kept thinking, one day I'll get over the guilt. Maybe he had convinced himself that he had gotten away with murder. But God knew and somehow Nathan knew. And now David is looking in the mirror at the man he has become. He examines himself and admits what Nathan has revealed. He did it. He stole another man's wife. He had her husband put on the front lines where he would be killed. He had married her and acted as if he were still a man after the heart of God.

The greatest giant David faced wasn't named Goliath. It was a man named David. It was the man in the mirror. Everybody needs a Nathan. **Proverbs 27:6** *"Faithful are the wounds of a friend, but the kisses of an enemy are deceitful."* Those words remind me of Judas. He kissed Jesus, but it was a kiss of betrayal. Nathan didn't come to David as an enemy but as a friend. God help us to be a friend like Nathan. God help us receive the words of Nathan when he comes knocking at our door.

CHAPTER ONE DISCUSSION POINTS

Discuss the ways God may have used Nathan to influence David prior to his sin with Bathsheba. With that in mind, why did God choose Nathan to speak to David?

Discuss David's thoughts as Nathan began to tell him the parable, in 2 Samuel 12:1-4, of the rich man taking advantage of the poor man.

We often speak of someone having an agenda. What was Nathan's agenda? What was God's purpose in sending Nathan to David?

Think of a time when God sent a Nathan to you. How did God use that person to bring about change in your life?

WHO IS DEMAS AND WHO CARES?

2 Timothy 4:10 (64 AD)
Colossians 4:14 (62 AD)
Philemon 1:24 (60 AD)

Most everyone, even those unfamiliar with the Bible, has heard of King David. But have you heard about a man named Demas? The chapter you've just finished reading is filled with the sad details of David's sin. But I want to bring to your attention Demas. He was once a follower of Christ and served alongside Paul. We know very little about him. Also, knowing he's only mentioned three times in scripture, one could assume he must not be that important. So, who is Demas and who cares? I believe it is a fair question.

Below the title of this chapter, you'll see a list of scripture references and dates. I included those dates because I believe they reveal a possible pattern of drifting in the life of Demas. In Philemon 1:24, Paul mentions Demas along with men like Epaphras, Mark, Aristarchus, and Luke his fellow laborers. In Colossians 4:14, about two years later in writing, Paul mentions Luke and Demas in his greetings to the believers at Colossae. In 2 Timothy 4:10, some four years later than the mention in Philemon, Paul is writing and asking for help as Demas has forsaken him. I want to be clear this is only my opinion, but is it possible that over a four-year period Demas was on a gradual decline in his faithfulness to God? I believe falling away often happens quickly, but the drifting to that point may take a while. If Demas was on a four-year fade, that possibility causes me to take a careful look myself, my faith, and my walk with God. Am I drifting, fading, falling away from God? If so, what have I allowed to pull me away? We will think more about Demas' drifting later in this chapter. But for now, I believe it's important to be reminded, Demas didn't fall away overnight. Long before he fell, he drifted.

Chances are there is a someone like Demas in your family, in your circle of friends, and in your church. Either in a former life, their current situation, or in the future, they'll choose to walk away from God. They'll turn their back on what they have believed. They'll quit church. They'll reject their family. They'll surrender their convictions and blend in with complacency and compromise. This doesn't mean they're bad people. In fact, I would suggest Demas and those like him are good people who have made poor choices. And I believe it is of utmost importance how we, as believers, treat them.

Churches today still say they love everybody, that we should invite everybody, and welcome everybody to the house of worship. But the truth is, a scarred up, beat up, and messed up Demas isn't what we usually imagine as the ideal church member. David and Demas have a lot in common. Today, would any pastor invite someone with David's credentials to speak in their church? If David wrote a book today would anybody read it? Demas might be able to relate. He has lost his testimony. He has walked away from God. He loves the world. If he feels the slightest nudge of conviction, where's a guy like that going to go to church?

Demas is no ordinary sinner. I'm not suggesting there are special sinners compared to average, everyday sinners. But Demas has a story unlike many in his day. Some had never known Jesus - But

Demas knew Him and walked away. He had known the Lord and walked with Him. He had served with men like Paul, Luke, and Mark. He was included in the greetings in a couple of Paul's letters. He had seen things most believers had never seen, yet something drew him away. Again, I'll ask – Who is Demas and who cares?

Who Is He?

Alexander McLaren says Demas, "isn't a monster but a man..." Those words caught my attention. They are a warning against demonizing people because of their bad choices. When we paint people in a darker light than the sin they committed, we spread a version of their story that is nothing short of slander. Demas doesn't have horns on his head. He's not a monster. Demas turned his back on what he believed. He walked away from his ministry with Paul. He loved the world. But he's not some freak like you'd see advertised at a county fair sideshow. McLaren says, "A man either forsakes the world for Christ or forsakes Christ for the world." I would add, a man either loves the Lord or he loves the world. You can't love both. But you can try. And that's the problem with Demas and all of us who have ever walked a day in his shoes.

He was devoted. My imagination suggests Demas was one of many who was saved through Paul's preaching. I imagine he loved the Lord. I would like to think he loved Paul as a brother in Christ and served with zeal and passion. Maybe I am saying those things because, possibly, I can only imagine the thrill of serving alongside Paul. Little did he know that his travels with Paul would one day be used as scripture. Little did he know he was making history along-side the greatest Christian who would ever live. How could he have known that even his own personal blunder would be used as a warning to other believers?

Church membership rolls are filled with the names of men and women who were once devoted. After many years in the ministry my mind is filled with the memories of those who once followed the Lord faithfully. They preached, sang, taught Bible studies, led youth ministries, traveled as missionaries, served as deacons, led men's or women's ministries, loved the Lord, and faithfully lived their life for Christ. Quite honestly, the thought of all those who once served sold-out lives for the Lord is disheartening. While I am thankful for all those who finished strong and those who are finishing strong, one must wonder what pulled the others away. What sin or circumstance so competed with their loyalty to Christ?

We can only imagine about Demas and others like him. What we know for sure, however, is that he once followed Christ and served with Paul. It appears he was completely committed. It is a fair warning to any of us who believe, trust, and follow Christ, that if Demas could walk away, so can we.

He drifted. Like many of us have. Drifting from the Lord can be easier than devotion to the Lord. Devotion requires daily attention. Drifting doesn't demand much of anything. Devotion demands sacrifice. Drifting never looks at the clock. Jimmy Draper said, "You never drift anywhere worth going." Think about your own personal Christian journey. Think about the times you drifted. During that season of distance between you and God, how would you describe your life? Was your time away from God helpful or destructive? Did you become a better husband, a more loving wife? Maybe you drifted for weeks, maybe months, or maybe years. It could be that you're drifting from God even now. The good news is, while you can't go back and change how the drifting started – you can change how it ends.

Drifting often involves sinning. But before we paint that picture so dark and sketchy, let's look at ourselves during that time when we drifted. I am convinced that most Christians who are drifting from God are not in a bar or a club – they're in church. Some are sleeping in on Sundays, but others are in Bible study and worship as if all is well. As I think about Demas in this light it makes me wonder, toward the end of his time with Paul, was his heart already in Thessalonica? Was he going through the motions with Paul? Was He sharing the message of Christ routinely and reluctantly? Was he preaching from memory or from the heart? Most of us on any given

Sunday could sing, pray, agree with the sermon, give an offering, chat with other believers on our way out, get in our car, and head back home to another week of drifting and no one would ever notice. Drifting is so deceptive. It deceives others. And sometimes we deceive ourselves into believing we're in a good place. Demas drifted from Christ. He eventually turned away because he loved where he was drifting to more than he loved where he was. Be careful friend. Guard your heart.

He departed. Demas loved the world. Most of us, it appears, seem to at least like it a lot. It's attractive. It's fascinating. It's promising. It draws away anyone it can. The only resistance for believers is to love the Lord more. I have counseled with many people who were going through marital separation that eventually led to divorce. I wish I could tell you that, after all these years, I know just the words to say that will save their marriage. Wouldn't it be great if I had some magic solution? I don't know of anyone who does. In my experience, by the time most folks realize they need to talk to someone about their marriage they have already made up their mind what they're going to do. There have been times, in my conversations with couples, when I wondered if they were seeking some kind of pastoral permission to divorce. The truth is, God is the only one that can save a marriage. He may use pastors, friends, or family. But only God can repair a broken home. Only God can mend a broken life.

Could anyone have talked Demas out of walking away? We don't have any evidence that anyone tried. The Lord sent Nathan to David. Maybe he sent someone to Demas. But if he did, Demas resisted, and went the way of the world. During the great Welsh Revival, an old pastor was asked to stand and open a service in prayer. Baring his heart to God, the old man confessed his own wandering. He prayed, "Lord, I got among the thorns and briars, and was scratched and torn and bleeding; but, Lord, it is only fair to say that it was not on Thy ground; I had wandered out of Thy pasture" (help4today.org). I think it is fair to say Demas was not on God's ground. I don't want to judge him too harshly. I only want to make an honest observation. Demas, David, and I have some things in common, the greatest of which is we are all made of flesh and blood. We're all tempted. We're all drawn away by our own desires. The only thing that will keep you and me from loving the world too much is to love the Lord more. And more. And more.

What Happened?

We don't know what happened. But something happened, and some of us know, all too well, about things happening that change everything. Sometimes that *something* is a small thing that becomes a big thing that pulls us away from everything we hold dear. When something like that happens, everyone wants to know the details. I understand the questions and the intrigue. After all, inquiring minds want to know. But honestly, we really don't need to know. My dad was a good man. He was a common man with common sense. There were a few rules he lived by. One of them was to "mind your own business." If there was a disagreement at church or in the community, he distanced himself from the drama. I remember a time when there was a disagreement at our Sunday morning church business meeting. I asked him what we were going to do. He stated in no uncertain terms, "I don't know what everybody else is going to do but I'm going to mind my own business." That's good advice. Not knowing what happened isn't going to hinder our prayers. In fact, it might help. We don't need all the details; we just need to pray.

Astronomers tell us that a black hole in space has a gravitational pull so strong that stars, planets, and asteroids are sucked into destruction. If a star gets too close it disappears (science.nasa.gov). In a similar manner, it appears something or someone sucked Demas in. Did he get too close to someone in Thessalonica? Was he lured in under false pretenses? Did he succumb to a temptation he had never faced before? We don't know.

Does it really matter what happened to Demas? Maybe it only matters that it happened and now it matters how I treat him. If we knew all the whys and hows and whens, would it stop us from doing the same thing given the opportunity? Does knowing the possible consequences of our choices really make us stop and think about what we're doing? Sons often repeat the sins of their fathers. Daughters sometimes repeat the sins of their mothers. Given that sad possibility, we must ask the question, what do we do with Demas now? Brand him as worthless? Disqualify him? Write him off? Or pray for him as if were a son or daughter, a mom or dad? Truly loving him, forgiving him, and praying for him may be the most difficult things we'll ever do. It's easy to talk about forgiving. It's far more difficult to actually forgive. What are we going to do with Demas? Who is Demas and who cares?

Where Is He?

He's in Thessalonica. Where he is isn't as big a concern as why he's there. Why is he there and what is he doing? Thessalonica is more than a place on a map – it is a place of the heart. Thessalonica is like the Prodigal Son's far country. There is always a Thessalonica luring us and pulling us away. Something or someone there promises us better and happier.

Demas had been busy and on mission with Paul, Luke, Mark and others. He greets the brethren in the letters to Philemon and Colossians, and then something drew him away. Was it something or someone he had encountered on one of the missionary journeys? I have known many ministers who have made poor choices like Demas. Many of them lost their ministry and their family. They left a path of sad memories for themselves, their families, and for others. They knew better but did the worse.

Demas is in Thessalonica. Crescens is in Galatia. Titus is in Dalmatia. We know why Demas left. But why did Crescens and Titus leave? There is very little information about either one. But it appears they were sent out by Paul to continue the mission (Bible Knowledge Commentary). Also, the fact that he singled out Demas for loving the world gives us reason to believe the other two left for good reasons. I can't say with certainty that they left to continue the work, but if it is true, it begs the question, why didn't Demas go with them? Of all the men mentioned in those few verses, 2 Timothy 4:10-12, Demas is the only one who is said to have left because he *"loved this present world."* Maybe I am making too much of this point, but names and faces flood my mind as I think about ministers who have walked away from the ministry. We hear the stories, but we always learn there was more to the story. I wish we knew more of Demas' story.

Paul urges Timothy to bring Mark and to come before winter (2 Timothy 4:21). Why the urgency? Winter weather could hinder their travel and there's a good chance Paul might not live through another winter. In other words, come quickly. Only Luke is with him. Tychicus is in Ephesus. Crescens is in Galatia. Titus is in Dalmatia.

It is sad when kings like David and missionaries like Demas lose their testimony and forfeit their influence. The fallout is often great because, invariably, people put their trust in men rather than God. That shouldn't happen, but it does because Christians are generally some of the most trusting folks you'll ever meet. They trust the Lord and they trust their ministers, sometimes to a fault.

Country singer George Jones once sang, "Who's Gonna Fill Their Shoes?" Jones was singing about singers who were aging and passing away. When they were gone, who would fill their shoes? The same could be asked about preachers. While we certainly don't need another Billy Graham, we do need someone who'll continue his work. There'll never be another C. H. Spurgeon. There'll never be another D. L. Moody. There'll never be another John and Charles Wesley. There'll never be another Betsy and Corrie Ten Boom. Yet we ask, who will fill their shoes? While no one can completely take their place, may God raise up men and women who will continue their mission. I thought when I was a young preacher of nineteen years old that I might be the next Billy Graham. But I learned over time that God didn't need me to be Billy Graham, he just needed me to be me. And so, we thank God for men like Crescens, Titus, Luke, Tychicus, and Mark who stood by Paul and stood for Christ.

Demas may have walked away, but God was raising up men like Timothy to fill his shoes.

Where is Demas? That's a great question that I have tried to answer. The greater question is, where am I? Where am I in my relationship with God? Am I holed up somewhere in Thessalonica, running from God, wasting my time, and missing my purpose? Looking at David and Demas should cause us to examine ourselves. Am I in a place I shouldn't be? Have I walked away from the Savior I once held dear? Where is this road leading? If I continue down the path I'm on, where will it lead? Friend, the good news of the Gospel is regardless of where you are, there is a road that leads home. Come home. Come before winter.

Who Cares?

Who is Demas and who cares? It's a great question and deserves a great answer. Thankfully, there is such an answer in the Bible. Galatians 6:1 *"Brethren, if a man is overtaken in any trespass, you who are spiritual restore such a one in a spirit of gentleness, considering yourself lest you also be tempted."* The King James Version uses the word *fault* instead of *trespass*. No specific trespass or fault is mentioned. Could Demas' fault, be the fault of someone else? I don't mean to shift the blame away from Demas, but more than likely he's not alone in this trespass. If a person is going to sin, it helps to have someone to sin with. Misery loves company. Sin needs a buddy.

That verse begins with, ***"Brethren..."*** A believer. A Jesus follower. A brother in Christ. Someone who cares enough that they'll do something or say something. Even if it is nothing more than simply being present. A brother who will call, text, forgive, help, and if possible, restore. I'm not suggesting that the brother agrees with or overlooks Demas' choices. It just means, despite his *fault* or his *trespass*, Demas has someone there to act like and love like Jesus. Jesus said to the woman who was caught in adultery, *"Neither do I condemn you. Go and sin no more"* (John 8:11). Jesus didn't condone her sin, neither did He condemn it.

He confronted it and demanded she turn from it. Demas needs someone who will love him with tough love. Someone who'll point him to Jesus. Someone who has backbone enough to stay the course.

This won't be easy. Demas may disappoint you and go back to his sin occasionally. The brother who loves him enough to help must be tough himself. Demas may not appreciate your hospitality. Sometimes we must forgive sin. Again. And again. And again. Sometimes we must forgive foolishness. Sometimes we'll need to forgive his stubbornness. But when I look in the mirror, I'm reminded I've been guilty of all three. I've sinned. I've been foolish. I've been stubborn. If anyone told you forgiveness was easy, they lied.

"If a man be overtaken..." Meaning caught or suddenly overcome. Sin has a way of doing just that, and we have a way of allowing sin to have its way. Did Paul have someone in mind when he wrote these words or is this generally how sin works? We don't know who he is referring to, but Paul is clear on what to do regardless of who it is. My question: What is it that has overcome this person? Who is at fault? Again, we don't know and speculation about those details only generates more questions. Maybe he was done wrong or maybe he was the doer. Maybe he got in the wrong crowd or maybe he was the wrong crowd. At some point, as *"brethren,"* we must decide to help regardless of the details. The bottom line is they have been *"overtaken."* If we start asking whether or not he deserves our help, we may have to stop and do a quick self-inventory. Do I deserve anything – any grace – any goodness – any blessing? No. So if the brother in need doesn't deserve it, then he's in good company.

"Ye which are spiritual..." Meaning those who are saved, spirit-led, and sensitive to the needs of others. Those who have experienced the grace of God. Those who have believed God's word. Those who have been transformed and believed in God's power to transform others. If Demas is saved, he is a brother in Christ. If He is a brother in Christ, this is ministry. If he's lost, unsaved, and unbelieving, this is outreach. This is the Great Commission. It's a call to the godly, the mature, and the faithful, to go to Demas. Go to him because it's unlikely he will come to you. He loves the world. Those who believe in the power of the Gospel must go.

Somewhere over the years the church has stopped going to where Demas is. Somehow, we expect him to come to where we are. The Lord sent Nathan to David. He sent Philip to the Ethiopian Eunuch. He still sends people to reach people. He sent Peter to the house of Cornelieus. The Lord can certainly reach them without our help, but He often uses people like us to reach people like us. Sinners. Needing grace. Needing hope. Needing Jesus. May God help believers like us who, while worshipping, gathering, fellowshipping, and studying, get so busy in church that we forget about Demas.

"Restore such a one..." Meaning simply to bring back. Reclaim. Recover. It could also mean to furnish. That's a good idea. Imagine renting a furnished apartment. It has all you need. If we are going to forgive Demas, we must also be willing to furnish him. Invest in him. Stay in touch with him. Restoring doesn't mean we agree with what he did, where he went, what he said. Restoring Demas sees him as a sinner who needs a Savior. A foolish man who needs a faithful friend.

Restoring such a one as Demas could take a while. Could take a few days, a few weeks, months, maybe years. This is not an overnight success. Salvation happens immediately. Restoration takes time.

"Consider yourself..." Meaning, taking everything into account. In other words, all things considered. This is where personal experience at failure helps. If you've never really messed up, never failed miserably, never been ashamed of something you said or did, it might be difficult to forgive Demas, much less restore him. If you have ever failed, however, then you know from experience the value of forgiveness and restoration. Surviving difficulties and setbacks will save you a trip to the eye doctor. Suddenly you begin to see things differently. More clearly. Less judgmental. More mercy. Considering yourself will soften your heart toward sinners. Considering yourself will cause you to pray more and talk less. After you've

considered yourself, you'll care less about making your point and more about making a difference.

"Considering yourself" means checking your ego. Leaving your attitude behind. Praying. And then seeking to love someone who might have become unlovable. Caring about someone no one else cares about. Calling someone no one else is calling. Extending grace where it's undeserved. Realizing you are where you are because of God's grace and goodness.

Demas is someone's husband. Someone's dad. Someone's brother. Someone's son.
Someone's wife. Someone's mother. Someone's sister. Someone's daughter.
Demas is a fallen preacher or a disgraced pastor.
Don't be an elder brother to the prodigal son.
Forgive. Love. Restore.

CHAPTER 2 DISCUSSION POINTS

What do Demas and David have in common?

In light of what little we know about Demas, discuss his commitment to Christ and his gradual compromise. How does someone like Demas walk away?

Demas, a follower of Christ, turned to Thessalonica. David, a man after God's heart, turned to Bathsheba. Discuss how James 1:14-15 relates to them.

Discuss Galatians 6:1 and how *"you who are spiritual…"* can be used as a Nathan to bring restoration to people like Demas and David.

CHANGE IN YOUR POCKET

Proverbs 27:17

As iron sharpens iron, So a man sharpens the countenance of his friend.

I remember when I was a young boy asking my dad for a nickel. Back then, that's what it cost to buy a piece of bubblegum. Drop the nickel in the bubblegum machine at the department store, turn the knob, and out came the gum. The key to that process was my dad having some change in his pocket. He always did. My dad had change in his pocket in more ways than one. He was trustworthy. He was honest and believable. He was never dishonest with me. He never told me to do one thing and then he did another. My dad was not rich in worldly goods, but he had a wealth of integrity. I never had reason to doubt him. He, like Nathan, had change in his pocket. John Maxwell, in his book, *The 21 Irrefutable Laws Of Leadership*, compares trust to coins in a person's pocket. Each time you make good decisions, you earn more coins. Each time you make poor decisions you lose money. Nathan lived in such a way that his life jingled with the coins of character and integrity. With that in mind, David was bankrupt. He had no change in his pocket. He had spent it all on careless decisions.

What is accountability? How do you keep that change in your pocket for a lifetime? Good question. I went to the thesaurus to get some clarity about the meaning of accountability. Other related ideas I found there are liability and answerability. Basically, both of these words mean being responsible. Imagine those qualities in men and women today. We see it often in sports after a loss, a leader will step up and accept responsibility for the team's loss. We see it occasionally in ministry leaders, a pastor will admit his failure and accept the blame he deserves. We seldom if ever see it in politics, but we need to. This one quality would make our nation a better place to live, build families, and raise children.

Accountability…however you want to label it, David appears to have none. It appears David, at best, is reluctant to admit his fault and accept responsibility for what happened. But a close examination of ourselves might reveal some of the same reluctance. Not that we've been caught in the same sin as David, but I would suggest many of us, if not most, are hesitant to freely admit our shortcomings however great or small. Truth is, the spirit of David and Bathsheba is alive and well. Not many of us are eagerly willing to accept responsibility for our actions. David is still looking, and Bathsheba is considering the invitation. At the point of consideration there is some guilt of both parties involved. Certainly not to the degree of actually acting out the thoughts and imaginations, but guilt nonetheless that one would even consider being unfaithful.

It appears to me that we live in a time of little or no accountability. In fact, from watching news updates regarding politics, racial conflict, church decisions, and personal pursuits, few if any are willing to be held accountable for much of anything. The blame is placed on someone else. It's their fault. There is a need for personal and private accountability, without which we all suffer. Yes, we need our leaders, both religious and political, to be privately accountable but we also need mothers and dads who will practice personal accountability. What do I mean? D. L. Moody said, "Character is who you are in the dark." My take on that is to be accountable even when no one is watching. Watch what you do even when no one else sees. If King David had been accountable to God when no one was watching, the story of him and Bathsheba would have never happened. I'm not suggesting I have arrived or that any of us ever will. What I am suggesting is that while we never arrive at the destination, we continue the journey pursuing God, resisting the devil, and seeking to be faithful.

What David did is not new. Trying to cover up sin often leads to committing more sin. If a person lies to cover a lie, another lie is necessary to cover the most recent lie. At some point, because of no accountability, lying gets out of control...

David sent for Bathsheba.
They became intimate.
A baby is conceived.
David urges Uriah to go home.
Uriah is made drunk.
Uriah is placed on the front lines and killed.
David brought Bathsheba into his house.
She bore their child.

All appears to be well until accountability, in the form of Nathan, comes calling. Nathan came with a word from the Lord. Everybody needs a Nathan. Because, sometimes, we become so good at convincing others that our sin isn't really sin, we also convince ourselves. Nathan's words are like a pinch on the tender part of your lower back. That hurts. But David needed a pinch in the place that would hurt the most, his heart. His pride. His ego.

Change happens in the life of a believer because of the conviction of the Holy Spirit. He convicts of sin, righteousness, and judgment. Anything that hints of sin is brought to light. The Holy Spirit is always pointing toward righteous living. Believers are reminded that judgment always hangs in the balance. Blameworthiness comes through the power of God's Word that is *"sharp, quick, and powerful,"* and is also a *"discerner of the thoughts and intents"* of men's hearts (Hebrews 4:12). David didn't have a Bible, but he did have a Nathan. Everybody needs a Nathan. A necessary friend who will speak the truth even when the truth is unsolicited.

Iron Sharpens Iron

What happens when two pieces of metal are rubbed against one another? Sharpening. That's the point of Proverbs 27:17 – we can sharpen one another. We know how iron sharpens iron but how does one person sharpen another? How do we do that? Encouragement. Concern. Truthfulness. Nathan came because God sent him to tell David the truth. David had become dulled by his own sin. While it didn't happen immediately, Nathan's words restored David's heart to be sensitive to God's Spirit. Sharpening happens each time we gather as believers to worship, to pray, and for fellowship. But it can also happen each time we encounter someone who has been dulled by the hardness of life. When we speak words of life, and not death, our friends are sharpened. If you know someone who is a little rusty because of a storm, sickness, or some situation beyond their control, take the time to sharpen them. Speak life. Speak love. Lift them up.

When we're sharpened, we become better tools in God's hands. However sharp we are determines our usefulness for God's work. Our usability. To be useful for God's purposes should be the aim of every believer. We can become weapons in the army of God to defend and protect. Sharpening takes time and pressure. Before files and grinding stones, iron was rubbed against iron for the purpose of sharpening. But sharpening is not necessarily pleasant. Listen to this verse in Proverbs 6:4, *"Faithful are the wounds of a friend, but deceitful are the kisses of an enemy."* Would you rather be wounded by a friend or kissed by an enemy? Jesus knows about the kiss of an enemy. The sharpening of a friend may mean saying hard things that no one else can say. We say it because we love them. They receive it because we love them.

My dad always had a small garden at home. He began in late spring tilling the soil and then planting the seed. And then for a number of weeks, as the plants began to grow and produce vegetables, he would "hoe" the garden. But that hoe had to be sharpened. I remember, as a child, watching as my dad would put the hoe in a vice to hold it steady. Then he would take a file and, applying pressure, rub it along the edge of that old garden hoe. In just a few minutes that rusty garden tool had a shiny and sharp edge. Most of us have been sharpened by the Lord's grace at some point. And truthfully, there are many believers, who are less than useful for the kingdom, that continue to refuse the sharpening of the Lord. Nathan came to David's house as a file in the hand of God to sharpen the life of David. And, because David had been a man after the heart of God, he received Nathan as a brother.

Why do men and women like David fall? Why does someone drown in pornography, an affair, alcohol, addiction, bitterness, or anger? Maybe they have resisted the sharpening of God. Maybe they didn't listen to godly counsel. Maybe they believed they could control their sin, "I can handle it…I'm strong enough…I'm alright…No big deal…I'm good…No problem…Don't worry about me…" The Titanic sank after being warned about ice in the water. The Titanic was known as the unsinkable ship. If you think your ship won't sink, ask King David.

In his book, *Uncommon*, Johnny Hunt describes pride as an "anti-God state of mind." He was quoting C. S. Lewis who also said, "each person's pride is in competition with everyone else's pride." Hunt described three symptoms of pride: "Refusing to listen to wisdom or correction, refusing to submit to God's word, and refusing to admit wrongdoing." Each time, in my life, when I have refused godly counsel, inevitably I have experienced a downslide or detour away from God's blessing. An "anti-God state of mind" results with me taking matters into my own hands which never ends well. What can we do? Pay attention when God speaks to you through His word by the Holy Spirit. And if Nathan comes knocking, don't hide and act like you're not at home. Answer the door and listen to what he has to say.

For almost all of my life as a preacher I have had a father in the ministry, a mentor, someone who has invested in me. As iron sharpens iron, Brother Junior Hill sharpened me. I met him when I was twenty-five years old. I was a young pastor in my first church. Brother Junior was like a compliment to my dad who had raised me well, teaching me how to be a man, how to treat others, how to be responsible, and how to be a father and a husband. Brother Junior became a father-figure to me concerning the ministry of a traveling preacher. He taught me preacher-etiquette. Things like, how to communicate with the pastor, how to conduct the revival service, how to extend the invitation, and what to say and what not to say about the offering. Generally speaking, he taught me how to conduct myself in the ministry to which I was called. I needed him. I am what I am today, as a preacher, by the grace of God and by the influence of Junior Hill. Yes, there have been others who invested in me, and I thank God for each of them. But I owe a debt of gratitude to the Lord for sending Brother Junior to be a faithful friend to me. Both my dad and Brother Junior are in Heaven now. They ran strong and finished well. I pray that they might be the Nathan to someone else that they were to me.

Good preaching says, every Timothy needs a Paul, and every Paul needs a Timothy. I have been that Timothy. But now there is a transition taking place in my ministry. I have become a Paul to a few young men. I pray God uses me in their lives the way He has used men like Junior Hill in mine. Even though we've never had the conversation about accountability, I made myself accountable to Brother Junior. I imagined myself having to face him after some moral failure. I imagined confessing to him some financial indiscretion. I didn't want to hurt him like that. Add to that the hurt and humiliation of admitting some foolish fault to my wife, family, and friends. The thought of it all was just unbearable. Something special happens when iron sharpens iron, when one believer sharpens another believer, when one preacher sharpens another. Friends, I encourage you to keep sharpening and being sharpened. *"He that covers his sins shall not prosper: but whosoever confesses and forsakes them shall have mercy"* Proverbs 28:13. There is great value in having a friend who cares about you enough to hold you accountable.

God uses His Holy Spirit to convict us and draw us to Himself. He uses His Word to speak to us and show us our sin. Sometimes He uses people like Nathan to show us where we are and where we're headed. Everybody needs a Nathan. Yet while we all may need a Nathan, most of us would rather be numbed for a root canal than to have a conversation about our sin. The sudden clash of ego and embarrassment can be painful. Nathan's calls, texts, emails, and visits may be ignored. That unexpected knock at David's door was the beginning of the end of his pretense and a catalyst to his confession, forgiveness, and restoration.

Let's think about the conflict between ego and embarrassment. I have had ego issues since I was a young boy. Honestly, I believe it is something most men struggle with. As younger men we like to think we are faster, stronger, and better than others at some particular task. As a man I have had to resist the youthful temptation to see life as a competition. I have an idea David had ego issues too. It'd be hard for him not to struggle with pride. It was said, *"…Saul has slain his thousands and David his ten thousands"* (1 Samuel 18:7). That would be enough to cause a man to stumble over his ego. That declaration might cause a man like David to be so prideful that if he saw a beautiful woman bathing and sent for her, he would expect her to come immediately. But when that prideful spirit runs into the shameful humiliation of being caught and called out, there is the opportunity for either brokenness or bitterness. Thankfully, David didn't respond in bitterness toward Nathan or the Lord who sent him. He responded with brokenness. He admitted his sin. He had sinned against Bathsheba, Uriah, all those who respected him, the people of God, but mostly he had sinned against God.

The confession of his sin speaks of him being a man after God's heart (1 Samuel 13:14). I'm not overlooking David's sin. I'm not eager, at this point, to invite him to our church to share his testi-

43

mony. Like anyone in his shoes, David needs to marinate in the guilt and conviction of his actions. He needs to absorb the magnitude of his sin. He also needs to spend time in prayer and meditation soaking in the mercies of a gracious God who called him knowing what he was capable of doing. There are many ways David could have responded. He could resorted to self-defense, anger, blame, resentment, and the list goes on. He could have even questioned the integrity of Nathan. But thankfully, he responded with a broken spirit. He truly was a man after God's heart. We can learn a valuable lesson here. If a man like David can fall, can't we all? Truly, everybody needs a Nathan.

Nathan is dependable. Nothing suspicious about Nathan. No doubt about his integrity or his character. He's a man of God. He has influence and those who know him adhere to and abide by what he says. He's been in David's life as a role model and a mentor. His life wreaks faithfulness. His words are seasoned with truth. His walk with God is consistent. Nathan is like E. F. Hutton. When he speaks, people listen. Maybe you're not familiar with that reference. In the late 1970s the stock firm named E. F. Hutton gained notoriety through a series of TV commercials. One such advertisement focused on two men having dinner in a restaurant. As they were being served, they talked about their investments. One gentleman asked the other, "Who is your broker?" He responded, "My broker is E. F. Hutton, and Hutton says…" At that point everyone in the restaurant stopped what they were doing and leaned in to hear what Hutton had to say. The announcer at the end of the commercial said, "When E. F. Hutton speaks, people listen."

Think about the E.F. Huttons in your life. Why did you listen to them? Was it because they were foolish or because they were wise? Was it out of respect or disrespect? Chances are, you listened to that person because they had proven themselves to be authentic and consistent. My father was the first and greatest influence in my life. But I have had others who were intentional in having a positive influence on me. When they spoke, I listened. They were credible and believable. They practiced what he preached. They never exaggerated the truth. They were straightforward. They were old school. Many of these men had survived hardships and experienced blessings. Thinking back, they were careful with their words toward me. They never made me feel less-than. They never labeled me in some way that might haunt me in years to come. Like my dad, they spoke hard words at times, but I knew they loved me. When they spoke I listened, and I can still hear them today.

My E. F. Huttons have been coaches, teachers, pastors, friends, and short-term acquaintances. But all of them have had one common quality, they were believable. Not by coercive words but by consistent living that backed up everything they said. When they spoke I listened.

This talk about E. F. Hutton begs the question, am I living in such a way that anyone would listen to me? E. F. Hutton doesn't get people to listen to him by blaming others for his own faults. The people I have listened to were not those who had succeeded without compromise. They were men who failed, accepted responsibility, and learned from it. David Jeremiah told of the time he was asked to teach on the subject of time management. In a radio broadcast I heard, he described what he learned. He realized each person has the same amount of time in every day. We each have twenty-four hours to spend however we choose. After much study, Dr. Jeremiah realized the emphasis of his message should be on self-management rather than time-management (Turning Point Radio). When Nathan came knocking at David's door, God used him to bring David to a point of confession, admission of sin, and accepting the blame for what had happened.

Most of us who have influence on others also have scars. We failed, stumbled, and disappointed others. But we got up. Assumed responsibility. Accepted the blame. And were the better for it. Those of us who have a scar of some kind can speak from experience about the grace of God. We're not only quoting from a Book, The Book about God's faithfulness, we have lived it. When Nathan came to David, his words were like those of a battle-tested soldier. He had a few years on him, had traveled a few miles, and had proclaimed the steadfastness of God. When he spoke, David listened.

Nathan is discerning. In Proverbs 29:11 we read, *"A fool vents all his feelings, but a wise man holds them back."* He doesn't arrive at David's place on a whim…with an axe to grind…or a bone to pick. He went because God sent him. It's divine direction. He's there on God's watch. He's about the Father's business. His mind is on spiritual matters. I like to imagine he has prayed as he journeyed. He's been seeking God about what he will say. He's a prophet knowing what he says may be rejected. I'm sure "shoot the messenger" was a reality even in David's time.

Nathan could have vented his feelings. He could have told David how disappointed he was. But he stayed on point. I haven't been so careful. How about you? How many of us have ever vented our anger and regretted it? There have been a few times when I thought to myself in a heated moment – Don't say that. Sadly, When I had that thought I was already saying what I knew I shouldn't say. Can I get a witness? What I have learned is that I am not the Holy Spirit, and I can't do His job. All I can do is say what He leads me to say and then leave the results in God's hands. Nathan did that. He spoke as God led him and trusted the Lord to take a simple parable and use it to bring David to repentance.

The tongue is a fire and only God can control the tongue. Without His control we will speak words that will spread like fire and destroy everything in their path. Nathan got to the point. He didn't come for small talk. He wasn't there to talk about the weather. He came with one simple mission – speak to David about his sin. The verse from Proverbs describes a fool as one who *"vents all his feelings."* Maybe you've known someone like that. Hopefully, you've known someone like Nathan who doesn't vent all his feelings. A fool may act foolish because he is short-sighted, doesn't have all the facts, or is just easily provoked. But a wise man is discerning, focused, fearless, loving, caring, and discreet.

Harold Aldridge was one of the best men I have ever met. He was a member of the first church I pastored and proved to be a friend to me. Harold and I would go visiting together. We would visit the elderly, those in hospitals, prison, and nursing homes. I was a young man in my early twenties at the time and looked up to Harold as a mentor. We had many conversations about life, church, family, money, and struggles. I never heard him raise his voice. He never seemed agitated about anything. He never spoke of anyone in some disparaging manner. Almost every time we went out visiting, we would end the evening with a stop at the Dairy Queen for ice cream. Harold was like a Nathan to me. He spoke softly and care-fully. He was wise and patient. He was loving and caring. God give us more men like Harold Aldridge. Everybody needs a Nathan.

What Does Accountability Look Like?

Paul David Tripp said, "Accountability requires a willingness to roll up our sleeves and get alongside people as they fight the war between sin and righteousness." When Nathan went to see David, he went alone. He rolled up his sleeves, took responsibility for what God had sent him to do, and then proceeded in obedience to that commission.

We have already looked at King David's lack of accountability. His sin with Bathsheba could have been avoided if he had acted respon-sibly. But when other kings were at war he stayed behind in Jerusalem. He was a king with his armor removed. And in that vulnerable state of mind, he fell captive to his own lusts. He sent for the beautiful woman he had seen bathing, knowing she was another man's wife. There was no sense of obligation or liability on his part. He's king and he can do as he likes. And so he did.

David's story is a great lesson for anyone. David had been a seeker of God. He was a shepherd boy who became a king. He is described as ruddy and unlikely but was now seated on the throne. He had been a man after the heart of God, but in 2 Samuel 11 his heart was far from God and in pursuit of a wife that wasn't his. He was on the roof doing what kings do I suppose. Looking over his kingdom and domain. Prideful of what he has and who he is. Little did he know, like Cain's anger toward Abel, sin was at his door – a sin so vile it would drive him to do the unthinkable. He would dig a hole on that day of which he would never get out. He would never forget the foolish decision to send for her. He would live the remainder of his life in the shadows of what he had done. Yes, God forgives but sin never forgets.

You've got to live in the house you build...

There is a story of a wealthy landowner and home builder who was about to retire. But before he retired, he was going to build one more home. It would be the greatest and the nicest home he had ever built. For years he'd had an associate that helped him with all his building projects. His associate was younger than he and had been a loyal employee for most of his young life. The wealthy builder commissioned his associate to build the home. He instructed him to spare no expense. Use the best lumber, the finest stone, marble floors, oak and cedar on the walls. He was to build a home fit for a king. The wealthy man then told his associate he would be gone for six months, traveling abroad, and when he returned, he expected the home to be completed. The associate was unhappy and unmotivated. His boss was about to retire, and he would be out of a job. How would he provide for his family? Where would he live and what would he do? After these many years he thought, the boss is retiring and all I get is a handshake and a pat on the back. While his boss was away, the apprentice squandered his time. Most days he didn't even come in to work and when he did it was late. Time passed quickly. He realized his boss would soon be home in less than three months. He had much work to do. He gathered a crew and went to work building the home, but he was cutting corners, using second rate materials, ignoring uneven floors, and mis-matched painting. They hurriedly completed the outside with inferior land-scaping and a bumpy yet paved driveway. They finished the home just in time for the return of the boss. Upon his return, he and his associate stood in the drive admiring from a distance the large home that had been built. He congratulated his associate on what appeared to be a beautiful place to live. Then he turned to him and said, "It's yours! I hope you spared no expense. I wanted to do something for you after all these years of loyalty to me. This home is yours! You get to live in the house you built!"

What a powerful story. Just look around, we all live in the house we build. Some are living in the house of their dreams, while others find themselves living in a house that's more like a bad dream. But if we are just building a house, then let's order the lumber and proceed. But this is more than a house we are building; it is a home, a life, a family, and a future. David would live in the house he built. He could have avoided much of the heartache for himself and his children if he had held himself accountable to God and those around him. I want to suggest three kinds of accountability, especially for believers:

Internal Accountability

Let's think about internal or personal responsibility. This is looking in the mirror. This is having an honest conversation with yourself. This is personal examination. This is taking an in-depth look at yourself. This is internal integrity. Being accountable to yourself. The temptation is to lie to yourself. If you lie to yourself, you will lie to others about yourself. Did King David ever have a check in his spirit? David allowed his internal neglect to spiral him toward more than the sin of adultery, but the greater sin of denying God.

We are tempted to compare ourselves with others. "I'm not that bad... I'm not doing what they're doing... I would never do that... Did you hear what they did?" We're seldom honest with ourselves when we are comparing our bad choices with someone else's bad choices. But if I practice internal accountability as a believer I am listening to the voice of God, the work of the Holy Spirit. Under His influence I see myself as He sees me. Nothing is hidden.

In Romans 13:14 we read, *"Put on the Lord Jesus Christ and make no provision for the flesh to fulfill its lusts."* Paul doesn't give the believer any wiggle room. He says to put off the works of darkness and put on the armor of light, and then to put on the Lord Jesus. Be clothed in Him. John Wesley said this was a picture of abiding in Christ. I believe this is daily. This putting on and putting off is a daily discipline of the believer. If David had practiced internal accountability, Uriah would still be alive. Nathan would have never been sent. David made provision and gave opportunity for the flesh. He cracked the door and sin kicked it open.

In 2 Corinthians 13:5 we read, *"Examine yourselves as to whether you are in the faith. Test yourselves. Do you not know yourselves that Jesus Christ is in you? Unless indeed you are disqualified."* Those two words, examine and test, reveal the heart and character of a man. Those words reveal our motives. Too many are disqualified to serve and represent our Lord. Not because they out-sinned the grace of God, but because they continued to sin thus losing their testimony. They disqualified themselves by allowing unconfessed sin to ruin their witness for Christ. David failed to examine himself.

External Accountability

This is clearly what happened when God sent Nathan to David. Call it a divine interruption. Call it a shift in thinking. External accountability happens when someone or something from the outside disturbs us on the inside to the point of change. The result is vulnerable submission. An honest conversation with someone else about your plans or your dilemma brings about, in David's case, repentance and confession. David became transparent, allowing Nathan to see his heart.

This external accountability can be as dramatic as the story of Nathan and David, or it can be as common as a small group Bible study openly discussing struggles. And that open discussion stirs others to look at themselves in light of God's word. Personally, I have been challenged through conversations with others. God was using someone to bring change in my heart. And most often that person didn't even know the power their words held over me. In the first church I pastored I was also a full-time college student. I was 21 years old and struggling to make passing grades. I had gotten by in high school, never imagining I would one day go to college. I was ashamed of my grades and ashamed of what appeared to be my lack of ability. I went to see one of the leaders in that church who was my friend but also old enough to be my dad. I told him about my bad grades, about my inability to study and comprehend, and my plans to drop out. He looked me square in the eyes and said in no uncertain terms, "No you will not quit. You are going to study and pass and one day graduate!" Johnny McCay was a Nathan to me that day. He didn't tell me what I wanted to hear. He told me what I needed to hear. That is what a Nathan does. I went home with a renewed determination. I began to study. I began to make better grades. I graduated with an Associate's Degree, then with a Bachelor's Degree, then with a Master's Degree, and finally with a Doctor's Degree. Sometimes we all need a Nathan to push us in the right direction.

More specifically, we see this external accountability in Galatians 2:11-21 when Paul confronted Peter about his hypocrisy. According to Paul, Peter was frustrating, or annulling, the grace of God. He would eat with Gentiles unless there were Jews present. Paul said that Peter, *"feared those who were of the circumcision."* Paul continued his call to transparency by saying they *"were not straightforward about the truth of the Gospel."* To put this idea in my southern vernacular, God sent Paul to Peter that he might "straighten him out." My dad straightened me out a few times when I was a boy. I was straightened out in restaurants, at church, in public and in private. Sometimes he talked to me. At other times he punished me. A few times he grounded me. The end result today is a son who respects his father for not only speaking the truth but also living it. That is external accountability.

Eternal Accountability

This is living with eternity in mind. This is being so heavenly minded that your earthly impact is transformed. This is living with the judgement seat of Christ in mind. This is guarding your heart and tongue knowing that *"every idle word men may speak, they will give an account of it in the day of judgment"* (Matthew 12:36). This is living with the absolute certainty that in the here and now as well as then and there, *"at the name of Jesus every knee should bow, of those in Heaven, and of those on the earth, and of those under the earth, and that every tongue should confess that Jesus Christ is Lord, to the glory of God the Father"* (Philippians 2:10-11). This is where confession meets surrender. This is godly sorrow. This is Peter weeping after denying the Lord. This is giving an account to God. This is seeing ourselves stripped of name, accolades, degrees, accomplishments, and reputation, standing bare before God. It is admitting. It is submitting.

Whereas internal accountability is about calling myself into account, and external accountability is when God uses someone else to call me into account. Eternal accountability is the awareness that God will call me to give an account.

Nathan is direct. In 2 Samuel 12:1, the same verse where we read *"the Lord sent Nathan to David,"* we see that Nathan wasted no time. He quickly got down to the business for which God had sent him. We have looked at Nathan being dependable and discerning, but his direct approach is most compelling. It appears he didn't even ask how David was doing. There was no small talk. There are times when we must cut to the chase, be direct and to the point. Such is the case here. Nathan begins to tell David the story of a rich man and a poor man which is really the story of David and Uriah. The rich man had taken advantage of the poor man and David had taken advantage of Uriah. Nathan would eventually say with no uncertainty, *"You are the man."*

It is often said of preachers that they tell it like it is. My experience is that most congregations want their pastor to tell it like it is until *it* involves them. Nathan told it like it was. He's not there to win a popularity contest. He isn't trying to be politically correct. He's not fearful of David's response. He isn't self-serving. He's bold but he isn't brash. He went and spoke as God directed him. Everybody needs a Nathan.

As I bring this chapter to a close, let's go back to where we started. Nathan is accountable and God has sent him to hold David accountable. Nathan has change in his pocket. David listens without interrupting. Nathan's mere presence commands respect. He can be trusted.

Friend, how much change do you have in your pocket? If you were to talk to someone about trusting and turning to the Lord, would they listen, or do you have empty pockets?

Everybody needs a Nathan.
He has change in his pocket.
He's a man of integrity...
He's a man of character...
He's a man of principle...
He's a man of honor...
He's a man of his word...
He's a man of God...

CHAPTER 3 DISCUSSION POINTS

What does it mean to have "change in your pocket?"

Discuss the change in Nathan's pocket and how this earned David's respect for him.

Reflecting on the story about living in the house you build, how does that idea apply to Nathan and David?

Discuss the significance of internal, external, and eternal accountability.

4

DAVID AND CAIN

Genesis 4:12

G od told Cain that sin was at his door and that he should rule
over it. The imagery the Lord used is that of a predator at
Cain's door crouched and ready to pounce. But the killing of Abel
tells us all we need to know; the sin at the door ruled over him.

Likewise, sin was crouched at David's door, and he didn't recognize
it. The Enemy targeted David with the sole purpose of ruining his
life and wrecking his legacy. In many ways he succeeded. Like the
lion Peter described in 1 Peter 5:8, sin pounced on King David
intent on destruction and defeat. We must be alert to the sins
crouched at our door. We may not be looking for a demon around
every corner, but we must be spiritually alert, aware, and attentive to
the enemy's presence. I am not suggesting that we live in fear, but
that we live in the reality of who the Enemy is and what he does.

If you're looking for sin, you can find it. If you're interested in sin, it
will be interested in you. If you flirt you may not always get a
response, but there may come a time when you get more than you
bargained for. If you have wandering eyes there will come a day

when they will meet the wandering eyes of another. There is the biblical qualification for bishops and deacons that is translated, *"the husband of one wife"* (1 Timothy 3:2,12). Those verses describe a one-woman-man. That qualification has more to do with moral purity than marital status. A man who is the husband of one wife has a heart set on his wife and no one else's. His eyes are on his wife and no one else's. His thoughts are on his wife and no one else's. He is intimate with his wife and no one else's. He is a one-woman-man. King David was not a one-woman-man. He went after another man's wife. As far as we know he only did this once, but once was enough considering the ripple effects of his sin. David was a man after God's heart, but for a brief time he turned away from pursuing God and pursued the wife of Uriah. If you're looking for trouble, trouble is looking for you.

God is not the author of thoughts about sin, involvement in sin, or participation in sin. God's involvement in your sin is to lead you away from it. No need to blame your bad choices on God. David made the choice. If you turn from God to sin, God is not leading you, and won't bless what you're doing. God will never bless anything that is not His will. Paul wrote in 2 Corinthians 10:4 that they were to bring *"into captivity every thought to the obedience of Christ."* Why? Because thoughts have a way of leading to actions. David didn't suddenly have an affair with Bathsheba. He thought it out before he acted it out. Some have suggested that Bathsheba was the reason David tarried in Jerusalem while other kings went out to battle. We can't say that with certainty, but it is a possibility. Cain didn't suddenly kill Abel. He thought it out and then acted it out. What you're doing may seem like a small thing, just a glance in the direction of Bathsheba. Or a nod in the direction of David. But Satan will take advantage of small gestures and ignored weaknesses in the hopes of causing you to crumble.

I will talk more about this in the pages to come, but let me mention briefly what we find in Ephesians 4:27. Paul writes, *"Neither give place to the Devil."* Giving the Devil place is the first step in the wrong direction. How do we do this? Better yet, how do we not allow the

Devil to have a place, an opportunity, room to work? Again, there is an entire chapter to come on this idea, but may I suggest we first give him place in our mind. Our thoughts. Our imagination. How do we give place to the Devil? How did David do it? Lust. How did Cain do it? Jealousy. Moses - Frustration. Samson - Pride. Peter - Fear. Judas - Betrayal. Ananias and Sapphira - Greed.

How do *we* give place to the devil? When we allow our emotions to run wild. When we become complacent. When we are out of touch with God. When we are prideful. When we think we're in control. When we think we're invincible. Cain gave place to the Devil through jealousy, envy, and resentment. David gave the Devil place through lust, ego, and selfishness.

Cain was Warned

Cain was told by God in Genesis 4:7, *"Its desire is for you…but you should rule over it."* Cain had not been a murderer but suddenly became one. David had been a man after God's heart but in a matter of minutes he went after Bathsheba's heart. In Genesis 4:7, Sin is personified. God said, *"It lies at the door…"* We get the idea sin was crouched and looking for the opportunity to attack. It's as if sin was patiently waiting, tempting Cain, taunting him, teasing him. Both Cain and David had the know-how and the willpower to resist and rule over their sin, but it ruled over them instead.

Think about these comparisons: Cain and Abel, David and Bathsheba. What state of mind might Cain and David have been in at the time of their sin? Cain's offering was not received. David was not at battle where he should have been. At the point of committing murder and adultery what were these men thinking? It appears they were not thinking clearly at all. Call it having a weak moment, disregarding what they knew to be right, or battling temporary insanity. Whatever we call it, they failed. If we take Galatians 5:17 into account where we read of the battle between the flesh and the Spirit, with Cain and David the flesh clearly won. If we consider 1 Peter 5:8 we must admit neither Cain nor David was sober or vigilant. Proverbs 4:23 warns us to, *"Keep your heart with all diligence, for out of it spring the issues of life."* Our heart is a wellspring, a constant source of opportunities where we can find great joy or great sorrow. Friend, may we heed the solemn warning to guard our heart. How? Be a diligent student of the Word. Be a person marked by prayer. Consider the consequences of an unguarded heart.

Cain was Warned by God

My dad was not an unreasonable man. He was not an angry man. But he was a man that, when he spoke, I knew to listen carefully. Especially when he was speaking to me about what I should and shouldn't do. I don't mind telling you that my dad whipped me a few times with a belt. It was not severe punishment by any stretch of the imagination. All my whippings came before I was twelve years old. By then I had learned that my dad meant what he said. Usually, before the punishment, dad would tell me what he was going to do. He was going to whip me. He would fold the belt and then he would give me three or four whippings on my backside. As a boy I cried, not so much because it hurt my backside but because it hurt my feelings. But also, before he ever told me he was going to whip me, he told me what I shouldn't be doing. I had clear warning that if I acted in such a way, I would be punished. He was more than fair. And he was a patient man. But he also meant what he said.

Nothing has changed with God since the days of Cain. He still speaks clearly. He still speaks to us about sin. About choices. About plans that don't include Him. He leads. Guides. He directs. And He does it all through the work of the Holy Spirit. How does God speak to us today about sin that is at our door and how we should rule over it? By the conviction of the Holy Spirit. The Work of the Holy Spirit is described in John 16:8-11 *"He will convict the world of sin, and of righteousness, and of judgment..."* In this verse, "convict" means to convince, reprove, expose. It is a legal term, meaning pronouncing the verdict. Even though preachers do our best to convince, reprove, and even persuade, we cannot take the place of the Holy Spirit. There is a great difference between guilt and conviction. I may make you feel guilty, but only the Holy Spirit brings conviction. I may say something that causes grief. I may say something that stirs regret. But I cannot bring conviction of sin. I like what my friend Phil Waldrep said about this distinction. He said, "Conviction is forward thinking; guilt is backward thinking" (*Parenting Prodigals*, pg. 72). That idea helps me; maybe it helps you too. It reminds me how guilt can make me live in the past while conviction enables me to look to the future. Under conviction is a great place to be. Conviction is God's way of loving us and leading us in the direction we should go.

The Holy Spirit convicts the world of sin. Jesus clarifies, *"Of sin - because they do not believe in me…"* The word for sin means missing the mark. Unbelief coupled with deception is why so many miss the mark. If you can imagine a target with a bullseye. That's the idea. When we allow sin in our life and when we choose to live in unrepentance, we miss the mark. The Holy Spirit does His job of convicting of sin, pointing to Jesus, and drawing unbelievers, but ultimately it is our choice to trust Him or turn from Him. Make no mistake about it, because of sin we miss Jesus. He is the mark we're missing. Unbelief is the greatest sin with the most tragic consequences. Not trusting Jesus is the only completely unforgivable sin. God so loved the world that He sent His Holy Spirit to convict us, awaken us, and point us to Jesus.

The Holy Spirit convicts the world of righteousness. From Vines Expository Dictionary we learn the original spelling of this word was rightwiseness. Means doing the right thing and making wise decisions. Jesus clarified, *"Of righteousness – because I am going away and you will see me no more."* The temptation for the disciples after Jesus' death, burial, resurrection, and ascension would be to become self-righteous rather than depending on His righteousness. The sin of self-righteousness is still an issue among believers. And unbelievers. The lost often believe they don't need Jesus to save them, that they can save themselves. And believers often believe they can help Jesus in His work to make them righteous. Friend, clearly we can't save ourselves. If we could, Jesus' death was unnecessary. And believers can't make themselves righteous. He alone is our righteousness. The Holy Spirit convicts us to trust only in Jesus for our righteousness.

The Holy Spirit convicts the world of judgment. The Holy Spirit, once He is indwelling believers, would convince them of certain judgment. Jesus clarified, *"Of judgment because the ruler of this world is judged."* Satan is judged and is found guilty as the father of lies and the author of deception. The ruler of this world has been judged and so will we be judged. This conviction causes us to live with eternity in mind. We can and must live with an eternal perspective. Knowing that, according to 1 Corinthians 3:12, the works of believers will be revealed and likened to either wood, hay, and stubble or gold, silver, and precious stones. The choice is ours as to how we build. The Holy Spirit is also convicting the world about one day standing before God as unbelievers having rejected Jesus. What a sad day that will be.

Steve Farrar's Mission Statement

Steve Farrar has been one of my favorite authors for years. I have read many of his books and have always been challenged. I'd like for you to read his mission statement. It's a little crude but you don't have to wonder what he means. A mission statement like his might have helped David and Cain. It sure wouldn't have hurt. Farrar writes,

> "Several years ago, as I was edging gingerly through the door of mid-life, I decided to come up with a mission statement for my life. I'd been reflecting a bit about the first half of my life, and I was doing some hard thinking about the second part. You may find this odd, but it didn't even take a day. I didn't even have to go away to some island or retreat center to think about it. Quite frankly, it took me about two minutes. I've had this mission statement for years now and I haven't changed one word of the original two-minute composition. Here it is…Don't screw up. That's it. It's not real long, it's not real sophisticated, it's not real

polished, and it's not real religious. But it is real. As I look over the rest of my life, I don't want to screw up. Do you? Of course, you don't. I don't know any man who wants to screw up. Yet men screw up all the time. My goal for the second half of my life is not to screw up in a major way. I don't want to screw up my marriage. I don't want to screw up my relationship with my kids. I don't want to screw up my integrity." (*Finishing Strong*, pg. 47)

After reading Farrar's book I decided I would create a mission statement for myself. Mine was not as edgy as his but it has helped me continue this journey. My statement at that time was simply: Stay the course. This year I have tried to live by the mission statement: It matters. I have had a number of mission statements over the years. Statements that have helped me, driven me, protected me, and encouraged me. As I write these words, I am grateful to have stayed the course. But I must never forget - The Enemy is real and many have fallen. I chose the words "It matters" for this year because, honestly, it matters who I am wherever I am. It matters what I say, what I do, how I treat others, what I think, how I live, etc. Truthfully, everything matters. I want to finish well. I have a bracelet on my wrist that I have been wearing for at least six years. It just says, Finish Strong. I pray the Lord will continue to lead me in finishing strong.

Cain

Sin was at the door. That's what God told Cain. Don't miss the imagery. It's at the door. If nothing else the presence at Cain's door reminds us of the nearness of sin, the proximity, as Farrar said, of screwing up. What sin lies at your door ready to leap into your life? What is it that's stalking you? The opportunity for sin was brewing. Jealousy, envy, frustration, and rejection were on Cain's porch, just to name a few. For a brief moment in time Cain was consumed with rage. And then suddenly it was over.

Sin was crouched at David's door too. The lethal combination of pride and power proved too much for the shepherd boy that became a king. David should have looked the other way. He should have gone back inside. But instead, he sent for her. I believe David must have replayed that day in his mind over and over for years to come. There's no indication that he ever acted that way before or after. But we know for sure there was at least one day both he and Bathsheba lived to regret. In that one moment all that mattered was what he wanted. In that moment he became oblivious to his own sin. Sin had been at his door, and he never saw it coming.

Needless to say, if you have a heart for God, are interested in doing the will of God, seeking to know the word of God, and if you are being used of God, the Enemy will paint a bullseye on you with the intent of taking you down. As Peter wrote in 1 Peter 5:8, we must be *"sober minded"* and aware of the Enemy, because he roams about as a roaring lion seeking someone to devour. Your name and notoriety have no effect on the extent of Satan's attacks. If allowed, he will devour anyone, regardless of status or influence. Doesn't matter if you're King David, or Mr. Nobody – he roams about to destroy, destruct, and devour.

> ...David had Uriah killed, and then married his wife as if he had done nothing wrong.
> …Cain Killed Abel and responded as if his death was justified.
> …Ananias and Sapphira hid the money and lied about it.
> …Judas betrayed the Lord and took the money as if he got a good deal.
> …Peter stopped fishing for men and went back to fishing for fish.

All sin separates us from God, but some sins leave bigger scars. Some sins make a bigger mess. Some sins have a bigger impact on you, your family, and your future. Even though we have the Holy Spirit and the Word of God to guide us - sometimes we need a Nathan! A voice of reason. A friend who will speak truth to us. A mentor who will track us down and bring us back to reality. Someone who will tell us what we need to hear even when we don't want to hear it. Everybody needs a Nathan.

Imagine if there was a price tag on sin… I would love to have a new truck. Actually, I would love to have a truck, any truck. The price of a new truck is far more than I am willing to pay. But I often stop and look at the new models and dream of having one. The window sticker is amazingly detailed. I can read about the price of the basic truck, and then with all the options added. I have figured out, with the price of trucks these days, I can get a new one for around $400 a month… for the next forty years! After that calculation, I gladly walk back to my very used yet dependable Accord with the vivid reality, I cannot afford that truck. What if sin had a window sticker? What if you knew what sin would cost before you ever indulged? I am certain a window sticker on sin would prevent much heartache. If we knew in advance our sin would cost us our marriage, our family, our relationship with our children and grandchildren, would it not at least cause us to stop and think? Honestly, if you knew the price you would pay for the sin you might commit today, however great or small, would you reconsider? Sin always has a price. And it always costs more than we are willing to pay.

I thought about the price of sin recently as I watched an old interview with Billy Graham by Johnny Carson on The Tonight Show back in the early 70s. Both men were in their prime. Both were admired, popular, successful, but one was known for his life as a playboy and the other was known for his life as a man of God. Both would go on to live long lives and die having made a name for themselves and a difference in the world - but at what price? I'm sure Billy was tempted just like Johnny, and Johnny had the same opportunity to turn from sin as Billy. Two men. Big differences. I watched as Billy spoke clearly about having peace with God. I watched as Johnny questioned him. Johnny seemed intrigued. I wondered if he, like Felix in Acts 24, trembled at the possible reality of judgment to come. I'm glad to know God saved Billy Graham. And I'm glad to know God would have saved Johnny Carson if he had asked. I hope he did. Sin has a price. Jesus paid it in full. Our only response to the price He paid is to trust Him to save us.

In 1 Corinthians 10:13 we read, *"No temptation has overtaken you except such as is common to man; but God is faithful, who will not allow you to be tempted beyond what you are able, but with the temptation will also make the way of escape, that you may be able to bear it."* John Macarthur says temptation sometimes comes through disappointment (preceptaustin.org). The Enemy will take a shot at you while you're wounded. He'll wait till you've been thrown under the bus, then he'll back up and run over you. Along with the shame, guilt, remorse, and feelings of failure, Satan adds insult to injury. In my days of high school football, we called it piling on. He keeps throwing punches. He never ceases to tempt and distract. He is the Accuser. I am reminded, however, being tempted is not a sin. But I must be careful in the midst of disappointments to guard my heart and mind. As Peter says, *"be sober and vigilant."* Also, if the Devil will tempt Jesus when He's hungry, He will come after me when I'm discouraged.

As I bring this chapter to a close, I need to be clear, all our decisions matter. James 1:14-16 *"Every man is tempted when he is drawn away by his own lusts…When lust has conceived it brings forth sin…"* Birth always follows conception, but it takes a while. The birth of a baby takes about nine months. Sometimes it takes at least that long for a thought to give birth to an action. An immoral desire may sit idle for years before it conceives and gives and produces a shameful act. If permitted, lust will always bring forth sin. When we allow our lust to go unchecked, it will conceive and bring forth sin at some point. In 1:16 James writes simply, *"Do not be deceived…"* That's good advice for David and Cain. And for you and me. God help us.

CHAPTER 4 DISCUSSION POINTS

What do David and Cain have in common?

Cain was warned by God that sin was at his door. How does the Holy Spirit warn believers through conviction of sin, righteousness, and judgment?

Discuss the lethal combination of pride and power. And from another chapter the combination of ego and lust. How did these combinations affect Cain and David?

Discuss the price tag on sin: How some sins cost more than others and how some sins leave bigger scars.

GIVING THE DEVIL A PLACE AT THE TABLE

Ephesians 4:27

Charles Spurgeon said, *"I'd rather go to Heaven alone than go to Hell in a herd."* None of us who have a heart for God want to go to Heaven alone, Spurgeon included. But I get his point. We live in a herd-mentality culture today even among believers. People are doing whatever everyone else is doing. Believing what everyone else is believing. Accepting what everyone else is accepting. Applauding what everyone else is applauding. Much of society is running with the herd. Running in the wrong direction. And picking up speed. It appears we haven't heeded Paul's words. It appears we have given place to the Devil.

I believe we must do all we can to reach "the herd" for Christ. But much of the herd isn't interested in knowing Jesus. Considering the herd's mentality, I must take the initiative to guard my heart, guard my walk, and protect my fellowship with Christ. For me personally, that has meant creating my own herd of accountability. I have done that over the past forty years of ministry. Most of the men in my herd have never known they were members. I never asked them to join, and I never notified them of their inclusion. In fact, most of them are already in Heaven. But I chose these men to have influence on me. I have often wondered what they thought, how they would respond, and I have sought to learn what they believed. Well-known men like D. L. Moody, Billy Graham, John Wesley, Billy Sunday, George Whitefield, Adrian Rogers, Charles Stanley, Junior Hill, Don Wilton, Vance Havner, and Oswald Chambers have had great influence on me. I have also included in my personal herd of accountability, my dad, my pastors, several friends from college and seminary, and several not-so-well-known faithful men of God. I am grateful for this herd of godly men. Thus far, they have helped guide me, protect me, teach me, warn me, and inspire me.

Giving Place to the Devil

I'm sure Paul would have called this *"place"* a stronghold. And he would have said to tear this *"place"* down. In our culture, politics, the church, and in our homes, however, it seems we've given the Devil a place at the table. An opportunity to influence. A platform to shape and mold. We've given him elbow room. An opportunity to change the atmosphere. A place at the table happens by one of two ways: Either by invitation or intrusion. The Devil is either invited, or he intrudes. He's offered a seat, or he barges in. He's given a place, or he takes a place. God give us the discernment and the backbone to take back his seat at the table and burn the chair.

Oswald Chambers said, "There is no Heaven with a little corner of Hell in it." I have used this quote in my preaching and often asked what would happen if Heaven had a little corner of Hell? Overwhelmingly the response has been, Heaven would cease to be Heaven. Absolutely, when Heaven allows a little Hell, it immediately becomes less than Heaven. But Chambers was not talking about a corner of Hell in Heaven, he was making a point about allowing sin to take up a corner of our life. In this chapter I am talking about giving the Devil a place in our home, family, marriage, life. The world shouts back, *"Have an open mind!"* I'm okay with that. But if we're going to have an open mind, we must do so with an open

Bible. What does the Bible say about what I am allowing at my table?

Paul said, *"Don't give place to the Devil."* He also said, *"Don't grieve the Holy Spirit."* Those are fearful thoughts. As a believer, Satan can't occupy any ground in our life unless we allow him. As I mentioned earlier, in 2 Cor 10:3-5 Paul describes these strongholds, where *"place"* has been given to the devil in the form of thoughts, arguments, and imaginations that come against my knowledge of God. The Enemy will attack what we know about God, creating doubt and compromise. He creates a spin on Scripture and causes us to see it in a light we've never thought of before. Suddenly, loving our neighbor includes approving of their sin, agreeing with their choices, and accommodating their lifestyle. And any disapproval of our neighbor's choices is seen as condemning and judgmental. Isn't it possible to love someone and disagree about certain choices they make? Jesus loved the world. He didn't come to condemn it but save it.

Allowing sin to occupy a place in your life, your mind, or your home, is like driving with a snake in your car. Can you imagine driving, knowing there is a snake on the prowl somewhere in your backseat, your front seat, your seat? Several years ago, when I was a younger man, I sang in a local Gospel group. There were six of us and often we all traveled in one car to the places where we sang. One night while driving to the church where we were scheduled to sing the fella driving said, "Oh yea, there's a snake in here somewhere." The car belonged to him, and he loved snakes. He'd been playing with one earlier that day and it got loose in the car. Suddenly there was shift in the atmosphere. At that moment, all that mattered was finding that snake. He pulled over at our request, and all five of us bailed out as if we were on fire. We pulled out everything that could be pulled out. We cleaned out the trunk. We looked under the seats. We pulled out the floor mats. But there was no snake to be found. We all got back in the car reluctantly and proceeded to the church, but we all felt a little uneasy. No one drives with a snake on the loose in their car any more than they sleep with one in their home. If you know there's a snake in your car, and if you know the Devil's at your table - it's time to do some exterminating!

I read Pastor John Ed Mathison's blog about the Medusa jellyfish found in the Bay of Naples. There are also small colorful snails there, known as the Nudibranch. Occasionally the jellyfish will swallow one of the snails. The jellyfish can't hurt the snail because it's protected by a shell. But a slow death takes place as the snail connects itself to the inside of the jellyfish. In a short time, the snail consumes the entire jellyfish. One little snail, slowly devouring an entire jellyfish. When I read that story it reminded me of the scripture about giving place to the Devil. Even the smallest of sins can consume us. Don't be fooled by thinking some sins are innocent and harmless. We often preach against the great sins that destroy lives like murder, immorality, theft, and dishonesty. But how many people have been consumed by anger, unforgiveness, resentment, and jealousy? Sin is like that snail. It attaches itself to our heart and our mind and over time destroys us. How many people do you know who have been pulled away from God by what appeared to be some small, insignificant sin? Take note, Proverbs 14:9 says, *"Fools mock at sin."* Friend don't ever take sin lightly. If you crack the door, sin will kick it open. Paul reminds us in Romans 6:23, *"the wages of sin is death."* Like that snail, given the opportunity, given time, and given place, sin will consume you if you allow it.

But you might say, *"I have not given Satan my life"* - but have you given him a *place* in your life? Maybe you've not given him your marriage - but have you given him a *place* in your marriage? Hopefully you've not given him your home - but does he have a *place* in your home? Maybe not your heart - but does he have a *place* in your heart? Not your mind – but have you given him a *place* in your mind? If you've given him a place, you've given him opportunity. Room to work. A chance to interrupt and disrupt. You've given him a foothold, a place to dig in his heels.

Cain did it... When his offering was rejected. He gave the Devil place in the form of jealousy and pride. After which, he did the unthinkable. He killed his brother.

David did it... When he sent for Bathsheba. He gave the Devil place in the form of ego and lust. And thus began a domino effect of terrible choices that ended with the death of her husband.

Moses did it... When he struck the rock. He gave the Devil place in the form of frustration and unbelief. His journey ended at the border. He would see the promised land but never possess it.

Judas did it... When he conspired with the Enemy for thirty pieces of silver. He gave the Devil place through greed and pretense. He lost his mind and then took his life.

Peter did it... When he stood with the enemy. He gave the Devil place through doubt and compromise. He could have never imagined all that God had in store for him. To borrow a thought from Vance Havner, Peter was playing marbles with diamonds.

Ananias and Sapphira did it... When they hid the money and lied about what they had done. They gave the Devil place in the form of secrecy and hypocrisy. They lied to God and lost their lives. Secret sin often does more damage than public disregard. Guard your heart.

How do we take back the place we've given the Devil?

Put Off

In Ephesians 4:22 Paul writes, *"Put off...the old man which grows corrupt according to the deceitful lusts."* Paul paints a word picture of repentance. He describes it like taking off dirty clothes. Imagine Lazarus living in his old graveclothes. Putting off. Taking off, Turning off. Knowing you'll be better off.

Put On

In Ephesians 4:24 Paul writes, *"Put on the new man which was created according to God, in true righteousness and holiness."* Paul helps us visualize a man who has turned from his old ways, and now has a renewed desire to walk in the will of God. Like putting on new clothes… clothed in righteousness. The Gadarene demoniac, after being cleansed by the Lord, clothed himself immediately. One size fits all. You'll never put on righteousness, and it not fit. You can't buy these clothes – they are given by God.

Put Away

In Ephesians 4:25 Paul writes, "Putting away lying…" Following his admonition regarding lying he describes at least twelve sins from which we are to turn. I am sure you see the order in which Paul describes our living a life pleasing to God. We are to put off, put on, and put away. I would also believe this is an ongoing, daily putting off, putting on, and putting away. Paul is describing an active and intentional resisting of the Devil. This is putting away as in throwing away. Putting away as in turning away. It is a spiritual cleaning-out. Tearing down strongholds is never easy. If you think getting your house in order is easy, I doubt that you have ever actually done that. Putting off and putting away requires a lifetime of Jesus-loving diligence.

4:25 PUT AWAY LYING

Be Honest. And while we're being honest, can we agree that honesty isn't all that popular today? Paul writes, *"Let each one of you speak truth with his neighbor…"* Imagine all the drama that could be prevented if we were more honest in our dealings with each other. In fact, if everyone was more honest, there's a good chance the news outlets would have very little to cover. Imagine all the marriages that could be saved with honesty. Imagine all the political corruption that could be avoided if the people leading our country were honest. Imagine how carefree and guiltless our lives would be if they were lived more honestly. Imagine the impact on the family if our children could look at us as parents knowing we were men and women of integrity. The devil is a liar and the father of lies. Jesus is the truth, and the truth sets men free. We're either controlled by dishonesty and deception or we're walking in truth and transparency. It's been said that a lie has no legs, but it sure has wings. If so, may God help us clip the wings of the lie and give place to honesty.

4:26 PUT AWAY ANGER

Be Understanding. What if we, in the words of Glenn Campbell, were to "try a little kindness?" I am amazed at the anger today in and among politicians, political parties, families, marriages, and total strangers. If you disagree with someone today, it's not unheard of to take out your anger on them or their property. I graduated from high school in 1981. Most guys at that time carried a knife and many of those who drove a truck had a rifle or two mounted behind the seat. In my three years of high school no one was stabbed or shot. We had a few fist fights, but no one that I can remember ever pulled a gun. My, how times have changed. How do we go back to being more reasonable and less angry? Take away guns? Absolutely not. Turn our disagreements over to God? Yes. Paul writes, *"Be angry and sin not."* He is describing putting away the wrong kind of anger and controlling the right kind. The kind of anger that honors God doesn't throw a tantrum. It is patient and even kind. It disagrees with wrong but does so with a humble spirit. This anger may stand against someone or something, but it does so in obedience to God, and because it is morally sound, and because it is biblically sound. The Apostle Paul was no wimp. He wasn't soft. But neither was he mean spirited. Once the Lord changed his heart, he learned to agree with James who wrote, *"Be swift to hear, slow to speak, and slow to anger"* (James 1:19).

4:28 PUT AWAY LAZINESS

Be Trustworthy. I know I've already mentioned my dad a few times in this book. But he was a great example to me as a father, a husband, and as a man. He worked for a living. He never expected a handout. He didn't stand in line to get something free. When housing was slowed in the late 70s, instead of receiving a check from the government, he went to work at a cabinet shop for $5 an hour. He worked that job until the home building industry picked back up. He could have easily depended on someone else to take care of him. But he had something that is severely missing today – he had a work ethic. He had character. He was a man of integrity. If he owed you money, he would pay what was owed. I admire him for many reasons, but his willingness to work when he could have coasted causes pride to swell within me. Surely some of that resilience rubbed off on me. As I sit at my desk and type these words, it's just after lunch on a warm, sunny Wednesday. No one is watching over my shoulder to make sure I am working. Something beckons me to work. Something calls me to be worthy of my hire. I consider these urgings to be a combination of conviction of the Holy Spirit and the example of a good father. We have raised up a generation that don't and won't work. A generation that feels entitled, expects to be fed and clothed, and demands to be paid with the money that another man earns by the sweat of his brow. Jesus helped people who couldn't help themselves and we should too. Paul admonishes believers to provide for themselves, and for *"him who has need."* He is far from mean spirited. He has the Holy Spirit and good sense. We desperately need both. Paul wrote, *"Let him labor, working with his hands..."* The greatest cure for theft and laziness is hard work.

4:29 PUT AWAY CORRUPT COMMUNICATION

Be Considerate. Paul is not speaking only of profanity; he is dealing with any kind of corrupt communication. In most churches the problem with bad language is not the use of profanity, but that of a gossiping tongue. More damage has been done through gossip than profanity. A gossip is someone who knows what they're saying isn't the truth. Surely gossip must be a form of profanity because it certainly brings no glory to God. Jesus said in Matthew 15:18, it's not what goes into your mouth that defiles you but what comes out of your mouth - because what comes out of your mouth begins in the heart. If you speak profanity, it comes from your heart. If you speak slander, it comes from your heart. If you spread gossip, it comes from your heart. Guard your heart. Pride demands we tell others what we know about someone or something. Or what we think. Or what we assume. Paul motivates believers to not only abstain from corrupt language, but to speak that which imparts grace to those listening. May God help us guard our heart that we might speak words that please the Lord.

4:30 PUT AWAY GRIEVING THE HOLY SPIRIT

Be Surrendered. Paul also warned about quenching the Holy Spirit in 1 Thessalonians 5:19, and in Acts 7:51 Stephen spoke of resisting the Holy Spirit. But here Paul includes this reprimand in his lengthy list of things to put away. Do not grieve the Holy Spirit. Quenching the Holy Spirit is when we attempt to do God's work without His power. Resisting the Holy Spirit is just that, resisting that which is not irresistible. Grieving the Holy Spirit, however, is different in that we acknowledge Him but don't allow Him to lead. Some define this phrase as "disappointing God," and rightfully so as the word means to make sorrowful. Alexander MacLaren described this sin as - not cooperating with God. Jesus said the Holy Spirit would guide believers into all truth. When we refuse to cooperate with the Holy Spirit, we are choosing to live in less than the truth. I don't have a horse, but I have a friend who does. When he rides, he talks about letting the horse run. Grieving the Holy Spirit is like holding back on the reins. As believers, we hold back on the reins of the Holy Spirit because we want to be in control. And because, if we let go of the reins, we don't know where the horse will run. Yet when we hold back on the reins and grieve the Holy Spirit, we are missing the adventure of allowing Him to take us where we need to go. We can only imagine what we miss by holding back on the reins. God help us to do as my friend and let the horse run!

4:31 PUT AWAY BITTERNESS, WRATH, ANGER, CLAMOR, EVIL SPEAKING, AND MALICE.

Be Forgiving. Wow, that's quite a list of things to put away. It appears Paul had preached too long and decided to sum up the remainder of his sermon in one verse. He warns in one simple verse of six actions to take. But these six exhortations all have one thing in common; they are places we give to the Devil. Places where we give him room to work. And over time, these sins become burdensome. Get rid of bitterness – let go of unforgiveness. Put away wrath – stop walking around with a chip on your shoulder. Put away anger – stop looking for a fight. Put away clamor – why be so demanding? Stop with the slander – stop tearing other people down. Put away malice – put away evil intentions. I would imagine Paul's sermons fell on both receptive hearts and dull ears. Even in our day there are those who want their preacher to preach the Bible – until he does. These are hard warnings and verse 31, in particular, feels confrontational. But is it? Not if you continue reading into the next verse. Could it be Paul is writing with the heart of a pastor? Could it be he is writing to protect and care for these believers? Could it be these hard words are written for their own good?

Think about living the kind of life Paul wrote about. Someone might ask you, Did you lose weight? Did you get a haircut? Is that a new dress? Is that a new shirt? You might reply, no… I just put away lying, anger, laziness, corrupt communication, grieving the Holy Spirit, bitterness, wrath, anger, clamor, evil speaking, and malice. I stopped being a troublemaker and started being a peace maker. I got over myself. I forgave my neighbor, and I asked forgiveness from those I had hurt. I sought holiness and found happiness

So, if we're not going to give place to the Devil, what should we do? I'm glad you asked. I think Paul gives us clear directions how we can give place to Jesus.

Give Jesus Place!

4:32 *"Be kind…tender-hearted…forgiving one another."*
Imagine what your life would look like if Jesus had first place. What if you gave Him first place and everything else was at least second? What if, instead of giving the Devil room to work, we give Jesus all the room He wants?

Give Him place…And He will give us the power to do all He commands us to do. What if we sought first the kingdom of God? What if we acknowledged Him in all our ways?

He Took Our Place!

Romans 5:8 *"…While we were yet sinners Christ died for us."* We should give Jesus place because He took our place. He took a place that didn't belong to Him. He bore sin and guilt that was not His. He who knew no sin took up the cross, took our shame, and then took our place.

He's Prepared For Us A Place!

John 14:2 *"I go to prepare a place for you…"* We should give Jesus place because He's gone to prepare for us a place. There may be many roads that lead to Chicago, but there's only one way to get to Heaven. There is no other name by which we are saved. He's prepared a place for us and prepared a way for us to go there. He is the Way. All we must do is trust Him.

Give Jesus Place. Give Him First Place.

CHAPTER 5 DISCUSSION POINTS

How does a person give *"place"* to the Devil?

In Ephesians 4:22, 24, 25 Paul wrote about *"putting off,"* *"putting on,"* and *"putting away."* How is this spiritual warfare?

Concerning all that Paul says believers are to *"put away,"* discuss how each of these can be a *"place"* given to the Devil.

From Ephesians 4:32, discuss what giving *"place"* to Jesus looks like.

6

THE DEVIL'S PLAYBOOK

1 John 2:15-17, Matthew 4:3-10

W hy make such a big deal about the Devil? I believe that is a great question and I have a great answer: Because Jesus did. Jesus believed in the Devil. If Jesus believed in him, so should we. Billy Sunday said, "I believe in the Devil because the Bible says so, and because I've done business with him."

Peter said the Devil seeks to devour. 1 Peter 5:8

Paul said the Devil wars against believers. Ephesians 6:11

Paul wrote that Satan transforms himself as an angel of light. 2 Corinthians 11:14

Jesus said the Devil would sift Peter like wheat. Luke 22:31

Jesus said Satan was the father of lies. John 8:44

God said Satan is more subtle than any creature He made. Genesis 3:1

Paul wrote that Satan blinds the minds of unbelievers. 2 Corinthians 4:4

Jesus said the Thief kills, steals, and destroys. John 10:10

James reminded us that Satan believes in God and trembles. James 2:19

Satan is good at what he does: tempting, deceiving, accusing and more. He is more subtle, craftier, and more cunning than any creature the Lord made. 1 John 2:16 describes the tools of his trade. They are used by him in every tempting opportunity. These are what I call the power-plays of the Devil. John describes these power-plays as the lust of the flesh, lust of the eyes, and the pride of life. I like to imagine Satan has one playbook yet only three plays. He keeps running the same plays because - they work. He does whatever is necessary to deceive, disrupt, and destroy. In the wilderness, Matthew 4:3-10, Satan threw the book at Jesus, so to speak. Our Lord faced every temptation that any of us will ever experience. And He refused them all. He resisted the power-plays of the Enemy by standing on the Word of God. James 1:12 tells us, *"Blessed is the man who endures temptation."* There is so much to learn from Jesus' response to the Devil in the wilderness. But we must acknowledge that even Jesus stood on the authority of Scripture. If Jesus stood on the Word, how much more should we.

The Lust of the Flesh...is the Temptation to DO Something.

The lust of the flesh is the desires of our sinful nature. How does that look in real life? Remember Samson? He was the strongest man in the world, but he couldn't control his own sinful desires. Given the opportunity, the lust of our flesh will confuse our knowledge of God and compromise our fellowship with God.

Jesus' temptation in the wilderness is the perfect example of what it is like to be tempted with the lust of the flesh. In Matthew 4:3 Jesus was tempted to, *"Turn these stones into bread..."* Why was this such a fiery dart for the enemy to throw? Because Jesus was hungry. He had been fasting. He was the Son of God, yet he was hungry like any of us would have been. As a believer in Christ, saved by God's grace, and filled with the Spirit I need to be reminded - the flesh is not dead. Sin is not dead. The Devil is not dead. But as Paul said, we are to *"reckon ourselves to be dead unto sin…"*

Galatians 5:17 describes the battle. How does this battle work? It's like that well-known dog fight, we've heard about, within us between the flesh and Spirit. It's our choice, every day, which dog we feed. It is our choice whether we obey the flesh or the Spirit. None of us will ever be tempted to turn stones into bread because that's something none of us can do. But we will be tempted with something we <u>can</u> do. I don't think the Devil will ever tempt me to steal an airplane. Why? Because I don't know how to fly one. I don't think the Enemy will ever tempt me to rob a bank. Why? Because I don't know how. I believe the Devil will tempt us with opportunities to do things that we can do, things that are accessible, things that are available, things that I know how to do and have the ability to do. Things like lying, lust, greed, revenge, slander. Jesus could have turned the stones into bread but if He had He would have been less than Lord, and Satan would have won. Jesus stood on the Word and resisted the enemy. God help us stand with Him.

The choice is ours as we read in Galatians 5:16, *"Walk in the Spirit and you will not fulfill the lusts of the flesh."* Someone has well said being a Christian would be easier it wasn't so daily. Daily walking with Jesus. Daily resisting the Enemy. Daily listening to the Spirit. Daily denying the flesh. Daily in God's Word. Daily in prayer. Paul wrote, *"Walk in the Spirit…"* That's every day. All day. Walking in the Spirit is like getting an alignment on your car. If we don't walk in the power and under the leadership of the Holy Spirit, we will veer to the right or the left. Walking in the Spirit means aligning ourselves with God's will.

The Lust of the Eyes…is the Temptation to HAVE Something.

It is desiring what we see. Remember Achan? He took of what was accursed and brought defeat on the whole camp of Israel. In Joshua chapter six, before he led the nation of Israel to destroy Jericho,

Joshua instructed them specifically, in 6:19, not to take for themselves any of the spoils of war. But Achan disobeyed God.
According to his own words in Joshua 7:21, he took, *"…a beautiful
Babylonian garment, 200 shekels of silver and a wedge of gold weighing fifty
shekels."* Following their amazing victory at Jericho they were driven
away and defeated by a much smaller army at Ai. Why? There was
sin in their midst. God clearly spoke to Joshua saying they would not
be able to stand against their enemies until the accursed thing was
removed (7:13). What was Achan thinking? I believe we all know
what he was thinking. He was thinking no-one-will-ever-know. That
has to be one of the greatest lies the Devil has ever told. He must
have thought, who's going to miss a garment, some silver, a little
gold? The truth is the garment was worthless, but the silver and gold
were consecrated to the Lord and would be brought into the trea-
sury of the Lord. But the issue at hand is not the value of the silver
and gold or even the consecration of it to God – it was an act of
disobedience to the word of the Lord. This power play of the Devil
is hard to resist. This lust of the eyes is one of the Enemy's greatest
tools. This lust drives us to pursue what we see regardless of the
rules. Achan couldn't un-see these spoils of war. The problem,
however, was not in the seeing but in the lusting. And in the taking.
And in the hiding of these things in his tent. For a while he was one
of the richest men on earth. For a few days he had silver and gold.
Sin often brings immediate happiness, but never leads to lasting
fulfillment. Achan's sin brought defeat to Israel. And it brought
death to him and his family. Guard your eyes against the lust of the
flesh.

But Achan wasn't the first one to follow after the lust of his eyes and
he won't be the last. King David did the same, causing him to go
after Bathsheba. Judas lusted with his eyes, making a deal for thirty
pieces of silver. Ananias and Sapphira did it and lied to God about
the money they kept back. It's the lusting of our eyes that breeds
covetousness and gluttonous living and keeps us from walking with
Jesus. It is desiring and pursuing anything contrary to the will of
God. Achan was probably making plans as to how he would spend
his newfound wealth. I imagine David was already making plans for

romantic evenings with Bathsheba. Judas may have been planning his life after Jesus. Ananias and Sapphira probably thought they had made a good business decision. But all of them gave into the lust of the eyes. But what about me? What about you? Where is it in my life that I have been drawn away by the lust of my own eyes?

How do we resist? Jesus is the perfect example. In Matthew 4:8 Satan showed the King of Kings all the kingdoms of the world and promised it could all be His if He would "fall down and worship me." While this is not a funny story, we must not miss the humor in it. Satan is offering Jesus something He already possessed. He is offering the King of all kings and all kingdoms that of which He is already Lord, King, and Master. This was certainly not one of Satan's best moments. He had met his match and much more. Jesus quoted scripture and the Devil left Him alone. For us it is often the greener grass of bigger and better that lures us away. Notice it was what Satan showed him. What is it Satan is showing you? What is the Enemy promising you? Just keep this in mind, that greener grass is most often artificial turf. Stay where you are.

Matthew 6:22 describes the problem. Jesus said the eye is the lamp of the body. *"If your eye is bad, your whole body will be full of darkness."* Eyes of lust, greed, and covetousness darken the whole person. In Matthew 5:29 Jesus said, *"If your right eye causes you to sin, pluck it out and cast it from you; for it is more profitable for you that one of your members perish, than for your whole body to be cast into Hell."* But thank God the good news application for this verse is this: You can keep your eye if you'll just give Jesus your heart. Give him your life and surrender to Him your eyes. In the following verse, 5:30, Jesus makes the same point about cutting off your hand. Again, I believe the greater call is to keep your eyes and hands and use them for the glory of God. Give Him your heart and life, use your eyes to see His goodness, and use your hands to serve His purpose.

The Choice is Ours. In Job 31:1 we read, *"I have made a covenant with my eyes not to look lustfully on a woman."* John Gill said, "Job entered into a solemn engagement with himself - not to employ his eyes in looking on objects that might ensnare his heart…" Job was already in agreement with God, but he went further and made an agreement with himself. If this sin were only a lust for material objects, the remedy would be simpler. This sin seldom confines itself to material possessions only. This sin seeps its way into unhappy marriages causing men and women to lust after someone else's wife or husband.

Too often, like Achan's sin in Jericho, we see it, want it, take it, and hide it. I have learned over these many years of ministry few of us, if any, are very good at hiding our sin. What's done in secret somehow always becomes public. The public knowledge of private sin begins to wreck homes, divide families, destroy character, and derail future plans. David's sin was covered as well as anyone's could have been. Then Nathan knocked on his door. God told him to go and told him what to say. Nathan may not have known the intimate details of all that happened between David and Bathsheba, but he went and delivered the message. God has a way of bringing to light what had been held in secret. Friend, if you have followed the lust of your eyes to a place you shouldn't be – run for your life. Go home while you can.

How does this lust of the eyes progress? Better yet, how does it begin? Most likely it begins with an innocent, unintentional glance. If that's the case, we must look the other way. If the glance becomes an imagination we must, as Paul said, catch our thoughts. If these thoughts begin to interrupt our life to the point of controlling us, we must have an honest conversation with ourselves. But it's hard to be honest with ourselves when we are involved in something that makes us feel so good. Yes, sin makes us feel good – it is the satisfying of the flesh. Our ego is inflated, our confidence is abundant, our outlook is bright. Oh, but it is only for a season. The brightness will eventually fade to darkness. Reality will set in, and like David, we will weep over our sin. But an honest conversation with ourselves could prevent us from ever going down that road. The prodigal son had that talk with himself after he came to his senses. He soon went back home. Along with that honest conversation about what you can and cannot do because of your faith in God, and because of who she is and who you are, and because it's morally wrong, and because it's biblically wrong, and because you're making decisions based on fantasy not reality – you should also make a covenant with your eyes. Job did. Again, in 31:1 we read, *"I have made a covenant with my eyes; Why then should I look upon a young woman?"* I believe Job not only made a covenant with his eyes, but also a promise to himself, and a renewed commitment to God. I would do well to be like Job and not only make a covenant with my eyes, but also my mouth, my ears, my mind, and my heart.

The Pride of Life...the Temptation to BE Something.

I'd like to begin this section with a unique spelling of the word pride. The I in the middle of the word is uppercase and looks like this: **prIde**. Why emphasize the letter I? Because pride always caters to what I want and what I need. David Allen says the pride of life is like standing in front of one of those multi-sided mirrors in a department store so you can see yourself in that new suit or dress. When you look into that mirror, everywhere you look - you see you. The pride of life is me-centered. My wish is my command. The pride of life ignores the needs of others. The pride of life makes me the priority. The pride of life couldn't care less how badly others are treated. The pride of life crowns us either king or queen and bows to all we want, dream, wish, or expect.

Tony Evans told the story of Muhammad Ali and his refusal to wear a seatbelt on an airplane. As the story goes, Muhammad Ali and a few of his friends were on a plane about to take off. The stewardess came by and asked him to buckle his seatbelt. Ali responded, "Superman don't need no seatbelt!" The stewardess then responded, "Superman don't need no airplane." Touché. The pride of life makes a man think he's Superman. Makes a woman think she's Wonderwoman. The pride of life will try and convince us we are invincible.

David Allen says the pride of life is the "...arrogant spirit of self-sufficiency. It expresses the desire for recognition, applause, status, and advantage in life. This word in Greek translated pride describes the pretentious braggart." Wow, what a description. Sounds like the man or woman who can't stop talking about themselves. They love to hear themselves talk. But the truth is like the proud preacher who asked his wife, "Just how many good preachers are there?" She responded, "One less than you think."

The pride of life is an exaggerated view of pleasure, possessions, and position. Pride in and of itself is a good quality to possess. Think of the father and mother who are proud parents, proud of their children, and proud of their children's accomplishments. Think of the pride in a job well done. The pride that comes by finally graduating from college. There is so much good pride such as that of American pride, pride in your favorite team, being proud of a new home or a new car. But this pride of life isn't referring to being proud of your life. This pride is a demeaning, arrogant, selfish attitude that causes one to feel superior to others. From the *Jamieson-Fausset-Brown Bible Commentary* I found this description of the pride of life: "arrogant assumption; vainglorious display." As you think about those words, do they in any way describe you? What a sad state of mind in which to be. That assumption is two-pronged in that it assumes the worst in others and the best in ourselves. This pride never ends well. Adrian Rogers said, "There has never been an argument, a war, a divorce, or a church split—which was not caused by pride." The vainglorious display mentioned earlier is that of domineering and condescending assurance that I am right and you are wrong. Oh, my friend, the Devil is good at what he does. In arguments, wars, divorces, and church splits where the pride of life is calling the shots, nobody wins – everybody loses.

Pleasure

2 Timothy 3:4 warns about being *"lovers of pleasure rather than lovers of God."* Think about the pleasure of winning – and the pleasure of someone else losing. I'm not referring to a ballgame or a race. The pride of life mentioned in scripture is that which rejoices when someone else loses in life. The pride of life intends to win at all costs.

Losing is not an option. Their car is not only fast, but also faster than yours. Their job is not just good, it's better than yours. Honestly, this is a sad condition for any of us who find ourselves bound by it. The times when I have been guilty, the pride of life was actually a cover for some other inadequacy I felt at the time. This pride shows up at little league baseball tryouts, job interviews, junior high school talent shows, community beauty pageants, political races, husband and wife disagreements, and church business meetings just to name a few. Maybe you know of someone who always has to be right even if it means losing a friend. And maybe you know someone who is always chasing happiness but never finds joy. That, my friend, is a person consumed with the pride of life.

Possessions

In Revelation 3:17 we read that the church of Laodicea boasted about being *"rich, increased with goods, and needing nothing."* Not only is that an accurate description of Laodicea, it is also a clear picture of where America and the church is today. It appears, even though we need nothing, we're always wanting something. We may even refer to what we have as "living the good life." Someone looks at what another person possesses and says they've got it made. What did Jesus say about accumulating possessions? In Luke 12:15, Jesus said to them, *"Take heed and beware of covetousness, for one's life does not consist in the abundance of the things he possesses."* Preach that in most churches and you'll get a hearty amen. But go home with many of those who said amen and you'll see an abundance of possessions. The truth is, many of us live as if life really does consist of the abundance of the things which we possess. Our extra bedrooms are filled with more than enough of everything. Our garages are filled. Our closets are filled. Our attics are filled. We even build extra buildings to store our possessions. We have things that belonged to parents, grandparents, and great, great grandparents. We don't need what is passed down to us, but we don't want anyone else getting it. The pride of life beams as we describe to others all we possess. If you know of someone that is always accumulating but never finding contentment, you know someone who is bound by the pride of life.

Position

In Acts 8:9-24 we read of Simon the Sorcerer who tried to buy the power of God. Peter described him as being *"poisoned by bitterness and bound by iniquity."* I wonder how many today are as the sorcerer was, poisoned by bitterness and bound by iniquity? I have been saddened to see good people sacrifice family and values for a better position in life and at work. They've climbed the ladder to the top only to find out it wasn't worth the price they paid to get there. What benefit is a bigger title, a larger office, a greater expense budget, and a company car if you lose your family and forsake your values to get them? Certainly not everyone who succeeds in business sacrifices their family. But rising to the top often means something must play second fiddle and sadly, it's often the family. I have a feeling when each of us is facing eternity we won't be wishing we'd spent more time at work. We will embrace the time we have and thank God for family, friends, and faith to cross over to the other side. May God help us guard our heart against sacrificing what matters for what doesn't. If you know of someone who has climbed to the top of the ladder and they're still not fulfilled, learn from their emptiness. Being on top of the world isn't all it's cracked up to be.

Again, Jesus' temptation is the perfect example of the pride of life. In Matthew 4:5 we read about Jesus being tempted to throw himself down. He was told the angels would be summoned to catch him. Someone has said if God tells you to jump off a cliff, He will either catch you or teach you to fly. But this isn't God telling Jesus to jump. It is Satan himself. Jesus had no reason to jump, nothing to prove, and nothing to gain. He was already Lord and to jump would not have made Him any more King than He already was. To jump would have been an act of tempting God. Jesus responded with the scriptures, *"You shall not tempt the Lord your God."*

Satan is still tempting people to jump off a cliff. And people are still jumping. There's something exhilarating about the initial jump. Something exciting about leaping into temptation. There's even the thrill of the flight. But you and I know the hardest part about the jump is the landing. I hear of so many, who after years of faithfully serving God take the leap into temptation. Believing they're invincible. Believing the lie of the Devil. Friend, if you're on the pinnacle, about to take the leap into what you know to be wrong, please step back from the edge. Cry out to God for help. Walk away from the temptation. Run for your life. Fall on your knees and thank God that He gave you strength to turn from doing the unthinkable.

This temptation to throw Himself down was unique in that Satan also quoted scripture by paraphrasing Psalm 91:11-12. Talk about being more subtle than any creature that God made, Satan is good at what he does. He's using scripture to tempt Jesus. He's using the Word of God to temp the Son of God. He's using the spoken Word to bring down the living Word. If the Devil tempted Jesus with scripture back then, don't think he won't use the Bible to fit his agenda to bring you down today. Matthew 4:5 begins, *"Then the Devil took Him up..."* I feel compelled to point out the obvious – the Devil couldn't have taken Jesus up if He was not willing to go. The Devil may have taken Him, but Jesus went submitting Himself to temptation just as He would submit Himself to the cross. The Devil couldn't take Jesus anywhere outside of the Father's will. Jesus was tempted in all points as we are and still, He did not sin (Hebrews 4:15).

Satan tempted Jesus to be what He already was. Lord. Master. King. He was tempting Jesus to tempt the Father. Jesus didn't take the bait. For us, I believe this is the temptation to be significant, important, to have rock-star status, and to gain the applause of the world. It is the defying of God, shaking our fist in His face while surrendering our values and convictions. We see it in politics. Sometimes we see it in ourselves in the prevailing attitude of not needing God, not seeking God, not trusting in God. The temptation is to rely on ourselves, our name, our wealth or at least the appearance of it. The pride of life is alive and well.

The Choice is Ours. 1 Peter 5:6 *"Humble yourself under the mighty hand of God that He may exalt you in due time."* Our job is to humble ourselves. Exalting us is God's business. Exalting ourselves never leads to humility. But humility before God leads to the blessing and favor of God. I have a simple choice to either humble myself or exalt myself. Those in the Bible who promoted themselves reaped a harvest of heartache and disappointment. Pursuing humility is like chasing a greased pig; it's hard to get your hands on it. Once you finally get to the place where you have humility, the admission of your victory causes you to lose the thing you so treasured. The great preacher Charles Spurgeon said, "Pride is so natural to fallen man that it springs up in his heart like weeds in a watered garden…It is an all-pervading sin, and smothers all things like dust in the roads, or flour in the mill. If killed it revives, if buried it bursts the tomb. You may hunt down this fox, and think you have destroyed it, and lo! your very exultation is pride" (Spurgeon.org). No one sins against God without first submitting to the pride of life. It hinders the preacher from preaching and the singer from singing. It hinders the church from growing. It hinders the Gospel from spreading. It's like fuel on the fire of divorce, unforgiveness, resentment, and jealousy. It is as relentless as the Devil himself. He never takes a day off and neither does the pride of life. Buckle up and, as Alistair Begg said, "Keep your chin up and your knees down."

Friend, we've covered a lot of ground these last few pages. Ground that I fear many of us are not afraid to walk over. These power plays of the Devil are so prevalent that we've become accustomed to the compromise they bring. I wish somehow, I could convey passion as I type these words – brother and sister in Christ, guard your heart! Guard your family! Guard your home! The Enemy is on the warpath. You might ask, what can we do? I have a simple response as I close out this chapter. Simple, yes. But simply powerful. Look with me at three power-positions of the believer.

Power-Positions of the Believer... Standing on the Word. Kneeling in Prayer. Lifting your hands.

What do we do when the Enemy throws the book at us? When we're on the receiving end of his fiery darts? When his power-plays are coming at us full-speed? When the hounds of Hell are on our trail? When we're on the front lines living for God dodging bullets left and right, what do we do? Is there any hope?

Stand on the Word

When the Devil begins to hurl his fiery arrows at us, do we stand on the Word or run for our life? When I was younger it was common to hear someone referred to as a godly man or a godly woman. Where are the men and women of God today? Where are those godly saints who are walking with the Lord and standing on His word? In Hebrews 4:12 we read, *"The Word is living and powerful and sharper than any two-edged sword."* A two-edged sword cuts both ways. Obviously, it is a weapon, but it is also a means of protection. A sword, in and of itself, has no conscience. It cuts whatever it touches. The Word of God, like a sword, affects whomever it touches. The word of God not only calls the lost to be saved, but it also calls the saved to repentance. It cuts both ways. May God help us stand on the Word of God. The Word of God is the will of God. We will never know the will of God outside the Word of God. God's plans are different for each of us, but His will is the same for all of us. Stand on His Word and you are standing in His will.

Kneel in Prayer

There is no substitute for humbling ourselves in prayer. My fear is we talk more about prayer than we actually pray. We sing about prayer, have conferences on prayer, preach sermon series on prayer, and even have nights and places designated in our churches for prayer. But with all that said, are we praying? Are we seeking the plans of God? Are we lifting up our children and family and friends to be saved? Are we humbling ourselves as we petition the Lord for direction in making decisions? Are we interceding on behalf of those who are sick or suffering? Are we praying? I know most of us believe in prayer especially when there's sickness, when there's a crisis in our nation, and when there's an urgent need in our families. But what about when we face the Enemy in battle? Do we take matters into our own hands or leave the battle in God's hands?

George Mueller was a prayer warrior with a heart for God. He said, "I live in the spirit of prayer. I pray as I walk about, when I lie down, and when I rise up. And the answers are always coming" Mueller was an unusual man. He lived what he believed. One morning at the orphanage he coordinated in Bristol England, he faced a crisis that has become a well-known story of his great faith. This account is found at georgemeuller.org: "'The children are dressed and ready for school. But there is no food for them to eat,' the housemother of the orphanage informed George Mueller. George asked her to take the 300 children into the dining room and have them sit at the tables. He thanked God for the food and waited. George knew God would provide food for the children as he always did. Within minutes, a baker knocked on the door. 'Mr. Mueller,' he said, 'last night I could not sleep. Somehow, I knew that you would need bread this morning. I got up and baked three batches for you. I will bring it in.' Soon, there was another knock at the door. It was the milkman. His cart had broken down in front of the orphanage. The milk would spoil by the time the wheel was fixed. He asked George if he could use some free milk. George smiled as the milkman brought in ten large cans of milk. It was just enough for the 300 thirsty children." When the Enemy throws you a curve, take it to the Lord in prayer. As Psalm 95:6 says, *"Oh come let us worship and bow down; Let us kneel before the Lord our maker."*

Lift Your Hands in Praise

Lifting our hands in praise is a sign of surrender, not to the Enemy but to God. With both hands raised high we declare that we lay down our weapons and we lay down our life to the One who is worthy of our praise. Hands lifted in surrender signifies I am yielding my will to God's will. It shows submission. It is turning over all I have held onto. It is trusting God with all my fears. It is bowing myself to the only King. In my preaching travels over the past few years since the pandemic, I have witnessed more lifted hands than ever before. As I see both young and old lifting their hands in worship, I get the idea people are desperate for God. The fear of dying has become greater than fearing of what others might think. And following the pandemic, the shift in our culture has been such that we feel compelled to worship or the rocks will cry out. The church is under attack along with the family. May the Lord be our source of strength in these troubling times. May we lift our hands, our hearts, and our hopes to Him. This is no time to compromise. There is no reason to hide. God help us, in response to the attacks from the Enemy, to surrender to the One who fights for us – Jesus our Lord. Lift your hands in praise! Lay down your weapons and trust the Lord to fight your battle! May we gladly embrace Psalm 134:2 that says, *"Lift up your hands in the sanctuary and bless the Lord."*

Finally, after looking at the power-plays of the Devil and thinking about the power-positions of the believer, I want us to place our confidence in the one powerful name that is above all names.

One Powerful Name...

Jesus, the name above all names

Spurgeon said, "I have a great need for Christ; I have a great Christ for my need." Our need is not greater than His name. Our sin is not greater than His salvation. Our guilt is not greater than His grace. When the Devil is on the warpath and you're in his crosshairs, call on the name of the Lord! Cry out to God in Jesus name! Pray with reckless abandon trusting God with an answer than only He can provide. I also love this quote by Augustine, "Christ is not valued at all unless He is valued above all." Oh, that we might place the greatest value on Him and our walk with Him. Lordship is a word that's thrown around often and sometimes carelessly. Lordship is when Jesus is first place in my life and everyone and everything else is at least second place. Put Him first before the fire, in the fire, and after the fire. Call on His mighty name when things make sense and when they don't. Love Him, live for Him, and leave the battle in His hands. Be reminded of what Philippians 2:9-11 says, *"Therefore God has highly exalted Him and given Him the name which is above every name, that at the name of Jesus every knee should bow, of those in Heaven, and of those on the earth, and of those under the earth, that every tongue should confess that Jesus Christ is Lord, to the glory of God the Father."*

Jesus is the One who silenced the Devil. Walked out of the grave. Took our sin and shame. Ascended to the heavens. And will one day come again. There is Victory in Jesus' name.

CHAPTER 6 DISCUSSION POINTS

Discuss how the *"lust of the flesh, lust of the eyes, and the pride of life"* are the power-plays of the Devil.

Discuss Galatians 5:17 and the practical daily application for believers.

From Job 31:1, how do we make a "covenant with our eyes?"

From 1 Peter 5:6 discuss the need for and the results of humbling ourselves *"under the mighty hand of God."*

Discuss the power-positions of the believer and how they prepare us for the Enemy.

THE DOMINO EFFECT OF SIN

Genesis 3:1-8

I n the Garden of Eden, one thing led to another. Sin works that way. The Devil may tempt you in some small matter that leads to something larger. But remember the Enemy is never interested in small victories alone. His goal is complete dominion. In the Garden of Eden, it all began with the enemy questioning what God had said. That's a red flag for sure, but the Devil is the adversary of Christians. We shouldn't doubt the lengths to which he will go to deceive believers. A popular term these days used in political conversations is the word propaganda. It's a big word with an ugly meaning. Propaganda is when a lie is dressed up as the truth. The Devil has been doing that since the Garden. *"Has God said…"* was a gateway temptation for Adam and Eve. Marijuana is a gateway drug. It opens the door for other drugs. Doubting God's Word is the gateway to complete unbelief. If Satan can cause us to doubt the authority of God's Word, he is doing that so we would ultimately doubt God Himself.

The domino effect had its way in the life of King David as well. One thing led to another and suddenly, like a tornado, a path of destruction was left behind. David's sin against God, Uriah, and Bathsheba began with a look. From 2 Samuel 11:2-4 we read that…He saw her…He inquired about her…He sent for her…He lay with her. Yes, there's more to the story. We also read, *"It happened in the spring of the year, at the time when kings go out to battle that…David remained in Jerusalem."* We can only guess why he chose to disengage himself. There is speculation as to why he remained behind. Some suggest a depressed spirit, some say he was weary of war, and some assume he stayed behind because of Bathsheba. Possibly he had seen her before, but no one knows. Assuming is a dangerous mental activity because the assumption lacks proof. Many a good man and woman have had their reputation tainted because of someone's assumptions. Still the fact remains, David wasn't where he should have been. If he had been at war with Joab, his servants, and all of Israel, chances are this sad event would have never taken place. The domino effect began as David was in a relaxed state of mind, thus making himself vulnerable.

The dominoes continue to fall. After their visit, Bathsheba is *"with child."* David set up a scenario where it would appear that Uriah was the father of the expected child. Twice, David tried to get Uriah to go home. As I have stated before, Uriah was more loyal to his priorities than David. Uriah wouldn't go home believing it was not the honorable thing to do. David then puts in play the unthinkable – He will make sure Uriah is placed on the front lines of the hottest battle so that he would be killed. Did David ever imagine doing this on that spring day when he saw Bathsheba and sent for her? I believe we can say with certainty, it never crossed his mind. The Devil is good at what he does. A man after God's heart took another man's wife and then took that man's life. Everybody needs a Nathan. God will use Nathan to help David see through the fog of his sin and his need to repent. David would be restored but he would never be the same. Sin takes its toll on a man.

In the history of God's Word being spoken and written, it has been questioned, doubted, hated, despised, burned, banned, and mocked, but it has never been silenced. Adam and Eve doubted what God had said. And nothing has changed. Satan is still tempting us to question what God has said, and we're still listening to his distractions. Sin is powerful. Once you allow sin, regardless of how small, you have allowed the Enemy access into your life. The Devil knows what he is doing. He is more subtle than any creature God made. What seemed so simple like fruit on a tree led to the tragic fall of man. Adam and Eve started a battle that still rages today. The choices they made continue to have an effect on all mankind. Call it the domino effect.

I remember some time ago watching a domino championship on TV. It wasn't a championship game of actually playing the game of dominoes, but a championship of players setting up thousands of dominos up in various designs and then watching them fall. The winner was the team that set up the most dominoes and had the most creative designs. As the team leader pushed that first domino over it was the beginning of several minutes of watching them fall one by one. As I watched I thought about the subtle power of sin – the domino effect of sin. Since the Garden of Eden, the Devil has been tempting man to commit just one sin at a time. One subtle thought. One innocent conversation. One insignificant act. But over time, oh the result. The great philosopher Andy Griffith said it well, "Oh what a tangled web we weave, when first we practice to deceive." When Andy said that he was quoting Sir Walter Scott from his poem, Marmion: A Tale of Flodden Field. The saying means what you might think: When we act or speak dishonestly, we create our own personal domino effect of complicated results that often lead to misery and heartache. As Scott so clearly pointed out, it is a tangled web of deceit. Once tangled, it is almost impossible to straighten out.

I have chosen four rhyming words to outline my thoughts for this chapter on the domino effect. We will look at the source of sin, the course of sin, the remorse sin brings, and the force of sin when allowed to continue. The force of sin led Jesus to die for the sin of all who would ever believe. In doing so He began a domino effect of another kind – that of confession, repentance, forgiveness, salvation, joy, peace, and eternal life. To God be the glory.

The Source of Sin
Genesis 3:1-5

Sin originates in a mistrust of God. Think about it, every sin that someone commits is an act of not trusting God. Whether it is a sin of something I shouldn't be doing or a sin of something I should be doing, I am not trusting God's help and direction. Adam and Eve trusted the query of the Enemy rather than trusting the Words of God. They weren't the only ones. Think about both Abraham and Isaac when they lied saying their wives Sarah and Rebecca were their sisters (Genesis 20:2, 26:7). Think about Jacob taking Esau's birthright and blessing (Genesis 27:36). Think about David taking Uriah's wife Bathsheba (2 Samuel 11:3-4). Think about Peter's denial (Matthew 26:69-74) .Think about Judas' betrayal (Matthew 27:3). Think about Ananias and Sapphira's dishonesty (Acts 5:3,9). Each of these well-known people in the scriptures acted out of mistrust in God. They knew better and did the worse. They knew right and did wrong. Sin, great or small, begins as an act of disobedience to God. Others may get hurt in the crossfire, but it is ultimately a sin against God. Regarding the source of sin, let's look at three things the serpent said that caused Adam and Eve to doubt God.

He asked a loaded Question: *"Has God said..?"* (Genesis 3:1). Satan doesn't hesitate to question what God has said. It is an effort to cause doubt and create confusion. He knew what God said, yet the temptation was made as if he didn't. We must learn from these verses, what God says is absolute truth. God's word doesn't change to fit a progressive culture. God's word doesn't change fit a political agenda. God's word doesn't change to fit a liberal theology. A hundred years ago in the early twenties most folks were still traveling in horse and buggy, some had automobiles, and many walked. We've seen so many changes over the years. It's true, times have changed, but people haven't. And the Devil hasn't changed one bit.

He's still tempting us to doubt God. But God hasn't changed either. The Devil is still a liar and Jesus is still Lord.

He made a subtle Suggestion: *"You will not surely die"* (Genesis 3:4). Isn't it amazing how Satan works? Often, we're lured into sin by the simplest of suggestions. The mere possibility of eating the forbidden and not dying opened untold realms of possibility. They must have imagined if God wasn't honest about the tree and the fruit, what else has He been dishonest about? If what the serpent said was true, then all barriers were removed. There was nothing forbidden. All trees were accessible and good for food. Not only does Satan promise you won't die, but he also promises you won't get caught. It's almost as if he opens new ideas and new opportunities. Satan is busy today in the sacred arena of sexuality. He's still lying. He's telling men they can be women and telling women they can be men. Telling men they can marry another man and telling women they can marry another woman. Telling men and women if they don't want the child they've created they can abort it even in the last moments of birth. He's still busy promoting every kind of sexual sin imaginable. Sexual standards based on the Word of God have been all but obliterated. Little girls and little boys are being told they're neither boys or girls. One day when they're older they can decide their gender. Oh, my goodness, may God send revival. The Devil is busy seeking to erase the unchanging truth of God's Word. *"Has God said…?"*

He captivated their Attention: *"For God knows that in the day you eat of it your eyes will be opened, and you will be like God, knowing good and evil* (Genesis 3:5). There is something captivating about the possibility of experiencing what was previously forbidden. The Devil works in the same way today he did back then. Do this and you will be rich! Do this and you will be happy! Do this and you can have anything you want! And our imagination is prone to run wild. We want to be happy with no regrets. Imagine this: What if the Devil was honest? Imagine a fisherman being honest with a fish he's trying to catch. He drops a bare hook in front of him and says, "Hey Mr. fish, I want you to bite this hook. When you do it's going to sting for a minute. After you're hooked, I'm going to yank on the line, pull you up out of the water, remove the hook from your lip then put you in what we call "the live well." After that, I'm going to put you on ice. Then we're going to cut off your head and remove your insides and then we're going to have what's known as a fish fry. You will be our honored guest. No! The fisherman isn't honest with the fish. He deceives him with a lure. He dresses up the hook to look like anything but a hook. He lies to the fish and makes the hook look innocent. And so does the Devil. He is a liar and the author of confusion. He seeks to devour. He dresses up a lie to look like the truth.

The Course of Sin
Genesis 3:6

The domino effect of sin not only hurts you, but it also hurts those around you. Sin in your life causes others around you to also rebel against God. It's been said, you have to let sin run its course. And if you do, sin will run its course and take down everyone in its path. Someone must stop the advance of sin. Someone must demolish the stronghold. In Genesis 3:6 we read of Eve who, "...*took of its fruit and ate. She also gave to her husband with her, and he ate.*" The course of sin is when we not only partake but encourage others to do the same. Sin is seldom if ever self-contained. If a father is prone to alcohol, don't be surprised if the son shares his father's bad habit. If a mother is not interested in church, don't be surprised if the daughter has no interest as well. Most men who drink have a drinking buddy. Birds of a feather flock together. We seldom sin in isolation. Dad and Mom, you're either leading your children to God or pulling them away. You can't walk with the Lord and hold hands with the Devil. You cannot serve two masters, but you can try. Adam willingly took the fruit. He offered no resistance.

The course of sin, the domino effect, encourages us to go along with what everyone else is doing, what everyone else is believing, and where everyone else is going. I remember an incident from my third-grade year in school. I was caught going along with the crowd. I remember it like it was yesterday. One of buddies suggested we walk out of the lunchroom and take a stroll down the sidewalk in front of our school. There were four of us and for a few minutes we were free as birds, no longer captive to Mrs. Prince and Mr. Thomas. In a matter of moments, however, that freedom was taken away. We were all marched back into the school, not to the lunchroom but to the principal's office. In Mr. Thomas' office I was asked why I walked out of the lunchroom. I had a brilliant idea, blame the other guys. I responded quite cleverly I thought, "They told me to." The principal then asked me something I had never thought of before, "If they told you to jump off a cliff? Would you jump?" Suddenly we had gone from walking out of the lunchroom to jumping off a cliff. I never realized walking out of the lunchroom with a few friends could lead to jumping off a cliff. But today, some fifty years later I know for certain, Satan will tempt us to jump off a cliff. He told Adam and Eve to jump. Convinced them they could fly. The course of sin takes you and your best friends, your family, your children to the edge of the cliff and whispers - jump and see what happens. Mr. Thomas paddled me, and I decided to never walk out of the lunchroom again.

Eve was drawn away by her Appetite... *"So when the woman saw that the tree was good for food..."* (Genesis 3:6). In Genesis chapter 2 we read that, *"God made every tree grow that is pleasant to the sight and good for food."* But there was one forbidden tree and its fruit. Genesis 2:17 describes it as *"the tree of the knowledge of good and evil..."* It appears all the trees were pleasant to the eyes, and all the trees were accessible except the tree in the midst of the garden. Because of my free will, I am free to go and do as I please. And while I am free to choose what I do, I am not free to change the consequences. I am in control of what my mind thinks, what my tongue says, where my feet go, what my hands do. My appetite may desire something forbidden, but God has given me the will and the ability to turn away. Satan knows the heart of man, and there are times when our appetite cries out. I try to never shop for groceries when I am hungry. Because, when a person is hungry enough, they'll eat anything. In the spiritual realm, Satan is well educated regarding hungry souls and forbidden fruit.

She was lured away by sin's Attraction... *"that it was pleasant to the eyes..."* (Genesis 3:6). If someone talks about the ugliness of sin, they're describing the end result. Sin always has a sad ending. But on the front end, sin is quite attractive. Delilah must have been alluring, even seductive. Her appeal caused Samson to walk away from the Nazarite vow, his devotion to God, and his parents. For Judas, thirty pieces of silver must have been hard to turn down. A bag of money lured him away from what he had seen, heard, felt, and known. The sins we commit are always attractive to begin with. It's amazing how we are drawn to the forbidden. The Garden of Eden was filled with beautiful trees that were good for food – but Eve was tempted with the one tree which was off limits. Like an old preacher once said, "Sin distracts, attracts, and attacks." Sin makes you look, look, and look again and then pursue and partake. But it's expensive. Sin will cost you everything that matters.

She was coerced by her own Ambition... *"a tree desirable to make one wise..."* (Genesis 3:6). If I had been in their shoes I might have asked, how could something that looks so good be so bad? How could this fruit be forbidden when it looks so innocent? Mark Twain said, "There is a charm about the forbidden that makes it unspeakably desirable." Twain also suggested if the serpent had been forbidden, they would have eaten it (goodreads.com). This temptation was at least three-fold. It was attractive, good for food, and would make them wise. Honestly friend, if something sounds too good to be true it probably is. How could something that looks so good be so bad? Just read Proverbs 6:26, *"For by means of a harlot a man is reduced to a crust of bread..."* That verse has intrigued me since the first time I read it. I have watched many people over the course of my life be reduced to a crust of bread. They pursued wealth, acceptance, popularity, possessions, notoriety, multiple lovers, and the thrill of the moment. Far too many of them were reduced to nothing. Over time they became broke, embarrassed, humiliated, and shamed. Don't be so blinded by sin's beauty that you overlook its bondage. Don't be so blinded by sin's attraction that you miss its seduction. Abraham's nephew Lot saw the plain of Sodom, but he never imagined the pain it would bring. Billy Sunday said, "I believe there is a

Devil for two reasons: One, the Bible says so. Two, I've done business with him." Friend, guard your heart from doing any business with the Devil.

The Remorse of Sin
Genesis 3:7-8

Up until the point of eating the forbidden fruit, there had been no shame, no guilt, no embarrassment, and no reason to hide from God. But sin separates us from God. Sin drives a wedge between us and fellowship with the Lord. Sin builds a wall between us and peace with God. Thank God, Jesus built a bridge. Sometime back I was preaching in a church and in attendance was a lady in her early eighties. I know that because she told me her age, along with a story about her life almost seventy years earlier. In her teens she had gotten pregnant and faced the shame of her mistake. She feared ridicule and rejection by her family. She resorted to secretly having an abortion. She confessed she didn't know what would have been worse, the public shame of having the baby or the private shame of having the abortion. She had lived most of her life ashamed of her decision to end the baby's life. I preached that night about God casting our sin as far as the east is from the west. I added he not only saves you from your sin, but also from your shame. She wept that night as she, for the first time in years, enjoyed true freedom from her sin and her shame.

Their Innocence was replaced with Guilt. *"The eyes of both of them were opened..."* (Genesis 3:7). They saw what they had never seen. Felt what they had never felt. Just what many of us do when we're brought face to face with our sin. For the first time, they were ashamed. I remember the first time I felt shame and conviction of sin. Although I didn't know what I was feeling at the time, my seven-year-old heart was broken over what I had said. I had called my sister a name I had heard at school. In a heated disagreement after school, I called her a fool. I didn't know what a fool was. We didn't use that word in our home. But I repeated to her what I had heard someone else say that day at school. I didn't think a thing about what I had said until that night at our church's Wednesday night Bible study. Wouldn't you know it – the preacher read that evening from Matthew 5:21-22 about the dangers of calling someone a fool. *"…Whosoever shall say thou fool shall be in danger of Hell fire"* (KJV). For the first time in my life, that I can recall, I felt conviction. It felt miserable. And the worst part of it all at that time was, I didn't know what to do about it. I didn't know about confessing my sin. I didn't know about repenting. I was an unsaved young boy who didn't know about forgiveness. That must have been some of what Adam and Eve felt. The heaviness of what they had done with no idea how to be freed from the shame they carried. Thank God friend, we don't have to live in and under the guilt of our sin. We have a Savior, not so we can sin, but for when we do. And He is able to take away our shame. Thank God for Jesus.

Their Joy was replaced with Grief. *"And they heard the sound of the Lord God walking in the garden in the cool of the day, and Adam and his wife hid themselves from the presence of the Lord God…"* (Genesis 3:8). For the first time they dreaded standing in his presence. When we're caught, our first instinct often tells us to run and hide. Since the beginning of time, we have been trying to hide from God. Some of us choose a hideout among the most vile and evil places known to man. And, sadly, some of us hide in the church. We sing the songs, dress the part, give the offerings, and speak the right words, but we are far from God and living in sin. The Devil has not changed and neither have we. He still steals, kills, and destroys and we still let him. I am so glad I don't have to live my life hiding from God. I am glad I can live openly and honestly dependent on Him and His grace. I'm glad I can confess my sin and know forgiveness and cleansing (1 John 1:9).

Their Freedom was replaced with Bondage. Up until the bad apple, Adam and Eve had lived a life of openness and honesty. Now they resorted to secrecy and blame. In Genesis 3:21 we read that the Lord God, *"made tunics of skin and clothed them."* They had always been naked but then suddenly, because of their sin, they recognized their nakedness. Now they saw themselves through the eyes of sinners. Immediately they felt shame. In 3:7 we read, *"Then the eyes of them both were opened, and they knew that they were naked, and they sewed fig leaves together and made themselves coverings."* They tried to cover their shame and so do we. They tried to hide and so do we. But there are some things that we can't cover. Our guilt. Our sin. Our shame. God so loved the world that He sent Jesus to the cross to cover our sin and take away our guilt. God's clothing of Adam and Eve reminds us that our salvation does not come through our own effort but by God's grace. When we come to God by faith in Christ, believing in His forgiveness for our sin, He clothes us in His righteousness. In Philippians 3:9 Paul wrote, *"...not having my own righteousness, which is from the law, but that which is through faith in Christ, the righteousness which is from God by faith."* Adam and Eve knew nothing about what Paul described, but they were given a glimpse of what it was like to have their unrighteousness covered by the Father. We have our bondage replaced with freedom when we trust Him with our sin.

The Force of Sin
Genesis 3:12-13

As I begin to bring this chapter to a close, I want to remind you of what we have covered so far. We have looked at the source of sin. It begins in a mistrust of God. We looked at the course of sin. It is like the domino effect where one thing leads to another. We have thought about the remorse of sin, the grief and heartache that sin inevitably brings. I'll conclude this chapter writing about the force of sin. Speaking of force, I am referring to the power of sin and how we often feel led forced or compelled to follow our heart, trust our own counsel, and lean on the arm of flesh and the strength of common sense. Faith and common sense seldom agree. Faith and your flesh never agree. When we take a step of faith something in our flesh, something in our common sense will disagree. Paul writes in Roman 14:23, *"Whatever is not of faith is sin."* The power of sin is undeniable. The force of sin causes people to go deeper in deception. It is the force of sin that causes the addict to take one more drink. It pushes the adulterer to see his mistress just one more time. It caused David to have Uriah killed. It causes the depressed soul to swallow the pills. It encourages the sinner to rebel, resist, and run. But thank God, the power of sin caused our Heavenly Father to provide the Cross. There was no other way to save sinners from sin. There is only one hope: Jesus.

Shame always leads to Blame. In Genesis 3:12 we find these words, *"Then the man said, 'The woman who you gave to be with me, she gave me of the tree and I ate.'"* If you'll allow me a little liberty with my words here, I'd suggest Adam may have thought something like this: It's that woman! She made me eat the fruit. I don't even like fruit! She basically forced me to eat it against my will. It's that woman's fault…that woman you gave me. Adam blamed God for giving him the woman and then blamed the woman for giving him the fruit of the tree. In 3:13 God asked the woman, *"What is this you have done?"* She replied, *"The serpent deceived me, and I ate."* Adam blamed Eve. Eve blamed the Devil. Shame leads to blame.

Compromise always brings Consequences. Adam and Eve and the serpent were forever changed. The curse of sin would cost Jesus His life on the cross. Sin always carries a price tag. The price is always higher than advertised and often has unexpected consequences. David Jeremiah told about a Seattle man, for example, who tried to steal gasoline from a motor home. Attaching a siphoning hose to the vehicle, he started to work; but police found him shortly afterward writhing in agony in the street. Seems he had attached the hose, not to the gasoline tank, but to the motor home's sewage tank! (Preaching.com). Know anybody like that? The unintended consequences of sin are often seen in the toll that our sin takes on those we love the most. It is seen in the price our family pays for our foolishness. And the sad reality is many of those living in sin have no concern as to the effect on their family. As long as they're happy is all that matters. Listen to the story about a pig: A pig ate his fill of acorns under an oak tree and then started to root around the tree. A crow remarked, "You should not do this. If you lay bare the roots, the tree will wither and die." "Let it die," said the pig. "Who cares as long as there are acorns?" (familytimes.net). And such is life. Many a good man has been wrecked by the power of alcohol. Yet he continues to live the life of the pig just mentioned unconcerned about future consequences. I'm not above compromise. At my age, the Devil would love nothing more than to cause me to stumble. I must, like a sheep, stay close to the shepherd. I have watched from a distance countless men and women live out the consequences of their compromise. The stories are sad and most are very similar. Their sin began as something small and seemingly insignificant. But over time, their sinning grew. It's the domino effect of sin. One sin opens the door to another. And all compromise has consequences. Guard your heart.

Disobedience always brings Death. In Genesis 3:21 as I have already pointed out, the Lord covered Adam and Eve with the skins of an animal. *"Also for Adam and his wife the Lord God made tunics of skin, and clothed them."* This death was the beginning of death for sin throughout the Old Testament of lambs, rams, bulls, and goats. They were killed as a sacrifice to satisfy the demands of the law. But they were never enough. Until the day God sent Jesus to the cross as a final, once-for-all sacrifice to end death for sin. On the cross Jesus put an end to sacrifice. We are forgiven through Christ's death. He died so we won't have to. He didn't destroy the law. He fulfilled it. He finished it. And as far as our sin He covers it. He cleanses it. He forgives it. Because of Jesus, death has died and, whosoever believes has life – life eternal.

Satan Kills, Steals, and Destroys. John 10:10

Satan will do what's necessary to destroy you.

The gift of God is eternal life. **Romans 6:23**

God did what's necessary to save you.

CHAPTER 7 DISCUSSION POINTS

Discuss the domino effect of David's sin that led to the death of Bathsheba's husband Uriah.

How is doubting the authority of God's Word the source of all sin?

Sin ultimately brings remorse and regret. Discuss the difference in guilt about sin and conviction of sin.

What does the sin of Adam and Eve have in common with David's sin?

THE HIGH COST OF SIN

James 1:14-16

The old Gospel song says, "Sin will cost you more than you want to pay." My, is that ever true! Some are still paying for their sin. Some are sitting in a prison cell paying for their sin. Some are sitting on a church pew paying for their sin. The prison grief is obvious. But why would a person on a church pew be in such a grieved state of mind? As a good friend of mine said, "They think they have to clean themselves up. They can't forgive themselves for their past failures." He continues, "I don't recall ever seeing in scripture where we are supposed to do that." Amen. If we have truly repented, we can fully rely on God to forgive us. The reason I asked my friend is because he spent about three years behind bars. I spoke on behalf of him at his hearing and would do it again. He has a perspective on life now that I don't. Truth is, our prisons are packed with folks paying for their sin, but our churches are just as filled with those who haven't fully trusted God to take away their guilt. We aren't capable of doing what only God can do. Repenting is what I do. Forgiving and cleansing is what He does. So, friend, unlock and open that prison door and walk out into freedom. The freedom that is found only in Jesus and the price He paid. This chapter is about the high cost of sin. King David knew something about that. He paid the price. He never knew Jesus who would pay the highest price, with his own life, to set the captive free, save the sinner, and bring home the prodigals. The cost of sin is high – and Jesus paid it all.

What if you knew the cost of sin before you ever bought into the temptation? Would it change your decision? The devotional, *Our Daily Bread*, illustrates the price of sin in a story about a misplaced comma. "It was only a little comma, but it cost the Lockheed corporation millions of dollars! An error was made in a contract with an international customer—a misplaced comma in a crucial number. The company insisted that the manufacturer honor the contract as written. Unfortunately for Lockheed, the error was made in an equation that adjusted the sales price, and it cost them $70 million." That's a crucial mistake that cost millions. But friends, there are countless men and women who have lost things money can't buy. Peace. Contentment. Happiness. Family. While $70 million is more money than I can imagine, I can tell you of those who would pay that and more to have their family back. To have peace of mind. To live without guilt and heartache (odb.org).

Sin is a stealer of time. Sin robs a person of their youth. Fast and foolish living opens the door for sin to slip in taking away innocence, character, and integrity. Sin comes in like a thief in the night, and by morning light all that's left is a shell of the man who used to be. His smooth complexion has been stolen and replaced with a wrinkled face. His thick, dark hair has been stolen and replaced with thinning gray hair of a much older man. The spring in his step has been replaced with a shuffle. The gleam in his eye has been replaced with squints that struggle to recognize faces. His strong back is now bent, Sin has taken its toll. Why didn't someone tell him? They probably tried. But when you're young, it's difficult to take advice. When you're young, days are long and sleep is sweet. But oh, how quickly time slips away. Sinful living has a high cost, even though at the time it may seem so small. Seemingly harmless decisions can end up doing great damage.

Sin will cost you...

In Jonah 1:3 we read that he ran from God, went to Joppa, boarded a ship bound for Tarshish, and paid the fare. He planned to go down to Tarshish and then went down into the ship. Sin always goes downhill. The scriptures record, *"He paid the fare."* We don't know the amount he paid for the fare, but we know what he paid for his sin. Whatever the amount, we can almost guarantee he wanted his money back. This was a boat ride Jonah should have never taken. But you don't hear him regretting. He complains. But he doesn't offer any prayers of regret or repentance. He paid the fare in more ways than he could have predicted. Everybody needs a Nathan. Even Jonah.

David should have learned from Jonah's example. But not even a personal God-sent Nathan could stop the momentum of sin David had created. Jerry Vines said, "Isn't it a shame that when we think about David we think about his greatest victory and his greatest defeat? We think about his victory over Goliath, but we also think about his sin with Bathsheba" (sermonsearch.com). Sin will cost you your reputation. Hundreds of years after the fact when we remember David, we still remember his sin. F. B. Meyer said, "This is the bitterest of all - to know that suffering need not have been - that it has resulted from indiscretion and inconsistency; that it is the harvest of one's own sowing; that the vulture which feeds on the vitals is a nestling of one's own rearing. Ah me! This is pain!" (Meyer as quoted by Charles Swindoll in *Living Above the Level of Mediocrity*). Sin will cost you your peace of mind. Though your sin may be forgiven and by grace abound, the mind is an amazing recorder that keeps track of all we said, all we thought, and all we did. And sometimes our conscience presses play, and we remember – as badly as we want to erase the recording, it remains. At that moment we must turn our thoughts over to the Lord and ask Him to help us remember that the sin is covered and forgiven by the blood of Jesus.

> Adrian Rogers said, "The most miserable man is a child of God who is out of fellowship with God. He is far more miserable than an unsaved man! When God saves you, He fixes you so that you cannot sin and enjoy it anymore (Hebrews 12:8). David's sin **wearied** him (Psalm 38:3). His sin is on his heart. He cannot sleep. Guilt will sap the strength out of your life — strength that ought to be given to productive purposes. His sin **weighted** him. *"For my iniquities have gone over my head; like a heavy burden they are too heavy for me"*(Psalm 38:4). His sin **wounded** him. *"My wounds are foul and festering because of my foolishness"* (Psalm 38:5). He is talking about spiritual gangrene. Guilt is a dirty wound — until is cleaned, it only festers. His sin **worried** him (Psalm 38:6). Every time David saw people talking, he wondered, 'Do they know?' He had no peace. His sin **wasted** him. *"For my loins are full of inflammation, and there is no soundness in my flesh"* (Psalm 38:7). He is not talking poetically now. David's sin **weakened** him (Psalm 38:8). He used to be a mighty warrior; now he is broken in body and spirit. In the next few verses of Psalm 38, David speaks of himself as being blind, deaf, and dumb—blind to blessing, deaf to danger, no longer singing praise to God" (lwf.org).

Yes, the scriptures are accurate about Jonah in stating, *"He paid the fare."* Yes, he did. And in many ways, he continued to pay. He paid with his heart, soul, and mind. Bitterness is a cruel friend. Bitterness and his brother Revenge find their resting place in our hearts. They seem to arrive just when we're at the point of forgiveness and reconciliation. They prod and poke the mind to remember what was said and done in days gone by. Jonah was in no mood to be kind to the ruthless people of Nineveh who were some of the enemies of Israel. He felt no obligation to repay their cruelty toward the people of God with the grace of God. Running from God is expensive. It costs your peace of mind, a clean conscience, and pleasant memories. I would imagine there are folks who live most of their life on edge waiting for an opportunity to retaliate. What a sad way to live. They have what many old timers would call, an axe to grind. As Jonah sharpened his axe, God was relentless in pursuit to send the message of saving grace to Nineveh. Jonah was a prophet of God. His failed trip to Tarshish was more than an attempt to run from God, he was also running from Nineveh. He simply didn't want to go where God was sending him. I am convinced that many who appear to be running from God, are running from other things even more so. Many who are running believe in God, they're just not ready or willing to trust God. Such is the case with Jonah. Running may bring initial feelings of freedom. But in the long run, the price of sin is bondage to grief and guilt.

Romans 6:23 states, *"For the wages of sin is death…"* There's an old saying, "What doesn't kill you will make you stronger." That's not always true. What doesn't kill you may leave you scarred and crippled for life. What doesn't kill you may haunt you for years to come. Jonah's attempt to run from God didn't kill him, but it certainly scarred him. At the end of the book of Jonah we see him pouting over a plant that had died, more than being thankful for a people who were spared. The scriptures record a brief conversation between God and Jonah in Jonah 4:9. God asks, *"Is it right for you to be angry about the plant?"* Jonah responds, *"It is right for me to be angry even unto death."* Oh, my! If this wasn't so tragic it might be somewhat humorous. As tragic as it is, however, I believe Jonah's sin and his state of mind is typical today. We often feel justified in our running. When we are running from what God wants us to do, we are clearly and simply – running from God. Jonah *"paid the fare."*

Your sin will cost others…

In Jonah 1:5, *"Then the mariners were afraid; and every man cried out to his god, and threw the cargo that was in the ship into the sea, to lighten the load…"* We can only imagine the value of the cargo that was thrown overboard. No one knows how much they lost or how much it cost. What we do know is Jonah's disobedience cost them. His rebellion caused them great loss. In Jonah 5:13, even after Jonah had confessed his sin and offered himself to be thrown into the sea, the men on the ship *"rowed hard to return to land but could not…"* Jonah was learning he could not out-run the will of God, and the mariners were learning they could not out-row the displeasure of God. After praying to the Lord, *"They picked up Jonah and threw him into the sea and the sea ceased from its raging."* The mariners threw their cargo into the sea to lighten the load, but the only cure for the raging sea was to toss Jonah overboard. Afterward they feared the Lord, offered a sacrifice, and took vows. What a turn of events – Jonah was running from revival in Nineveh and created revival on a ship bound for Tarshish. How many men were on board we do not know. But it appears they all turned to God and believed.

Husbands and wives, when you run from God, the cost of your sin is often paid by your wife, and ladies by your husband. Dad and Mom, when you run from God, the cost of your sin is often paid by your children. Sometimes the cost of your sin is your home, your family, your future. The pandemic of unhappiness is running rampant today. Folks like Jonah, running in the opposite direction of God causes their families and children so much heartache. Jonah was going to be happy even if his contentment cost everyone else their peace of mind. The lives of the men on the ship and the salvation of the Ninevites hung in the balance. He ran, knowing the will of God was calling him to Nineveh. Friend, you may be enroute to Tarshish today, running, and resisting God's appointment for you. If you actually make it to where you are bound, when you arrive you will find God is already there. You may run, but God runs faster. You'll also find that Tarshish isn't all you hoped it would be. You'll discover it is the prodigal son's far country. You'll yearn for home.

Will you examine yourself today? Are you running from God? What is your running costing you and those you love? Jonah…if God is sending you to Nineveh, please go for your sake, and for the sake of others. And King David, if Nathan is knocking on your door bringing you a word from the Lord, don't turn him away. Because, when you run from God, and when you sin against God, your sin will cost you and those you love the most. We have some friends who are foster parents. One of the children they fostered was just an infant. That sweet baby was born into this world needing detox because of her mother's choices. Thank God that baby is now a healthy child because of loving parents and amazing grace. How many dads are leading their sons to sin? How many pastors, teachers, and coaches have shamefully sinned against God and against someone who respected them, only to reap the consequences of their foolish decisions? And to scar some young person for life? Our sin will cost us, but it will also cost others.

God knew the price of sin. He paid the debt for anyone who will believe and call on the name of the Lord. You don't have to live life bound by the power of sin, past or present. Romans 6:23 says, *"... the gift of God is eternal life in Jesus Christ our Lord."*

All Our Decisions Matter - James 1:14-16

Some decisions have more of an impact than others, but all our decisions matter. If we hope to be pleasing to God, faithful to God, and a living testimony to His grace and goodness, all our decisions matter. This is not an encouragement to be a legalist, but to be Spirit-filled, and if necessary, use a little common sense. You don't have to be Spirit-filled to know not to play with fire. Joseph knew to run from Potiphar's wife. No one had to tell him. I thank God for the Holy Spirit that guides me and warns me. But even if I were not a believer in Christ, a good dose of common sense would serve me well. Sometimes the best thing you can do is run from sin. James writes, *"...Every man is tempted when he is drawn away of his own lust and enticed. Then when lust hath conceived it bringeth forth sin; and sin when it is finished, bringeth forth death."* I like the King James Version of this verse because it uses the word lust instead of desire. I understand that to lust means to desire, but there's something about the word lust that captivates me. The edginess of the word lust helps me understand what draws men away is not some casual, complacent desire, but a hunger, a thirst, a craving, a pursuit for something outside of God's will.

Oswald Chambers wrote, "Lust means, I must have it at once" (utmost.org). Chambers was referring to a spiritual lust, but this idea of immediate satisfaction also thrives in the physical realm. Leonard Ravenhill said, "Lust means, I will satisfy myself; whether I satisfy myself on a high or a low level makes no difference, the principle is the same. It is the exercise of my claim to my right to myself..." (sermonindex.net). Richard Foster observed, "The sin of covetousness is the inner lust to have" (seedbed.com). Over the years I have been on a regular diet of Chambers and Ravenhill. God used these men and their writings, early in my life, to shape me and my faith in Christ. These two, along with Foster, paint a vivid picture of the power of lust. More than just desire, but an inner drive, an immediate demand, an intense desire to have what I want when I want it. And in that regard, James writes that every man is tempted, not some or a few, but we are all tempted when we are drawn away by our own lusts and enticed.

Everybody needs a Nathan because everybody is tempted when they are drawn away by their own lusts. Nathan is like a spiritual compass. An actual compass always points to true north. The Holy Spirit always points to Jesus. Nathan was a tool in the hand of God to point David in the right direction. What did David do in response? He repented. He confessed his sin. And, as far as we know he never sinned in that way again (1 Kings 15:5). Everybody needs a Nathan.

"Drawn away of his own lust..."

Lusts. We all have them. They're shameful, seldom admitted, often secretive. While most of us know when we're being drawn away, pulled away from what's right to what's wrong, obviously some of us like being pulled away. Whether you're tempted with a car you can't afford, or a relationship you can't have, the possibility is tempting. We imagine driving a car like that. And we wonder what it would feel like to be loved by someone like that. Before you buy, have an honest conversation with yourself. If you can't afford it, admit it and move on. Otherwise, you may be driving a car that is the envy of your friends, but you'll be eating ramen noodles three times a day so you can make the payments. And, regarding that man or that woman who's already married – If you were to find yourself eventually married to them and the possibility becomes reality, you'll discover that even Mr. Wonderful snores at night and Mrs. Amazing sleeps in a flannel gown.

I heard the story of two older men, in their late eighties, taking an early morning walk. It was a beautiful morning as they made their way around the lake and the conversation was light. Suddenly they noticed up ahead, sitting right in the middle of the path, a frog. As they got closer the frog began to talk to one of the men. The frog said, "Sir, I know I look like a normal frog, but if you'll pick me up and kiss me on the head I'll turn into a beautiful princess. You can take me home and I'll do anything you want me to do." The gentleman to which the frog had spoken reached down, picked up the frog, held it close to his face, examined it closely, then gently put the frog in the pocket of his jacket. The other gentleman had watched all this in unbelief. He said to his friend, "Did you hear what that frog said? She said if you would kiss her, she would turn in to a beautiful princess, go home with you, and do whatever you asked her to do. And you are just going to put her in your pocket and keep walking?" His buddy responded, "At my age I'd rather have a talking frog." Life is filled with talking frogs and such, making promises that are hard to believe. Guard your heart. Guard your lusts. And if you encounter a talking frog, just keep walking.

"And enticed..."

Enticed. Tempted. Captivated. I believe we have underestimated the power of enticement, which also means to charm, bribe, or persuade. Enticement seems to be a veiled form of temptation. It's no less powerful but its ugliness is disguised. The enticement in the Garden of Eden follows this line of thinking. Adam and Eve were made to believe the fruit was good for food and would make them wise. They must have thought about what God had said and wondered, how could something that looks so good be so bad?

Enticement has not changed. It is the reason marriages break up. It's the reason lives are wrecked through addiction. It's the reason gamblers gamble. It's the reason our prisons are filled. It's the reason our churches are empty. Enticement brings out the worst in us. We think we can resist it. We think we're strong enough. Old enough. Saved enough. But the truth is, there are many who are being controlled by sin, as the old saying goes, like the tail is wagging the dog. Like the man who no longer controls his anger, his anger now controls him.

Billy Sunday said, "Temptation is the Devil looking through the keyhole. Yielding is opening the door and inviting him in." What a powerful thought. I believe the Enemy is roaming about looking through all the keyholes he can, seeing all he can see, enticing as many as possible. May God help us shut the door and keep it locked.

"When lust hath conceived…"

Conceiving means to make a plan or premeditate a course of action. When we begin to act on our lusts, desires, thoughts, imaginations, we are following the narrow path which leads to destruction. If we could only get a glimpse of where the road we're traveling leads. If we could see the end result of the choices we are making today. Cain would have brought an acceptable sacrifice. Esau wouldn't have sold his birthright. Samson wouldn't have gone down to Timnah. Jonah wouldn't have run from the Lord. Judas wouldn't have betrayed Christ. Peter wouldn't have denied Him. Time is a great teacher. We look back and see all the time we squandered while living in sin. We think to ourselves, "If I only knew then what I know now." So how do I prevent myself from following the course of temptation that will cause me to live in regret over decisions I am making today? Live for Jesus now. Trust in Jesus now. In every decision, *"Acknowledge Him and he shall direct your paths"* (Proverbs 3:6).

Before the Prodigal ever left home, he was already there - in the far country where the course of enticement and temptation had taken him. Before Jonah ever paid the fare and boarded the ship, his imagination already had him sailing on the high seas. Long before David ever sent for Bathsheba, his thoughts were already set on taking what was not his. Before Ananias and Sapphira hid the money, in their minds it was already spent. Before the Prodigal left home, he was already gone. The course of temptation doesn't end until it is finished, and we are wrecked.

"When it is finished…"

Sin always takes the life of something. Sin will kill your joy. Sin is the death of contentment. Relationships have died because of sin. Sin will take the life of your marriage. Sin will even kill a church. It was sin that killed Jesus. Jesus paid the wages of our sin by dying on the cross. Sin's goal is to *Finish…* to kill, steal, destroy. Sin isn't interested in only putting a dent in your fender – it seeks to wreck your life. From his reading of Psalm 51, Alexander MacLaren describes David's remorse like this: "A whole year had elapsed between David's crime and David's penitence. It had been a year of guilty satisfaction not worth the having; of sullen hardening of heart against God and all His appeals. The thirty-second Psalm tells us how happy David had been during that twelvemonth, of which he says, *'My bones waxed old through my roaring all the day long. For day and night Thy hand was heavy on me.' Then came Nathan…"* (MacLaren, *Expositions of Holy Scripture*). Wreckage and ruin – that's what the Enemy seeks – to wreck your life, your joy, your peace. To ruin a man who had been a seeker and lover of God. David is a broken man in Psalm 51. Three times in the first two verses he takes responsibility for his sin. He confesses *"my transgressions…my iniquity…my sin"* David was chosen as king because God had sought to find a man who was after His own heart. David was that man. And in Psalm 51 he still is. I'm not making light of his great sin, but I am certainly making a big deal of his great repentance. Only a man after God's heart would be broken like that. A hardened man would shirk off the

121

notion of any wrongdoing. A callous man couldn't care less about his iniquity, his sin, his transgressions. But David isn't hardened. He's broken over his sin against the Lord, Bathsheba, and Uriah.

Oh, the remorse that sin brings to a heart that has known yet rebelled against God. From Psalm 51:1-15, I call your attention to David's pleas:

"Have mercy upon me, O God."
"Blot out my transgressions."
"Wash me thoroughly from my iniquity."
"Cleanse me from my sin."
"Purge me with hyssop."
"Wash me, and I will be whiter than snow."
"Make me hear joy and gladness."
"Hide your face from my sins."
"Blot out all my iniquities."
Create in me a clean heart."
"Renew a steadfast spirit within me."
"Do not cast me away from your presence."
"Do not take the Holy Spirit from me."
"Restore to me the joy of your salvation."
"Uphold me by your generous spirit."
"Deliver me from the guilt of bloodshed."
"Open my lips and my mouth shall show forth your praise."

Nathan was sent by the Lord to tell David he was *"the man"* who had sinned. But Nathan was also there to acknowledge the forgiveness and mercy of the Lord. In 2 Samuel 12:13 after David had confessed his sin, Nathan spoke these words, *"The Lord has put away your sin; you shall not die."* Nathan was there to speak truth and in doing so took control of the conversation in the room. Folks like Nathan have a calming effect on a room filled with tension. Nathan came as a peacemaker, not a troublemaker. Without Nathan, I wonder how much longer David would have continued the charade of innocence. Without Nathan, I wonder how much further David might have drifted into the pretense of normalcy. I also wonder how much greater the weight of his sin would have become. In his own words, *"his bones waxed old."* In his outward appearance all seemed well, but within he was racked with remorse so badly his bones hurt.

In Psalm 51 David is wrecked. He doesn't even want God to look upon his sin. But God saw it all. And He still sees it all – and as we confess our darkest sin, he extends His greatest mercy. Let me close this chapter with an observation and an invitation from Alexander MacLaren: "Know that thou art utterly black and sinful. Believe that God is eternally, utterly, inconceivably, merciful. Learn both, in Him who is the standard by which we can estimate our sin, and the proof and medium of God's mercy. Trust thyself and all thy foulness to Jesus Christ; and, so doing, look up from whatsoever horrible pit and miry clay thou mayest have fallen into, with this prayer, 'Create in me a clean heart, O God! and renew a right spirit within me, take not Thy Holy Spirit from me, and uphold me with Thy free Spirit.'"

The high cost of sin is too much for us to pay. Thank God Jesus paid it all. He paid our sin debt with His own life. We love to sing of a grace that is amazing. But there would be no grace so amazing without a loving God who is equally amazing, forgiving, and sustaining.

CHAPTER 8 DISCUSSION POINTS

What did David's sin cost him? Discuss the possible long-term effects of his sin.

How does your sin cost others? Discuss the effects of David's sin on his children.

Discuss the power of enticement. *"Every man is tempted when he is drawn away of his own lust and enticed…"*

From Psalm 51, discuss the prayerful pleas of David.

ESAU'S BIRTHRIGHT AND A BOWL OF SOUP

Genesis 25:21-34

Talk about getting a raw deal - Esau was swindled out of his birthright. Hungry and feeling faint, he traded his privileges of being the firstborn for a bowl of homemade soup. Jacob, taking advantage of the situation, made the most of the opportunity and walked away with an honor he didn't deserve. I've had a few bad deals in my life. I've had some bad haircuts. I've been given some bad advice. I've received some bad directions. But Esau's bad luck trumps anything I've ever experienced. He traded his rights as the elder brother for a bowl of soup. He traded something that money couldn't buy for momentary satisfaction. People do it every day, but Esau's story found its way into scripture.

I wrote extensively in another book, *Deep Dark Holes*, about Esau. That chapter is titled, "Esau: The Man Who'd Give Anything for a Bowl of Soup." Talk about needing a Nathan – Esau could have certainly used a friend like Nathan. The one thing Esau had that was rightfully his from the moment of birth, he gambled away for a bowl of temporary relief. Not receiving the blessing of his father was not his doing. But trading his birthright was all on him. Jacob was a deceiver, a heel-grabber, and a supplanter. He did what deceivers do – he tricked, manipulated, bribed, and deceived Esau right out of his greatest possession. This is indeed one of the saddest stories in scripture. His foolishness and David's senselessness have much in common. They both acted on impulse. Neither of them considered future implications. They both lived to regret their choices.

Living in the moment is a good thing. Living in the moment means making the most of the circumstances you're in. Instead of constantly looking forward to something down the road, just enjoy the moment, soak in every second with those you love. But if you change one small word in that idea it becomes - living *for* the moment, which often ends in regret. Living for the moment caused Esau to trade his birthright for a bowl of soup. Living for the moment led David to send for Bathsheba. Living for the moment caused Abraham to lie about Sarah and Isaac to lie about Rebekah. Living for the moment opened the door for Adam and Eve to eat the forbidden fruit. Living for the moment caused Peter to deny the Lord. None of those I just mentioned gave any thought to the future consequences of their decisions. They acted on impulse.

Living for the moment is good soil where regret begins to grow.
In that moment we say things that can never be unsaid.
We do things that can never be undone.
We buy things we can't afford.
We go places we shouldn't go.
We leave when we should have stayed.
We stay when we should have left.
We do wrong when we knew it wasn't right.
We lie when we should have told the truth.
Esau traded his birthright for a bowl of soup.

In these next few paragraphs, I want to remind you of three stories in scripture that capture and reveal the truth of what I am attempting to say. But more than just simply saying something, I feel these stories are more of a warning. Warnings about living for the moment with no thought of God or the future. The first, of course, is about Esau and his bowl of soup. The second is about Judas and his bag of silver. The third is about Ananias and Sapphira and their buried treasure.

Esau's Bowl of Soup

As I have already discussed, James had it right in his own letter, 1:14-16, when he wrote about being drawn away and enticed. Imagine with me as we see Jacob overhearing Esau as he says, I'm starving to death - I'd give anything for a bowl of soup. What he actually said in Genesis 25:30-32, *"Let me eat some of that red stew, for I am exhausted... I am about to die, of what use is a birthright to me?"* I also imagine Jacob saying, have I got a deal for you! The scripture records in Genesis 25:34 that Esau *"despised his birthright."* Despise is a powerful description of how he felt. That being said, I wonder how many today have despised their new birth, their salvation, their hope for eternity? I wonder how many, like Esau, have foolishly gambled away their peace with God for some temporary solace? I wonder how many have despised their marriage, home, and family and walked away in desertion like some prodigal looking for greener pastures and bluer skies?

This is more than a bowl of soup. It is a state of mind. It's a condition of the heart. To have no regard for what is priceless, to have no appreciation for and treat as worthless the grace of God is almost criminal. Certainly shameful. That is what Esau did. That is what people are doing today. Disposable families and marriages are only the tip of the iceberg. If something or someone stands in the way of our happiness, it has to go. It seems as though the anthem of the world has become: Make me happy or else! Esau got his bowl of soup. But I would imagine the next morning he was hungry again.

Shopping with a credit card, when you're broke, is dangerous. But no worries, you can pay off your new wardrobe in monthly installments. Need new shoes but have no money? No problem! Buy the boots and pay them off for only a few bucks a month. The harsh reality sets in when you realize you have too much month at the end of the money. Buying things you can't afford is akin to gambling with things you can't get back. Both demand that you act foolish and irresponsible. Welcome to a day in the life of Esau.

Esau traded his future for some food.
He traded his birthright for a bowl of beans.
He traded a lifetime for one moment in time.

I think it's worth noting what Esau gave away. The Hebrew birthright included being the spiritual leader of the family (Genesis 27:29). Also, the elder son would receive a double share of the father's inheritance (Deuteronomy 21:15-17). And, his birthright was part of a covenant blessing (Genesis 12:3) (biblestudytools.com). Also, I think it's a pretty big deal if your name is not included the genealogy of Jesus. Jacob's name is there. But Esau's is nowhere to be found. Matthew 1:2, *"Isaac begot Jacob, and Jacob begot Judah and his brothers."*

Why would Esau despise his birthright? Why do people today treat their family, friends, and faith as if they are unnecessary? Comedian Jerry Seinfeld said, "Everybody is looking for good sex, good food, and a good laugh, because they are little islands of relief in what's often a very painful existence." While I wish he wasn't right, I believe he is. Many live a painful existence because of sickness, debt, failure, and heartache, just to name a few. Many are looking for just a brief interlude of happiness, and it seems some will trade all that matters for all that doesn't matter. These little islands of relief that Seinfeld mentioned are everywhere. Little islands with big consequences. Friend, guard your heart! And like Job, make a covenant with your eyes.

Judas' Bag of Silver

In Matthew 26:15 Judas asked the chief priests, *"What are you willing to give me if I deliver him to you?"* Evidently Jesus was worth no more to them than an Old Testament slave (Ex 21:32). Again, James had it right when he wrote about *"When lust has conceived, it gives birth to sin..."* In Matthew 26:14 we read, *"Judas Iscariot went to the chief priests..."* I have an idea Judas already had a price in mind. I believe Judas already had a premeditated plan. I imagine if they had offered him fifteen pieces, he would have taken it. He probably had a bottom dollar he was willing to take. I sold a used car recently. I parked the car in front of my home near the highway and placed a For Sale sign in the window. On the sign I wrote down the model, year, mileage, and price I was asking. Even though I was asking a certain amount, I was prepared to take less. I waited for an offer. I believe Judas was made an offer he couldn't refuse. A bag of silver looked like enough to last a lifetime. The Bible doesn't say they shook hands on the deal. But it clearly says they gave him the money and from that time forward Judas sought an opportunity to betray Him. He got what he wanted, or so he thought.

This was Judas' opportunity to join the opposition. Instead of belonging to a rag-tag group of disciples, Judas was stepping up his game so to speak. He was now hanging out with the big-shots, hob-nobbing with the chief priests. He had pockets filled with silver and a heart full of the Devil. Jesus once asked, *"For what shall it profit a man, if he shall gain the whole world and lose his own soul?"* (Mark 8:36). The simple answer to Jesus' question is, nothing. Not a thing! For Judas, I must ask, what did he gain? Temporary wealth. Temporary pleasure. Temporary ego. But mostly nothing. His life was short lived. He eventually threw the money down in the temple, ran away, and hanged himself.

Judas lost the silver. He ran to the enemy. He could have run to Jesus, but instead he ran to the very ones who had bought him to begin with. In Matthew 27:4 he went to the chief priests and elders admitting he had sinned and confessed to them he had betrayed an innocent man. They responded callously, *"What do we care...that's your problem"* (NLT). What will Judas do now? He's been used by the chief priests. Caught in their trap. Having betrayed Jesus, he can't go back to following Him as if nothing ever happened. He can't show his face among the disciples. On impulse he runs away in despair and takes his own life. I imagine the chief priests must have laughed and I think the Devil applauded.

Judas lost his mind. In those last few minutes of his life Judas must have asked, "What have I done and what am I going to do?" In John 17:12 Judas is described as *"the son of perdition,"* meaning the one who was bent on squandering himself, bound for destruction. Warren Wiersbe says in that regard, "It is prophesied that one of Messiah's close associates would betray him. The fact does not relieve Judas of his responsibility. We must not make him a martyr because he fulfilled this prophecy" (christianity.com). No one forced Judas to betray the Lord. He wasn't forced to take the silver. He wasn't backed into a corner against his own will. He, of his own volition, led the chief priests to where Jesus was. It was he, by his own choice, who went back to the chief priests and threw the money down. It was he alone who ran to the place where he would hang himself, and it was there that he ended his life. Wiersbe is right – Judas was no martyr. He was the betrayer of Jesus. All for a bag of silver.

Judas lost his soul. Judas died remorseful but unrepentant. He ran to the chief priests but never came to Christ. Judas blended in but had never bowed down. There's no evidence whatsoever that Judas ever repented and turned to Christ as a believer. In John 13:27 at the Last Supper we read of Judas, *"Satan entered him."* Friend, if you are a believer in Christ, Satan cannot and will not enter you. He may influence you, but he cannot indwell you. While we know the Holy Spirit had not yet been poured out on the Day of Pentecost, it is clear that Judas was indwelt by Satan himself. He was not a saved man. He was not a repentant man. He may have been sorry for what he had done or maybe he was just sorry he got caught. There is no indication he repented for betraying our Lord. Judas threw the money down, but he should have thrown himself down repenting and begging God for mercy. Judas died without Jesus and without hope. Hell is not a place of annihilation where souls cease to exist. It is a place of eternal separation apart from God and His grace. Judas lost his soul. What a sad ending to the life of Judas, a disciple of Christ.

Ananias and Sapphira's buried treasure

In Acts 5:4 Peter asked Ananias, *"Why have you conceived this thing in your heart?"* Peter makes it clear in those verses that Ananias knew what he was doing and was in control of the decision he had made. Peter tells him, *"You have not lied to men but to God."* While this is no bag of silver like Judas had, evidently they thought it was worth jeopardizing themselves to keep it back. James had it right again. He wrote, *"And sin, when it is finished, brings forth death."* There are many theological questions and arguments surrounding the story of Ananias and Sapphira. My emphasis is on the practical rather than the theological. My focus is on their decision to keep back the money and lie about it.

My imagination has them taking part of the money and hiding it somewhere in their home or on their property. When I was a young boy back in the seventies, I remember hearing of older folks in the community who had money buried in old coffee cans at various places on their property. The reason for it I was told, they didn't trust banks. When I read this story of Ananias and Sapphira hiding the money, I wonder if they buried it somewhere in their backyard. Recently it was reported of a man locally, who was remodeling an old home he had purchased. When tearing out some of the existing walls, he found several thousand dollars hidden near the fireplace. I wonder if Ananias hid the money in the walls of their home. The truth is, it doesn't matter where they hid the money. What matters is they hid it and lied about it. They lied to fellow believers, but mostly they lied to God.

Rick Burgess observed a distinct difference in what happened after the death of Ananias and Sapphira, and what happened after the death of Stephen. In Acts 8:2, after Stephen had been falsely accused and stoned to death the Bible says, *"And devout men carried Stephen to his burial, and made great lamentation over him"* But in Acts

5:6,10, after the deaths of Ananias and Sapphira we read this: *"And young men wrapped him up, carried him out, and buried him."* And with Sapphira, *"And the young men came in and found her dead, and carrying her out, buried her by her husband."* Burgess asked, "How will they carry you out?" With Stephen devout men carried him out. When Ananias and Sapphira died, young men, most likely some young fellas who were there and available, carried them out and buried them. When Stephen died great lamentation was made over him. They wept at his passing. With Ananias and Sapphira, we read of no one weeping or lamenting their passing.

Needless to say, how we live profoundly impacts how we will be remembered. Devout men buried Stephen and cried at his funeral. Not so with Ananias and Sapphira; they were just taken out and buried. Sin not only affects how we live here but also how we leave here. Don't live in such a way that the world will be a better place when you're gone. Live a life that honors God. Live a life of loving, giving, and serving. Live For Jesus! And then when this life is over you can go live with Jesus!

In 1865, during a morning service at the Monument Street Methodist in Baltimore, Maryland, pastor Schreck's prayer went longer than expected. While he prayed, Elvina Hall scribbled words as she thought about sin, salvation, and the cross. After the service she gave those words to her pastor. She didn't realize that Pastor Schreck had received a few days earlier, from his organist John Grape, a new tune with no words, titled All To Him I Owe. Through a series of conversations, Hall and Grape merged the words and the tune. The end result is the wonderful hymn, Jesus Paid It All (Google various sources).

I hear the Savior say, "Thy strength indeed is small;
Child of weakness, watch and pray, Find in Me thine all in all."
Jesus paid it all, All to Him I owe; Sin had left a crimson stain, He
washed it white as snow.

Thank God for Romans 6:23, *"For the wages of sin is death, but the gift of God is eternal life in Jesus Christ our Lord."* Esau's bowl of soup, Judas' bag of silver, and Ananias and Sapphira's hidden treasure are no match for the grace of God. If any one of them had turned to God in repentance, He would have forgiven them completely. Friend, trust God with your past mistakes. And trust Him with your future hopes. Eternity is too long to be lost. Trust Jesus today!

> The price of our sin is death. Jesus paid it.
> The gift of God is eternal life. Jesus gives it.

CHAPTER 9 DISCUSSION POINTS

Discuss the dangers of living for the moment. Consider Jerry Seinfeld's quote, "Everybody is looking for good sex, good food, and a good laugh because they are little islands of relief in what is often a very painful existence."

Discuss which may have been more tempting for Judas: Thirty pieces of silver or the significance in being included in the overthrow of Jesus.

Discuss the difference in and the importance of the way Ananias and Sapphira were carried off after their death compared to that of Stephen.

What similarities do you see between the actions of Esau, Judas, and Ananias and Sapphira, compared to that of David.

10

SERVING TWO MASTERS

Matthew 6:24

Jesus said it can't be done. *"You can't serve two masters."* The problem with this simple verse is not a lack of understanding. The problem is, even though we know we can't serve two masters, we still try. And inevitably, if you try to serve two masters, Jesus said you will love one and hate the other. You can love only one.

You can't walk with the Lord and hold hands with the Devil. I heard a preacher say this years ago and I've never forgotten it. How true it is. Holding hands with the Devil pictures someone courting the Enemy. It pictures a spiritual impossibility. No one can serve two masters. But I also believe it presents another great truth – If I am truly walking with the Lord, I won't hold hands with the Devil. I will resist the Devil. I will walk with God.

Imagine your life is 100 acres. Satan only wants one acre. Right in the middle. This is an Adrian Rogers quote. It paints a powerful picture. If Satan has an acre in the middle of my life it means I have given him access and he now has influence. I might say I am 99% committed, but what am I allowing to exist on the one percent? It becomes 99% neglect because the one acre gets all my attention. Satan isn't interested in small victories; he wants total dominion. He doesn't want one acre, he wants it all.

How married are you? 100%? 80%? 50%? This is a great question that creates personal examination. I heard this question while listening to a message to husbands and wives. I was taken back by the thought. I began to look at my commitment to my wife Dawn. I wondered, how can a person be 80% married. Well, no one can be somewhat married. If you're married, you are completely married. The question then becomes, am I completely committed to my wife and my marriage? Imagine a Valentine card that reads: Honey, I love you with 75% of my heart! While that Valentine's Day might be one to remember, the thought of being 75% married, or somewhat committed to your spouse is troubling. That question about marriage made me also look at my commitment to Christ. How saved am I? Can a person be 80% saved, somewhat saved, or a little saved? No. If you're saved, you're completely saved. The question is not how saved are you, but how committed are you?

Straddling the fence means - you want what's on both sides of the fence but you're not willing to commit to either. The old saying is, "You're living with one foot in the church and one foot in the world." Jesus said we can't live like that. We can't serve two masters. Fence straddling pictures just that. One foot in salvation, the other in sin. The call is to jump the fence. Get in or get out. Cold or hot. Right or wrong. Yes or no. I will or I won't. Fence straddling indicates a person wants what is on both sides of the fence but is committed to having neither.

Jesus said in Matthew 22:37-39, the first and great commandment is to *"Love the Lord your God with all your heart, with all your soul, and with all your mind…"* (Mark's Gospel adds *"strength"*). Those verses leave no room for a second master. Back to that Valentine card with a message that says, "Honey, I love you with most of my heart!" Guys,

EVERYBODY NEEDS A NATHAN

if you get your wife a card like that, you'll probably end up eating your own box of candy. I have a friend who says to me, "I love you with my whole heart." That's the idea. Loving God with your whole heart. The whole pie. The whole cake. Not a slice. Not a piece. The whole thing. Loving God wholeheartedly. Loving God with your whole heart enables you to love your wife/your husband with your whole heart. Loving God like that opens the door for me to love my children and grandchildren with my whole heart. I can love what God loves with my whole heart. I can love my friends with my whole heart. It's as if loving God wholeheartedly enlarges my capacity to love all that God loves.

Jesus said in Mark 12:30, *"You're either for me or against me."* This He said in response to the Pharisee's accusations that he was casting out demons by the power of Beelzebub. Jesus responded with truth and a bit of sarcasm. *"If Satan casts out Satan, he is divided against himself. How then will his kingdom stand?"* Practically speaking, Jesus is saying a person can't do right and do wrong at the same time. A person can't serve God and the Devil. No one can serve two masters, but they can try. If a person attempts to serve two masters, he will be loyal to one and despise the other. Matthew Henry said, "The more people magnified Christ, the more desirous the Pharisees were to vilify him." The Pharisees could never outsmart or outwit Jesus. Their arguments never held up against the Lord's reasoning. Jesus was operating by the power of God. Demon spirits were being cast out. The Pharisees, on a whim I suppose, said He was operating by the power of the prince of demons. This was an accusation that would have caused many to stammer. But Jesus, it appears, calmly responded that their argument made no sense. Satan would never cast out himself, for if he did his kingdom would crumble. Don't miss their allegation: They accused Jesus of operating in league with Satan. After dispelling their argument, He summed up their case by saying, *"He who is not with me is against me…"*

The Lord said to Moses in Numbers 33:51,52,55, *"Speak to the children of Israel, and say to them: 'When you have crossed the Jordan into the land* *of Canaan, then you shall **drive out all** the inhabitants of the land from before you, **destroy all** their engraved stones, **destroy all** their molded images, and **demolish all** their high places; But if you do not drive out the inhabitants of the land from before you, then it shall be that those whom you let remain shall be irritants in your eyes and thorns in your sides, and they shall harass you in the land where you dwell."* The application for us today is clear – Anything we allow in our life that competes with the Lordship of Jesus will be an irritant, a thorn, and a torment. What am I allowing to exist in my life, my home, my family, my marriage, that is hindering the presence of God? What is there that should have already been driven out, destroyed, demolished, for the glory of God? This passage in Numbers reveals Moses' directions to the children of Israel before they possessed the promised land. Moses has heard from God and is now passing along the imperative yet common sense detail about how they are to possess the land. While God's commands to them may sound harsh to us today, it was the only way the people of God could be the people of God. They could not serve two or multiple masters. The engraved stones, molded images, and high places were to be destroyed. The people who worshipped on these high places were to be driven out. Sadly, they didn't do as the Lord commanded. Time and again God's people allowed some of the pagan culture to remain and it was indeed a thorn in their side. May the Lord speak clearly to us once again about allowing sin to remain. About allowing anything that prevents me from serving God wholeheartedly. About anything or anyone that hinders my walk with God. *"Let God be true, but every man a liar"* (Romans 3:4.).

Alexander MacLaren warned: "The worst sin is not some outburst of gross transgression, forming an exception to the ordinary tenor of a life…. The worst and most fatal are the small continuous vices - Many a man who thinks himself a Christian is in more danger from the daily commission - than ever was King David at his worst. White ants pick a carcass clean sooner than a lion will." Read that again. Certainly, we fear the idea of being devoured by a lion. But MacLaren suggests a troupe of ants can do more damage in less time than a lion. Could it be, some of the greatest competition to the Lordship of Christ in us is not the lions that overpower us but the ants that undermine us? These ants, either undetected or simply allowed, eat away at our faith in God, our confidence in His word, our trust in His will. Slowly but certainly, we are devoured from within by the ants of unbelief, while we guard ourselves from the lions without. David was being eaten alive by the ants of overconfidence and underperformance. Some would disagree, suggesting David was worn down by weariness, worries, and war. No doubt, he had his load to bear. But there is no excuse for his compromise in sending for Bathsheba. Nor is there any excuse for my compromises. MacLaren is right, it's the consistency of a thousand ants that is more likely to destroy us than the strength of the one lion.

Imagine you are faced with some temptation. It's right before you. The decision is yours. We've all been there, faced with some temptation and wondering what if. But the real battle is not about what happens if we get caught, or what happens if someone finds out. The real battle is between us and God. We know we should walk away, but for some reason we linger. We hesitate. We give sin the opportunity to make a move. It's a sad game of spiritual chess. We've all played the game, and we all knew what we were doing at the time. But take this imagined scenario to another level. As you are faced with some temptation, seated next to your temptation is Jesus. He is not screaming "Choose me!" but you know you should. What will you do? It's just you, your sin, and Jesus. Even if you are not a Christian, you know something is telling you to walk away. But let me add to the imagined circumstance: to complicate matters, seated beside you are your mother and dad, your grandparents, your pastor, your Sunday school teacher, your coach, your best friend, all the people you've admired and respected; they're all there watching. What will you do? Think about it. You are faced with some temptation and everyone you trust and respect is watching. How will this story end?

It'd be a lot easier to choose Jesus with all those folks there. But most of the time it's just you and your temptation and Jesus. Alone in a room. Alone in front of a computer. In a place you shouldn't be with someone you shouldn't be with. Whether it's a little white lie or a big bold sin, you can't serve two masters. It is your decision. Whether the temptation is adultery, alcohol, anger, or apathy - it's your choice. Choosing Jesus and your sin is not an option.

The Word of God is the Will of God

Some would say that God's word reveals God's will. I don't dispute that. But I would go even further in saying God's word is God's will. I can never know God's will outside His word. If I meditate on His word, I begin to understand His will. His word is without fault as is His will. God's word is His will. Jesus said in John 17:17, *"Sanctify them by your truth. Your word is truth."* Paul wrote in 2 Timothy 3:16, *"All scripture is given by inspiration of God, and is profitable for doctrine, for reproof, for correction, for instruction in righteousness, that the man of God may be complete, thoroughly equipped for every good work."* God's plan for everyone is different, but His will is the same for everyone. Believers don't have to be confused about knowing the will of God. His will is not bound to a denomination, a creed, or a nation. His will is unwavering for everyone. When you understand God's word you are understanding His will. Praise be to God for providing His written word. Thanks be unto God for those who gave their life to translate His word and get it in the hands of all who have desired to have a copy. But now that we have His word, we must heed it.

God's word will always take precedence over:

What I Think about sports or politics might be interesting. But what I think about God always bows to scripture. If what I think about God and His will disagrees with scripture, then it really doesn't matter what I think. In that case the Bible is right, and I am wrong.

How I Feel about a choice, a decision, or a lifestyle is most likely rooted in how I was raised. I enjoy hearing people's opinions on certain cultural issues. But ultimately, how I feel about someone's decision is of no consequence if my feelings are not rooted in scripture.

What I Believe about certain religious practices in different denominations that varies from church to church, from state to state, and from nation to nation is an interesting topic of discussion. But the Word of God is the equalizer. All beliefs bow to the holy scriptures. Every knee will bow to Jesus and every tongue will confess He is Lord. And ultimately everyone will bow to the word of God which is the will of God.

What I Know about Heaven, Hell, God, Satan, creation, end times, miracles, gifts, salvation, and any other religious idea is subject to the word of God. Sadly, much of what we say we know is based on personal experience. We must take what we know and what we have experienced to the authority on all things concerning living and believing; the word of God is the will of God.

Two Choices

Serving two masters is impossible. If what I think, feel, believe, and know is contrary to the word of God, then it is also contrary to the will of God. God will not bless anything outside His will. Taking that idea a little further, we only have two choices according to Paul. In Galatians 5:19-26 we find a listing of the works of the flesh and the fruit of the Spirit. No man can serve two masters. Paul writes in Galatians 6:16, *"Walk in the Spirit, and you shall not fulfill the lust of the flesh."* Paul describes the works of the flesh beginning in verse 19: *"adultery, fornication, uncleanness, lewdness, idolatry, sorcery, hatred, contentions, jealousies, outbursts of wrath, selfish ambitions, dissensions, heresies, envy, murders, drunkenness, revelries, and the like…"* Beginning in verse 22 he lists the fruit of the Spirit: *"love, joy, peace, longsuffering, kindness, good- ness, faithfulness, gentleness, self-control…"* If no man can serve two masters, then we must also believe no man can walk in the flesh and walk in the Spirit at the same time. David was a man after the heart of God, but on at least one day in his life he walked in the desires of his flesh. That one day and that one act cost him dearly. God forgave him, but I'm not sure David ever forgave himself. Everybody needs a Nathan who will help us receive the forgiveness of God and live in its fullness.

In the second half of this chapter, I want to explore three ways of applying this great verse of scripture found in Matthew 6:24. These applications would have been relevant when Jesus made this point and I believe they still apply to any of us seeking to please God. First, I believe Jesus was questioning their loyalty to Him and His kingdom. Second, I believe Jesus was affirming His authority as Lord and master. Third, I believe Jesus was calling them to a life of purity and transparency.

Jesus Questioned Their Loyalty

I believe it was a legitimate concern for the furthering of the Gospel. We know Peter would deny Him and Judas would betray Him. Were they following Jesus for the free bread and fish? Would they be loyal in the face of adversity and threats of death? This one verse is a practical call to follow Christ. A call to follow Him when it'd be easier to go back.

To illustrate my point, Guys, what if you said to your future bride on the night before your wedding, "Honey, I love you and I can't wait to be married to you. I am so looking forward to spending my life with you. But, after we're married, I still want to see some of my old girlfriends. Nothing serious - just reconnecting every now and then. I just want you to know when that happens, I still love you." As the old saying goes, I'm pretty sure that would knock the honey right out of the honeymoon. Let me point out the obvious, any man that would say that to his future bride needs a psychological exami-nation. Any man that would dare think, let alone suggest such an idea doesn't need to be the husband of anyone. But I'd also like to make the point – His idea is no more ridiculous than those who say they love Jesus, yet they still love the world. His suggestion is no more absurd than the notion that a person can be saved and still live in their sin. As crazy as that sounds to even say it, there are countless folks today who say they love Jesus, but they have never stopped loving the world.

Concerning that future husband's plans after the wedding, I think we can all agree…That's not marriage. It appears he was planning a wedding with no intention of having a marriage. I would also point out regarding his after-marriage proposal…That's not commitment. There was a day when marriage meant loyalty to each other. There was a day when being saved meant being committed to Christ. I'll also point out, concerning what he said to his future bride…That's not love. She may have had his ring but she didn't have his heart. Finally, regarding what he said …That's unfaithful. Can you imagine the minister asking at their wedding, "Do you promise to love, honor, and cherish her, and keep yourself only to her as long as you both shall live?" And he responds, "Yes, but we've worked out an agreement." Call it what you will – it's insanity. But sadly, the insanity is not as insane is it once was.

In Matt.27:1-5 Judas allowed competition. He had tried to serve two masters. His attempt didn't end well. He tried to be a disciple of Christ and a friend of the Devil. He tried showing loyalty to Jesus, with a kiss of betrayal, and he tried to be a friend to the enemy by leading them to where Jesus was. His desires for acceptance competed against his discipleship with Christ. He loved money more than Jesus. No man can serve two masters – but he can try.

Jesus Claimed His Authority

Someone or something is your master. It's inevitable. Someone or something leads your decision-making, inspires your choices, controls your responses. In this simple verse, the Lord is saying it is impossible to be owned by two masters. It is impossible to be serving and loving two masters at the same time. Jesus is Lord. He knew who He was and what He came to do. No ego at work in Jesus – just a king who humbled Himself to die on a cross to save all who would believe. Jesus knew there was only one way to the Father, and He knew He was the way, the truth, and the life (John 14:6). he knew He was the Good Shepherd (John 10:14). He also knew He and His father were one (John 10:30). There's no need for any of us to try and make Him Lord. Our only response to His Lordship is to admit it and surrender to it.

Proverbs 3:6 has been my life verse since I was in my early twenties. I was given a cassette tape with a sermon on it titled, "Acknowledge Him." It was preached by Jack Hyles and given to me by my friend Steve Agee. I received the tape at a time when I was doing some deep soul-searching. I was pastoring a small Methodist church in Neel, Alabama. Those were some of the finest people a man could ever be privileged to pastor. I loved them and they loved me. I served there from the time I was 21 years old until I was 26. I learned a lot about God, myself, and what I believed in those five years. I recognized and answered my calling to travel and preach. And I also recognized that it was best for me and the Methodist church to part ways. Most of the reasons were theological, some were just preference. When I received that sermon of Jack Hyles preaching, I was on a mission to determine my place in the ministry. That simple cassette tape was an answered prayer. I listened to that message so much I almost wore out the tape. I memorized most of it. One thing Jack Hyles said that has stuck with me all these years was, Proverbs 3:6 has a fence right down the middle of it. He said one side of the fence is mine and the other is God's. One side is my job, the other is God's job. It is my job to acknowledge Him, and His job is to direct my paths. That's where most of us get in trouble. We try to do God's job rather than staying on our side and trusting Him. When I try to serve masters, I am straddling the fence in Proverbs 3:6. I am trying to do my job and God's job too. I am serving Him, but also attempting to persuade God. My job is simple: Stay on my side, acknowledge Him, go when He says go, and stay when He says stay. Just be loyal to His Lordship.

In Acts 5:1-11 Ananias and Sapphira surrendered to compromise. I want to suggest Ananias and Sapphira had a number of things going for them – position in the church, respect from their peers, and fellowship with believers. Chances are, they were leaders in the early church. Most of that is assumed, but there is one thing we know: They, like many others, were selling their possessions and giving the money to the church. But they had an idea. They would sell their land and give only part of the proceeds to the church. They would keep back some of the money, I would imagine, as a safety net in case the church they were a part of faltered. When we surrender to compromise, we bow to lesser loyalties. We must under-stand, Ananias and Sapphira had the wrong view of wealth as do many of us. They believed wealth could be counted. That value has a price tag. Rather than trusting the Lord with priceless riches, they trusted in the lesser loyalty of money in the bank. Now, I'm not against having money in the bank. But if our trust is in wealth rather than the riches of His grace and goodness, we are of all people most bankrupt. They were willing to lie about their gift to the church which reveals their true heart. They claimed Jesus as their Lord but sacrificed their testimony on the altar of wealth and prosperity. If we lie to God, there is no limit to how far we will fall. When we compromise in our walk with God, we will compromise anywhere, at any time, with anyone, about anything. James 1:8, *"A double minded man is unstable in all his ways."* You can't serve two masters.

Jesus Called Them to Purity

Jesus is speaking to the men who will be writing epistles, building churches, becoming missionaries, and taking the Gospel to the world. Purity in heart was a priority. One of Jesus' earliest admoni-tions about purity is found in Matthew 5:8, *"Blessed are the pure in heart for they shall see God."* Paul wrote in Romans 13:14, *"But put on the Lord*

Jesus Christ, and make no provision for the flesh, to fulfill its lusts." These verses, among others, call believers to stay clean in the midst of corruption. To stay pure in the midst of perversion. To strive for holiness in the midst of all that is unholy. The disciples needed this word of warning and encouragement. Many of them would die for their faith in Christ. A pure heart and mind would keep them on point. A pure heart and mind would enable them to live transparently with no hidden agenda and no secret ambition. When they spoke for Christ and against sin, their words would come from a clean heart. When they were attacked for political reasons and for religious reasons their response was credible. They were pure in heart. Practically, I cannot understand how anyone can live with themselves while having a Christian reputation yet having a secret life of sin. How do they sleep at night while privately serving two masters. No one can live pure and impure at the same time. The heart doesn't have enough space for double occupancy. If Jesus moves in, the Devil must move out. If Light comes in, darkness must flee. That being said, imagine your two potential masters, Jesus and your sin, are knocking at your door. Imagine walking over and answering the door. But because no one can serve two masters you can allow only one in. Which master do you leave on the porch? If you invite Jesus in, you must leave your sin outside. If you invite your sin to come in, you must leave Jesus outside. I believe Jesus is on the porch of many homes, churches, families, and marriages. He was once inside, but over time He was told to leave. If sin is alive and active in your life, Jesus isn't. No man can serve two masters. Not even King David.

In 2 Samuel 11:1-5 David drifted toward carelessness. David stayed at Jerusalem while other kings went forth to battle. What was he thinking? Did he ever imagine that his casual attitude would lend itself to compromise? Did he ever imagine his actions on this day in scripture would severely wound him for the remainder of his life? I don't think so. Like many have done, with no apparent consequence, he was being careless with his eyes, careless with his heart, and careless with his life. But there are always consequences. Bailey

Smith said when we become casual about sin and comfortable with ourselves, we are tilted toward tragedy. The tilting toward tragedy is subtle. No one notices. There's no apparent problem. But over time the tilting becomes a tragedy. No one can serve two masters.

David lost the battle in his MIND

Instead of being in the heat of battle, he was at home in bed.
In a relaxed state of mind, he became vulnerable to the Enemy's attack.
He wasn't where he was supposed to be which led to doing what he shouldn't have done.

He lost the battle in his HEART

Instead of being ready for war, he had removed his armor.
Instead of being suited up for battle he was dressed down for defeat.
Instead of being committed, he was compromised.

He lost the battle with his EYES

Instead of going after God's heart, he went after another man's wife.
Job made a covenant with his eyes. David coveted with his eyes.
He looked. He lusted. He lost.

No man can serve Two masters. You'll love and be loyal to One.

If you're like Judas, making deals with the Devil…
There's still hope. Your life is worth more than a bag of silver.

147

If you're like Ananias and Sapphira, dishonest with God…
There's enough grace for you. There's no sin He won't forgive.

∾

If you're like David, in a hole deeper than you ever imagined…
Don't give up. He will give you a clean heart.

∾

Let Jesus be the **One.**

CHAPTER 10 DISCUSSION POINTS

Consider the illustration – Imagine your life is one hundred acres. Satan only wants one right in the middle of your life. Discuss being 99% committed. Discuss the 99% neglect.

Discuss loving God will all your heart, soul, mind, and strength. How does a person do that?

Discuss Alexander Maclaren's quote, "The worst sin is not some outburst of gross transgression, forming an exception to the ordinary tenor of a life... The worst and most fatal are the small continuous vices - Many a man who thinks himself a Christian is in more danger from the daily commission - than ever was King David at his worst. White ants pick a carcass clean sooner than a lion will." Do you agree?

Discuss how the Word of God is the Will of God.

Discuss how our attitude about loyalty to Christ, the authority of God's word, and living a life of purity affects our walk with Christ.

THE FLEE FACTOR

...sometimes the best thing you can do is run.
1 Timothy 6:11

Muhammad Ali and some friends were traveling by plane. The stewardess came by, as they do on every flight, reminding the folks to buckle their seatbelt. Ali said to the stewardess, "Superman don't need no seatbelt." The stewardess replied, "Superman don't need no airplane" (unverified story @ Google). There's only one Superman and there was only one Ali. We all need to be reminded, there are no super men, just men. Men who need a Savior. Men who sin and sin again. Men who fail and fall short of the glory of God. Men forget birthdays and anniversaries, names and important events, and really important information our wife tells us, and we should have written it down, but we forgot to do that too.

We need some super men and women today. Super faithful to God. Super interested in knowing God. The Superman of old was faster than a speeding bullet, more powerful than a locomotive, and able to leap tall buildings in a single bound. For most of my life I have been less than even close to super. I have been mostly normal. Not really super at anything. I was not a great athlete. On my junior high school basketball team, I wore the number 00. That double zero summed up my basketball skills.

Neither was I a great student. When I finally began taking college classes in 1982, I was so behind in my education I took the better part of two years to catch up. One of my three classes during that first quarter of college was a How To Study class. One of them was 099 English. The third was Western Civilization. I failed the Western Civilization class. I took it a second time and failed it again. I took it a third time and passed with a C. I was not ignorant nor was I slow. I had been uninspired during most of my high school career. I had a bad case of I-Don't-Care. For most of my high school years I never studied for a test. I never wrote a paper. I never took a book home. I never tried. In the tenth grade my classes were typing, art, ROTC, agriculture, physical education, and English. Looking back, I am ashamed of my choices. I had no ambition other than graduating, getting a good paying job at a local GM plant, and living happily ever after. But God and His call on my life interrupted those plans. He saved me one year after high school, and called me to preach some three months later. Well, actually, God was dealing with me all through high school. I knew I needed to get my life right with God, but I knew if I did, I was also going to surrender to His call on my life to preach. I don't understand how that worked out, but I know now what I knew then – If I became a Christian, I was also going to become a preacher. Maybe that's why I lived so carelessly. Maybe I was hoping those feelings would go away. Maybe I thought I could outrun His call. Running seems to be a common theme in the stories of those who received some calling into the ministry. Running, accompanied with rebellion, leading many to end in ruin. Thank God I didn't end in ruin. In the spring of 1982, I went to a Christian youth camp and was forever changed. During that weekend, I surrendered to Christ quietly. And while I didn't make a big deal out of it publicly, I knew something in me had changed. I came home, bought a Bible and began reading it, began to listen to the sermons, and made a private yet real commitment to Christ.

In May of 1982, I was finishing up a semester of trade school where I was training to be a machinist. I was actually making progress. It was at that time God interrupted my schedule. Following that youth camp I mentioned earlier, I wasn't the least bit interested in becoming a machinist. I had God on my mind. He had placed preaching on my heart. On a Friday night after class at the trade school, I took the long way home. I felt led in the direction of a water park near Decatur, Alabama that also had an open prayer chapel. I drove up to the chapel, got out and took a seat inside. It was there I poured out my heart to God. After some time just talking to God about my life and the choices I had made, I made a bold statement that has shaped my life to this day. I said, "God, if this is you and if this is real, I want everything you have for me – save me." He heard me. He saved me. He forgave me. In a moment of time, I went from lost to saved. Needless to say, I stopped running. I began to tell my family and friends about being born again. And soon I was also announcing God's call and my commitment to preach the Gospel.

I know what it's like to run from God. Over the past forty years or so I have learned what it's like to run from sin. I have never been one to go looking for sin. If you look for sin, however, you can find it anywhere you are. I admit also, I have always been skittish when it comes to sin. I don't mind running from it. I'm likely to keep my distance from something or someone that might pull me away from what I know to be right. I don't think a person falls into sin like falling into a ditch. I have found it best to keep my distance from the ditches. I have not been perfect. I have come short of God's glory again and again. I have said things, thought things, and done things I shouldn't have said, thought, or done. And I must confess, after all these years, the Devil is still after me. I am made of the same flesh and blood that Samson and King David were made of. Woe is me if I think I am past the point of being tempted and wrecked. In this fourth quarter of my life, I am in no position to take off my armor and rest. I am still called to get up, stand up, and suit up as a good soldier of Jesus Christ. The Enemy is still hurling fiery darts. My only hope is my shield of faith. I'll keep running from sin. I'll keep fighting the Devil when I must. I'll keep living my life for the Lord - until I can't run anymore, can't fight anymore, and until my life is finished. I am His. And just like in 1982, I still want everything He has for me.

Joseph Ran

It was the best thing he could have done. The worst thing would have been to linger. The encounter with Potiphar's wife leads one to believe this entire episode happened quickly. In Genesis 39:6 we read that Joseph was handsome. Evidently his appearance opened the door for Potiphar's wife to be drawn to him. In 39:7 she *"cast longing eyes on Joseph."* Then she said in no uncertain terms, *"Lie with me."* In 39:8-9 Joseph refused her advances asking, *"How then can I do this great wickedness, and sin against God?"* In 39:10 she continued to pursue him day after day. And day after day he refused her. In 39:11-16 she caught him by his clothing and demanded he lie with her. But he fled. He ran for his life. She then accused him of trying to take advantage of her. He was caught and thrown in prison. But God knew and God was with him. Joseph ran from Potiphar's wife. Joseph knew if he sinned with her, it would not only be a sin against Potiphar and his wife, but it would be a compromise of everything he believed. I can see him now, running down the street, he may have been bare backed, but he was running with a clean conscience. He had lost his coat but not his character. When you run from sin you may lose some things but look at what you keep. Look at what you gain.

David Should Have Run

David should have run, not for his health but for his peace of mind. Should have. Could have. And if he had it to do over, he would have. But isn't that the story of so many? If I could just go back. If I could live that day over again. If I had one more chance. If I knew then what I know now. Life is filled with "ifs" and "what ifs." As I have already stated about David – He looked. He lingered. He lost.

Sometimes the best thing you can do is run. Run from sin. Run for your life. Run for your marriage. Run for your children. Run for your peace of mind. Joseph ran. David should have.

Here's the one-hundred-dollar question - Is there anything in your life not under the Lordship of Jesus? I remember hearing that question asked in a sermon. I also remember taking the question seriously and taking a good look at myself. I remember the conviction that question brought. I also remember the changes I made. On the TV show Gunsmoke, sheriff Matt Dillon was known to tell the troublemakers to, "Get out of Dodge and don't look back." There are times in our own lives when we need to make a clean break with our sin and don't look back. No time for discussion, just leave it, leave her, leave them, leave him, and don't look back. When Joseph was seduced by Potiphar's wife, there was no time for chit-chat. He knew there was only one thing to do - Run! Johnny Cash said, "Being a Christian isn't for sissies. It takes a real man to live for God - a lot more man than to live for the devil." It takes backbone, courage, convictions, and heart to run from sin. It takes someone willing to love God more than they love their sin.

I've just quoted Matt Dillon and Johnny Cash. Why not get a little insight from John Wayne too? He said, "Courage is being scared to death but saddling up anyway." I love that quote. Living for Jesus often calls us to saddle up even when we're scared of what we're going to face but believing God goes before us. Joseph saddled up and did the right thing when it would have been more convenient in the moment to compromise and sin. No one ever said following Jesus was easy. David should have saddled up and gone to battle like other kings. He should have armored up and gone to where his men were. He should have resorted to the courage of his shepherding days when he faced the giant and didn't flinch. If he had faced his sin like he faced the giant, he would have been a greater king and we would have a greater hero. Such is life. We learn from David's weaknesses lessons that help us deal with our own shortcomings.

Like most people I've watched the movie, *Forrest Gump*. Except for a couple of scenes, it is a great film. One of my favorite parts of the movie is early in his life when he's being chased by the mean boys on bikes. Forrest has difficulty outrunning them because of the braces on his legs. And then, miraculously the braces fall off. Jenny screams, "Run, Forrest, run!" The further he runs the faster he runs, and the freer he becomes. Sometimes the best thing we can do is run. As Forrest ran, the shackles fell off, and I think that's true for believers as well. Running from sin is not a sign of compromise but commitment. Running from sin is not a sign of cowering down but standing up. It's not a sign of being soft but strong. As I have mentioned before I am thankful for the consistent life that Billy Graham lived. But none of us know how many times he ran from sin. We don't know about the times, behind the scenes, when he refused to compromise. We saw him on TV preaching to thousands, but we never saw his resolve, when no one was around, to practice what he preached. Countless other well-known preachers failed where Billy was faithful. Sometimes the best thing you can do is run.

Early in my ministry when I was just a young man, I had pastors that warned me again and again about staying away from situations where I'd be tempted to compromise. I also read about the dangers of flirting with sin and the lasting effects. Professors in seminary warned us preacher boys about those dangers and the heartache that follows a life of yielding to temptation. The message was clear: don't fool around with sin. As Paul said, flee! But over time I have witnessed too many folks who, instead of fleeing, were fascinated. Instead of resisting the devil, they resisted the Lord. Instead of getting out of Dodge, as Matt Dillon said, they got in over their head. Paul told Timothy to flee. Several years ago, a friend of mine asked me to pray for him. And he asked using crude language. He said he needed prayer because the Devil was beating the Hell out of him. I assured him of two things – First, I would pray for him. Second, I guaranteed him the Devil wasn't interested in beating the Hell out of him – He wanted to beat the Heaven out of him.

You might say your problem is not the love of money. I understand that because, honestly, I have never struggled with an insatiable love for money. But, if I may be so bold to ask, what is your problem?

Your struggle? What is the one thing that consistently hinders you from being faithful to God? If I can honestly confess my sin to myself,, then I can move forward in confessing it to God. I will never be honest with God until I am honest with myself.

Why don't we run from sin? Why do we give it an opportunity? If we know what it is and what it could do – why give it a chance? Maybe we underestimate its power. Maybe we overestimate our ability to resist. And then there's the slight possibility that we enjoy the sin we're committing. Make no mistake about it, in the moment, sin satisfies. It satisfies the ego and satisfies the flesh. If there was no temporal satisfaction in sin, no one would be sinning. The forbidden fruit tastes good. If it didn't no one would be eating it. The affair, the addiction, and the anger all bring some measure of satisfaction. On the other hand, worrying, doubting, and stressing also bring satisfaction. As a traveling preacher I have had many conversations with folks about their sin. Most of these conversations were from people who knew I was passing through and they felt freedom in opening up to me about their sin. If I have heard it said once, I have heard it said a hundred times, "Brother Mike I know what I am doing is wrong. I know I need to stop. But I just can't." At that point, what can this preacher do? They know what the Bible says. They have felt the Lord convict them of their sin. They know they need to change. But they're not ready, or they're not willing to change. That being said, I want to make an educated assumption – Most people don't turn from their sin because they simply don't want to. I believe that to be theologically and practically sound. Needing to do something and wanting to do something are most often separated by action. Just because a person knows they need to doesn't mean they want to.

This chapter is titled The Flee Factor. Paul writes in 1 Timothy 6:11, *"But you, o man of God, flee from these things…"* Flee means run. In another translation flee means fly. You get the idea. Paul is referring to what he said about the love of money. In 6:10 we see those folks described in three ways:

157

People who love money too much...

The idea is greed. Earlier in verse nine Paul describes these people as those who fall *"into temptation and a snare, and into many foolish and harmful lusts..."* That's an amazing description that should make most folks run from such a temptation. Paul's description is that of people who are never satisfied, never content. We see these people today as those who are always wanting more, bigger, better, faster, nicer. These are the folks who are consumed with how to make more, have more, and get more. In Mark 4:19 we find Jesus' teaching about the deceitfulness of riches and how it chokes the word in believers and causes them to become unfruitful. So, how do riches deceive us? I have witnessed it and I have lived it. If we have a hundred dollars, we're not content until we have a thousand dollars. Having a thousand dollars makes us feel so secure we want two thousand. And the cycle never ends. Regardless of how much money we have, we are deceived into believing we need more. The same goes with having a nice home and a new car. Never content, we seek to have a nicer home and a newer car. Riches deceive us into believing the more we have the happier we will be. Riches deceive us into believing one day we will finally have all we need. But for many that day never comes. And if it ever does, we're deceived once again to wanting and needing even more. The truth is, only the Lord Jesus brings true contentment.

People who leave their beliefs behind...

In their greediness, some have *"strayed from the faith."* What does this greed look like? Adrian Rogers said, "Anything you love more, fear more, serve more, or value more than God is your idol." When you read those words in verse ten, notice Paul doesn't say their wealth had caused them to stray from the faith – it was in their greed. Being wealthy is not sinful. Being greedy is. I know a number of wealthy people who have used their money to help others, minister to others, and provide for others. The people that Paul describes are no longer firmly persuaded in God, planted in His word, and pursuing His plans. They have become a captive to their greed. As Adrian Rogers said, it has become an idol. At some point they became consumed with their pursuits and forfeited their faith in God. How does that happen? I think it begins with misplaced priorities. Somewhere in their faith journey their priorities changed. Rather than loving God first and foremost they began to slowly love money more than God. This doesn't mean they're bad people. It could mean they're good people who made some really bad decisions, the worst of which was to turn from God.

People who lose their peace of mind...

Paul writes in 6:10 that they *"Pierce themselves through with many sorrows."* Remember, Paul makes it clear that money is not the root of all kinds of evil. It is the love of money that is the problem. For those who love it too much, their life becomes painful with many sorrows. Maybe it is because of much debt. Maybe it is because of worries. Maybe they are pierced with the expense of keeping everything they own maintained. Could it be these folks are pierced, as they grow older, with thoughts of all they sacrificed because of their greed? Time has slipped away. Children and grandchildren have become adults. Youth has vanished. Death is imminent. And all they have to show for their time on earth is vanity. Why does Paul use the imagery of piercing? Because the end result is that painful – The end result of allowing something or someone other than God to lead you, control you, and be Lord over you. That, in and of itself, is painful.

Paul said to run from all that. "Flee these things." Run for your life. Why? Because, as he writes in 6:9-10, these things will *"drown"* you and *"pierce"* you. Run as if you're being chased by enemies that will pierce you through till death or hold you under till you drown. Don't try to be reasonable – Run! Don't try to work out a deal with the Devil. If you're David, put on your armor and go to war.

There Are Three Flees Paul Warned Believers About…

Flee Immorality 1 Corinthians 6:18-19 *"Flee sexual immorality. Every sin that a man does is outside the body, but he who commits sexual immorality sins against his own body."* This is one of the few sins that a person does which creates ripple effects that can last a lifetime. This sin is against yourself. Sexual immorality is a sin with your body and against your body. It is an act of adultery against yourself. It is an act of complete contradiction to who you are and what you know to be right. Paul is writing to the Corinthians, and as corrupted as they might have been they still had enough spiritual gumption to know the gravity of sexual sin. There's an old saying that goes something like this: "He shot himself in the foot," which means he created trouble for himself. He hurt himself. He's digging his own grave. King David created problems for himself. There are many today who, even though they are saved by grace, are separated from fellowship with God by their own foolish choices. Even though David was forgiven, he never completely recovered from his date with Bathsheba. Before we move on from this idea, let's back up and look at what Paul said in 1 Corinthians 6:13 *"…the body is not for sexual immorality but for the Lord, and the Lord for the body."* My body is to be used for God's glory. The Lord indwells me, lives in me and through me. I am His and He is mine. As a believer my body is a member of Christ (1 Cor.6:15). My body is a temple of the Holy Spirit (1 Cor. 6:19). He dwells in me. When I commit sexual immorality, it is a sin against the person I am with, against God, and against myself. Paul wrote, *"Flee immorality."*

Flee Idolatry 1 Corinthians 10:14-15 *"Therefore, my beloved, flee from idolatry."* While most of us today don't bow to images or idols, some are guilty of what Paul described as having *"fellowship with demons"* (1 Cor. 10:20). Also, we are guilty of attempting to *"drink the cup of the Lord and the cup of demons"* (1 Cor. 10:21). Paul makes it clear we cannot *"partake of the Lord's table and the table of demons"* (1 Cor. 10:21). And if we do, we are provoking the Lord to jealousy. I don't know about you friend, but I am a bit fearful of provoking the Lord. And while most of us understand that we are to shun the worship of any kind of idol, some of us are attempting to walk with Jesus and hold hands with the Devil. No one is somewhat saved. A person is either completely saved or completely lost. The question for the Corinthians and for us is not how saved we are, but how committed we are. I am completely married to Dawn, but am I completely committed to Dawn? I am completely saved but am I completely committed to the One who saved me? Too many of us have put God at the bottom of the list of priorities. He's just another box we check off the list. We believe Jesus is Savior, but we don't trust Him as Lord. Flee idolatry! Lordship means Jesus is number one and everything else is at least second.

Flee Impurity 2 Timothy 2:22-23 *"Flee also youthful lusts…"* Paul is writing about being a *"vessel for honor, sanctified and useful for the master, prepared for every good work"* (2 Timothy 2:21). In becoming such a vessel he writes to young Timothy about fleeing youthful desires. Why would the elder Paul warn the younger Timothy about such decisions? Because, as many of us know, the foolish, immature, and hasty decisions we often make as young men and women can haunt us the rest of our life. I imagine many of you reading these words remember a decision you made as a young person in your late teens or early twenties that has been a source of regret all your life. Maybe it involved alcohol, illegal drugs, sexual sin, or anger. Paul mentions disputes and strife in verse 23. He writes about refraining from quarrelling in verse 24. If that is the issue Paul is addressing, and it could be, think if all the heartache caused by disputes, strife, and quarrels. Think about all the anger and resentment, lifelong regret and heartache caused by a few moments of unnecessary anger. One of the greatest youthful desires is to win at all costs. Maybe Paul is warning Timothy about the dangers of prideful arrogance. Do any of you remember being 21 years old, feeling ten feet tall, and bullet proof? Most of us also know it doesn't take many years to pass before we're back down to six feet tall and gun shy. Spur of the moment decisions can become a ball and chain that a person drags around for the next forty or fifty years. Paul encourages Timothy to be gentle, able to teach, patient, and humble (2 Timothy 2:24-25). In my own personal Christian journey God has been molding me and breaking me of my youthful lusts. Even now, some forty years after being saved and called into the ministry, I still struggle with the young desire to win at all costs. The Lord is still working on me. I'm still fleeing youthful lusts. Sometimes the best thing a person can do is run.

The Flee Factors

We must Flee to Follow. 1 Timothy 6:11 *"Follow after these things…"* Fleeing and following is the practical life of a believer. So much to flee. So much to follow. So much to run from. So much to run to. Following the right things seems to fall in line with fleeing the wrong things. Like most dads, when my children were younger, I had a number of sayings that I repeated until I'm sure they became tired of hearing them. One of my most common sayings was: It's never wrong to do the right thing. Wherever you are, whoever you are with, do the right thing regardless. In these verses, I feel like Paul is being a father figure to his son in the ministry. He's encouraging him to do the right thing at all times. Paul mentions six priorities: Righteousness, godliness, faith, love, patience, and gentleness. Let's think about what these words mean:

> ***Righteousness -*** *The first five letters say it all. Do right. Live righteously. Pursue righteousness. Seek first God's kingdom and His righteousness.*
> ***Godliness -*** *Again, the first five letters say it all. Be godly. Live godly. Pursue godliness.*
> ***Faith –*** *Be a person of faith in a faithless world. Live out the well-known scripture that faith is the substance of things hoped for and evidence of things not seen (Hebrews 11:1). Without faith we can't please God. We walk by faith not by sight. Pursue a life of faithfulness to God.*
> ***Love –*** *Live according to the two greatest commands God ever gave; Love God with all your heart, soul, and mind. And love your neighbor as yourself (Matthew 22:37-39). Be*

162

> *loving. Love the unlovable. Live in such a way that you're easy to love.*
> **Patience** - *Patience is one of the fruits of the Spirit. Be patient with others. Wait on the Lord. Be patient as God is answering prayers.*
> **Gentleness** – *Be gentle with others. Possess a gentle attitude. Always give a gentle response. Speak with gentle words.*

I'd like to admit my struggle to live out those six admonitions I have just discussed. I often feel like Paul when he wrote about doing what he didn't want to do and not wanting to do the things he did. As long as I breathe, I will be pursuing all these attributes Paul wrote about. I will be a lump of clay in the potter's hands until the day I die.

We must Flee to Fight. 1 Timothy 1:18-19 Paul has talked about being patient and gentle, but he also encourages Timothy to fight. This fight is different because it is to be a *"good warfare having faith and a good conscience."* I have a pastor friend who lived a rough life before coming to Christ. He was known to be in a few bar fights in his day. According to him, people knew he fought dirty. What does dirty fighting look like? Again, according to my friend, dirty fighting means anything goes. More than fighting with your fists it means biting, gouging, pinching, pulling, and anything you can think of that might be dirty. Ever since he told me how he used to fight I have tried to be one of his best friends. I don't want to be the guy that causes him to go back to his old ways. I'm in no mood to be gouged. That being said, Paul encouraged Timothy to fight a good fight, having faith and a good conscience. Why does Paul emphasize having a faith and a good conscience? Because some, like Hymenaeus and Alexander, rejected such and *"suffered shipwreck"* (1 Timothy 1:19-20). There is very little information about these two men. They were not necessarily friends but most likely knew one another. They also most likely started out well but finished shamefully. Hymenaeus is most likely the person mentioned in 2 Timothy 2:17, while Alexander is most likely the coppersmith mentioned in 2

Timothy 4:14. I'd like to know more about these men, but the greatest information we have about them is inferred in the passage where their names are linked together. Evidently, they didn't have faith and a good conscience, thus causing them to fall short of waging a good warfare. Simply put, they didn't flee what they should have fled, which disabled them from fighting as they should have fought. As one preacher said, you can't fight the Devil if you're dating his daughter. If any of us seek to fight the Devil, the only hope we have of winning is to fight with faith and a clean conscience.

On his deathbed in 2 Timothy 4, Paul wrote that he had *"fought the good fight."* Some might say he lost the fight because his last words are written from a jail cell. Surely, if he had won, he would have finished well enough not to be spending his last days in jail. One might think that the man who wrote much of the New Testament would have lived out his last days in luxury, being waited on, being served, having life's best. But Paul didn't spend his last weeks and days living like that. He spent them in prison, still writing urging Timothy to come before winter and bring the *"cloak, and the books, especially the parchments."* Those last requests of Paul to Timothy always stir my heart. He's dying but he's still writing. Paul did much of his fighting by putting ink on parchment. He was writing what God would use as Holy Scripture. He knew something about fleeing. He had fled an old life of selfish living and had run to the Savior in hope and consecration. Paul didn't lose the race. He won and finished well. Maybe today we have the wrong view of winning. Paul fought and won even though he died in prison. Fighting the good fight doesn't guarantee a happy ending with wealth and luxurious living. Fighting the good fight doesn't mean you'll be applauded or even appreciated. Quite honestly, fleeing the Devil and fighting the good fight doesn't guarantee anything in this life other than the satisfaction that you fought with faith and a good conscience, which is pleasing to God.

We must Flee to Focus. 1 Timothy 6:12 *"Fight the good fight of faith, lay hold on eternal life..."* Paul urged Timothy to get a hold on eternal life. What a thought! Laying hold of eternal life takes my thoughts back to Jacob as he wrestled with God. In the wrestling, Jacob ultimately resorted to clinging or grabbing hold to God refusing to let go until God blessed him. Oh, my friend, if we could only lay hold to eternal life like that. Laying hold to hope, promises, joy, peace, like Jacob clung to the Lord. Lay hold and don't let go! Paul's focus was on things above. That eternal perspective was how he influenced Timothy. As I've mentioned, my mentor in the ministry for close to forty years has been a wonderful man named Junior Hill. He traveled the world preaching the Gospel and pointing people to Jesus, but he always had time for guys like me. His advice and counsel have never been what I would consider academic, but more practical with a commonsense approach. Brother Junior has also had an eternal perspective accompanied with real life applications. Due in part to Junior Hill's counsel I have, in some ways like Timothy, been able to keep focus on what truly matters, rather than being distracted by unnecessary concerns. My life is a product of the grace of God. My ministry has been enhanced and encouraged through the sound, practical, and down-to-earth direction from Junior Hill.

I absolutely believe that fleeing helps me focus. We are constantly hindered by distractions and potential detours. It's easy to get distracted by temporary pursuits, financial worries, and real-life struggles. Our focus should be on God's eternal promises and resting in Him, but life gets busy, and we get distracted. The lure of pursuing what looks like a better life can distract us from resting in God. The woe of financial concerns can distract us from trusting in God. And the common struggles of parenting, paying attention to our marriage, and plans that go awry can distract us from simple daily faithfulness. I have known struggles in my life, and I have seen them in the lives of others. There is a real distraction to look to what will be then and there rather than appreciating the here and now.

Distractions are a part of life. Detours are, too. Don't be discouraged when your life is derailed and suddenly you find yourself on a detour. There's a good chance your life isn't going to turn exactly as you think. You may have a five-year plan, a ten-year plan, a twenty-year plan, and even a forty or fifty-year plan for your life. It's amazing how a doctor's visit can change all that. You might be surprised how a company closure can change your plans. Hearing your husband or your wife say they want a divorce can take your life on a detour for sure. While it's easy for me to write about maintaining focus during these detours, I'm not just imagining what I would do. I have been there. I know what it's like to be detoured and wonder where the road is leading. My wife Dawn does too. Several years ago, she lost her husband. About that same time, I lost my marriage. Those were difficult days for us both. She began life without her husband, and I had to find my way after a failed marriage. Stay focused when God is allowing you to go through some road construction. Stay focused and trust that God is directing the traffic. He's building some bridges. He has you right where you need to be. And you might find that the detour is actually a part of the destination. Stay focused and flee anything that causes you to doubt His ability to get you where you belong.

We must Flee to Finish. 2 Timothy 4:7 *"I have finished my course..."* I love Paul's attitude in this verse and the verses that follow. No whining. No complaining. No wishing he had a do-over. He ran well, but for Paul, the race was almost over. He could see the finish line. We know how Paul finished. We know how many saints of old finished the race. How will you finish? What's it going to look like a few years from now when your departure is at hand? My dad died after an extended battle with dementia. He lived a long life and left a great legacy of faithfulness, loyalty, and integrity. My mother died a few years ago suddenly. She had battled heart disease for years and left us quickly and quietly. She left behind a legacy of love, kindness, and mothering behind the scenes. I'd like for my life to end quietly like theirs. But most of all I'd like to leave behind a legacy like theirs. I'd like to be able to say in advance, I have finished my course. But things may not work out like I hope. My race may end sooner than I expect. I may be in the last year of my life as I write these words. To borrow a line from an old country song, I should be living like I am dying. Because, the truth is, most of us will die like we're living. We will all face death with plans we were not able to complete. That's ok by me. I pray only that God will enable me to finish strong and finish well. May we all flee to be what God wants us to be.

Might we ask the Lord to give us a bad case of the "flees?"

James 4:7 *"Submit yourselves therefore to God, resist the Devil, and he will flee from you…"*

CHAPTER 11 DISCUSSION POINTS

Discuss the idea that sometimes running is the best thing you can do. Consider the John Wayne quote, "Courage is being scared to death and saddling up anyway."

Discuss the ripple effects of loving money too much, leaving your beliefs behind, and losing your peace of mind. How does one thing lead to another in this context?

Discuss the three "flees" mentioned in this chapter: Immorality, idolatry, and impurity. What boundaries can we put in place to protect our walk with God?

How does "fleeing" help us follow, fight, focus, and finish?

WHO'S AT THE DOOR

2 Samuel 12:1-9
Revelation 3:14-22

In 2 Samuel chapter 12 the Lord sent Nathan to the home of
David.
In Revelation chapter 3 the Lord is knocking at the door of the
church at Laodicea.
Jesus stood at the door and knocked, and I imagine Nathan did too.
David is compromised and Laodicea has grown lukewarm.

A s a pastor I knocked on many doors where no one ever
answered. But I knew they were there. I could hear them
inside. There's no hint of hesitation in answering the door in 2
Samuel. But I like to imagine, once David realized who was at the
door he would have rather not answered. If I am David, I am
wondering how does the prophet Nathan know what I have done?
What is he going to say? What is he going to do?

In Revelation chapter three little is left to the imagination. Jesus is
on the outside. The church is on the inside. He's knocking and
speaking. They're not responding. David and Laodicea have some

things in common. From the outward appearance all is well. David is married to the widow of Uriah, raising the child she and her husband were expecting. The church at Laodicea is wealthy, well-known, and in need of nothing. Nathan and Jesus are at the doors. What could they possibly want?

A Necessary Interruption

The knocks at the doors of David and Laodicea were necessary interruptions of a life and a church that had turned from God and become accustomed to living with distance between them and God. It was a necessary wake up call. David and the Church of Laodicea had developed the appearance of goodness and even godliness. Paul wrote in 2 Timothy 3:5 about having a *"form of godliness but denying its power."* That's another sermon for another day, but no doubt David and Laodicea were guilty of that sin. While we need to think about the false appearance of David in the aftermath if his sin, and the ongoing hypocrisy in Laodicea, I think we also must pause to examine ourselves. I like to think I am not a sinner like David. And I like to believe I am not lukewarm like Laodicea. But I am not always honest with myself. I find it easy to compare myself with the rest of the world, or even with much of the church. If I look the part, speak the part, act the part, and convince others that I am what I appear to be then what's to examine? That's the danger of relying on appearance.

On October 21 of 1966, the people of the Welsh village of Aberfan became part of a tragic reality after living for years next to what appeared to be a mountain-sized rock. Aberfan was a coal mining community in South Wales. Overshadowing the dust from the mines was the beauty of the rolling hills that beamed with color on this October day. In contrast to the beauty of the hills stood this black mountain at the edge of the village. On this day you could hear the chatter and laughter of at least 250 children as they made their way to the village school on Merry Road. This mountain-sized rock that stood out from the landscape of the village was a monument reflecting the many years of labor that made Aberfan home to the coalminers. But the mountain wasn't really a mountain. It was the result of about a hundred years of coalmining waste being dumped from bins that were carried to the site by overhead cables. This pile of slag had become a natural part of the landscape. It stood hundreds of feet high. That October of 1966, the valley had received unusually heavy rains turning the mountain of coal dust and the surrounding area into a huge sponge. On the morning of October 21, a maintenance worker climbed the hill near the waste pile to look into reports the giant mass of coal waste was moving. Suddenly the mountain began to melt. In a matter of minutes, the giant mound of rain-soaked coal dust covered the small school where 250 children were just beginning their day. In a matter of moments, an estimated two million tons of coal, rock, and mud flowed into the valley destroying the school and many homes. Of the two hundred people who were killed, most were children. Tragically, and in a matter of moments, an entire generation of Aberfan was wiped out. All because of a mountain that really wasn't a mountain at all. It was only a mountain in appearance. These were good people. Hard working people. Folks who were committed to making their village a better place to live. This tragedy didn't just suddenly happen on October 21, 1966. It was a disaster that had been in the making for close to a hundred years (Like A Rock - Andy Stanley -1997).

David and the Church at Laodicea were like that rock in Aberfan. They were not what they appeared to be. It had taken a while, but Laodicea had become lukewarm, and David had become compromised. At some point, and no one knows when or how, Laodicea veered off course. They allowed something. Permitted something. Surrendered something. David also, at some point, went somewhere he shouldn't have gone, dwelt on thoughts he shouldn't have had, and contemplated a life he should have never lived. Nathan and Jesus were necessary interruptions in lives that had become less than what God desired.

My dad was a painter. He spent the better part of forty years painting other people's homes. I learned from him the dangers of painting over bad wood. He was called on many times to repair what someone else had painted over. This is what I witnessed; no matter how many times a person paints over rotten wood, regardless of the color or the quality of paint, beneath the surface there's still bad wood. Some might compliment the beauty of the painting, but while we nod in agreement about the choice of color, a painter who paints over rotting wood knows what he has covered up. Beneath that beautiful paint is bad wood. David had painted well. Laodicea had chosen the right color. God used Nathan and Jesus to expose the bad wood.

A Necessary Inconvenience

Revelation 3:20, *"Behold I stand at the door and knock."* What an inconvenience! Stop and answer the door. I think most of us can relate. Imagine it's a Sunday afternoon, you've had a good lunch, the home is quiet for a few minutes, and it's a good time to doze off and enjoy a wonderful Sunday afternoon nap. Imagine about ten minutes into that blissful time of relaxation there's a knock at the door. And then another knock. And you're thinking nooooo! You get up off the couch, rub your eyes, open the door, and greet someone whose GPS isn't working and they're looking for the person across the street. Now the nap is ruined. It's over. How inconvenient! Oh, the inconvenience of a knock at the door. And for David and Laodicea it was the inconvenience of a knock at the door from someone they knew but never expected. Now everyone will know about David's sin. Everyone will know about the lukewarmness of Laodicea. How inconvenient. David is not what he had appeared to be. How inconvenient. Laodicea's red brick veneer can't cover their compromise. David's not a super-hero. He was a shepherd boy that God anointed to become king. He had been a man after the heart of God. Laodicea is one of the seven churches mentioned in Revelation. They have a great name. They're wealthy and influential. Now, the potential for being exposed is real. How will they go forward? Yes, sin and the confrontation of it is an inconvenient disruption of life. The only real and lasting remedy is repentance.

What does it mean to be lukewarm? In Revelation 3:15 the church at Laodicea is described as *"neither cold nor hot."* The idea that immediately comes to mind is complacency. The implication is they were interested in neither good nor bad, right nor wrong. They were neither cold nor hot. This is a picture of a church that's religious, rich, and reputable but drifting. Like a warm glass of lemonade or a cool cup of coffee, they're lukewarm. They were like the hot water that came from the hot springs in Hierapolis and cold water from Colossae; by the time these waters reached Laodicea they were both warm - neither cold nor hot. Laodicea is the only church about which the Lord had <u>nothing</u> good to say.

Think with me about their neitherness. Yes, I know neitherness is not a real word, but it clearly describes the Laodiceans. They were neither. They were neither cold nor hot. They were neither committed nor uncommitted. Neither convinced nor unconvinced. Neither believing nor unbelieving. Neither faithful nor unfaithful. Neither Christian nor un-Christian. Everything I have just written is a contradiction of terms. Isn't everyone either one or the other? Not necessarily. Lukewarm proves that point. The Laodiceans were neither cold nor hot which meant they were consistently lukewarm. Neither. Not either. James Emery White wrote a book titled, *The Rise of the Nones*. It's been a few years since he wrote the book, but the truth and the trend hasn't changed regarding the number of people in America who claim no religious affiliation. They are the nones. They are marked by neitherness. On surveys and questionaries when asked their religious affiliation they check the box designated None. They are Laodiceans and they are alive and well and growing. They are your neighbors. They believe in God, but they have no connection to a church. Or they are members of a church, but the church has no effect on how they live. The Laodicean church was active, but they were comfortably neither cold nor hot. God knew what was going on behind the closed door of the Laodicean church, among the lukewarm and consistently inconsistent; still He knocked. He knew they wouldn't answer, still He knocked. He knew of their neitherness still He knocked. His knocking at their door speaks far more about Him than it does them. Jesus was not "neither" nor was

He a "none." He was the one and only Son of God who did not come for the righteous but the sinner. He didn't come to condemn but to save. He was and is the Savior, fully committed to saving anyone who, at anytime and anywhere, would believe.

King David was in a "neither" state of mind the day he stayed behind while other kings went to battle. That day he noticed Bathsheba and sent for her was a day that has been remembered, researched, and reflected upon by numerous preachers like myself as to why David acted as he did. Honestly, I wish that day had never happened. If I could rewrite David's story, I would leave out that one chapter of his life. My sermon library would be a little smaller without that chapter. My go-to illustrations for men's events would be diminished for sure. David's story is a real-life adventure filled with the highest highs and the lowest lows. But that one day with Bathsheba became a turning point in his life. It changed his story and changed him. Just a quick reading of Psalm 51 tells us all we need to know about how his sin had taken a toll on him. This psalm is a window into the soul of David. He is still a man after God's heart. But his running after God has been hindered by a limp. His impulsive choices about Bathsheba and Uriah have overshadowed all the good he ever accomplished. He is begging God for restoration. He is a broken man. He is pleading for forgiveness, a clean heart, a new beginning.

This Psalm, this prayer seeks restoration that only comes from God. No more neitherness in David's heart. He is after the heart of God like never before. Brokenness will do that to a person. May God revive us from our lukewarm, neither, complacent state of mind.

A Necessary Interference

When I was a young boy being brought up in rural north Alabama, we had the modern convenience of receiving four channels on our television. We received these channels with the help of an antenna mounted on top of a thirty-foot pole that stood near the front porch of our home. On stormy nights our reception would be blurred

EVERYBODY NEEDS A NATHAN

because of the interference of the wind. I can't tell you the times I stood on the porch turning that antenna a little at a time to the right and then back a little to the left until the picture on the television was clear again. I adjusted that antenna in the wind and in the rain. Mother would stand at the front door and relay the message to me from my dad about the clarity of the picture on the TV. It was a process. I could have died if lightening had struck that antenna pole while I was turning it. But I reckon getting clear reception of the Carol Burnett Show was worth it.

I risked my life all because of interference. A disruption. A hindrance. When Nathan went to see David his words certainly disrupted David's life. But Nathan's visit was a necessary interference. When Jesus stood knocking at the door of the church at Laodicea He disrupted their routine, lukewarm, compromised Christianity. His knock was a necessary interference. Laodicea had grown complacent, compromised, and comfortably lukewarm. So had David. Nathan comes as a means of interfering, disrupting like a messenger with bad news. David's make-believe world of secrets was suddenly all too real. God uses people like Nathan to bring people like David back to reality. And the Lord Jesus has a way of interrupting schedules and interfering in people's lives. Especially when we get away from Him, out of His will, and uninterested in His word, He will knock at our door.

The church at Laodicea boasted of being rich, wealthy, and needing nothing. Sounds like a description of churches today. We like to be comfortable, don't we? I do. Comfort is good. But comfort can put distance between us and God. Especially when God calls us to do something uncomfortable. Laodicea had a comfortable religion. Oswald Chambers warned of "having comfort but no peace." His caution is to any of us who want comfort at all costs. It appears that Jesus' knock at the door was a much-needed interference. Like static on our TV back in the 70s, Jesus' presence interfered with their lukewarm Christianity.

We like comfortable churches. I am speaking for myself here. I like comfortable seating, enjoyable music, safe environments, and good preaching. My point is, we are all at times like Laodicea. We all need a knock at the door. We need Jesus to interfere with our routines. We have come to the place where we'd rather leave church charged up rather than challenged. We need preaching that demands a verdict, preaching that leaves us with no uncertainty about what we are to do, preaching that points us to the cross. Laodicea was comfortable. They *"did not know"* they were poor, naked, wretched, and miserable. David may not have recognized his spiritual drift either, but he certainly knew Bathsheba was a married woman. God used Nathan to awaken conviction in the heart of David. He used Jesus to awaken the Laodicean church to their compromised condition. May He awaken us.

CHAPTER 12 DISCUSSION POINTS

Discuss the "neitherness" of Laodicea. Discuss David's "neither" state of mind.

How was Nathan a necessary interruption in David's life?

Discuss how Psalm 51 reveals the heart of David. Even though he had sinned greatly he was still a man after God's heart. Do you agree?

Discuss the dangers of lukewarmness in Laodicea and complacency in David.

THE LORD SENT NATHAN

2 Samuel 12:1

"And the Lord sent Nathan..."

I remember many years ago hearing a preacher explain how God didn't need any help accomplishing His will. I didn't agree with all that was being said but I couldn't quite put my finger on why. I'm older now, which doesn't mean I have finally figured it out, but I do have more understanding than I did then. I agree that God doesn't need any help, but the Bible is consistently clear that He often uses people to accomplish His will.

The Lord sent Nathan. God did the sending, but Nathan did the going. God did the leading, but Nathan did the following. I'm sure if Nathan had not gone, God would have sent someone else. That preacher back then didn't believe that we have a choice in whether or not we do what God leads us to do. While it has taken me several years, I have come to believe in the perfect will of God as well as the free will of man. In fact, I believe His perfect will allows our free will. Our free will to choose is a necessary part of God's sovereignty. Nathan could have said no. Any of the disciples who were called could have refused. Paul could have turned away. Anyone at any time could have and can resist. And when that happens, God is big enough to direct and redirect and use it all for good. God has never needed help, but He has always sent, led, called, and directed. There has always been a response, to follow or not to follow, from those he sent, led, called, and directed. Isaiah 6:8 is clear in this regard. *"Also, I heard the voice of the Lord, saying, 'Whom shall I send, and who will go for us?' Then I said, 'Here I am! Send me.'"*

I'd like to tell you a story about four people named Everybody, Somebody, Anybody, and Nobody. There was an important job to be done and Everybody was asked to do it. Everybody was sure Somebody would do it. Anybody could have done it, but Nobody did it. Somebody got angry about that because it was Everybody's job. Everybody thought Anybody could do it, but Nobody realized that Everybody wouldn't do it. It ended up that Everybody blamed Somebody when Nobody did what Anybody could have done (Pinterest.com). If we don't do what God has told us to do, who will? And rest assured if you obey God in any matter Somebody will question your motives. Anybody will think they could have done it better. And Nobody will completely understand. Everybody may even make light of your faithfulness. Trust God anyway. May God send us a Nathan when we are like David. May God help us be a Nathan and go where God sends us.

The Lord sent Nathan to David. 2 Samuel 12:1

That's all we know – the Lord sent Nathan to David. That's all the information we have. We don't know how God spoke to Nathan. Was he praying? Was he dreaming? Was he preaching? We simply don't know. What we do know is that God sent him to David, and he went. Did he wrestle with God? Did he delay in going? Was he anxious about David's response? We don't know. All we know about the sending and the going is in one verse. David is king and Nathan is a prophet. David has sinned. Nathan is sent to confront him about his sin. Many of us have been in Nathan's position. We have felt the Lord leading us to do a difficult thing. We have walked into situations that we didn't know how they'd turn out. We knocked on doors when we didn't know whether we'd be received. We've had awkward conversations on front porches, in living rooms, and in parking lots because God sent us. We've prayed for God to go before us. We've prayed for God to soften their heart and to give us the right words. Finally, after praying and seeking the Lord – we went where we were sent. And honestly, sometimes it went well and sometimes it didn't. There were times when our David accepted us, prayed, repented, and reconciled. There were also times when our David was in no mood for conversation, prayer, or reconciliation. In both situations we left knowing we had gone where God had sent us and said what He told us to say. We drove away leaving it in God's hands. In that regard we say, to God be the glory.

The Lord sent Jonah to Nineveh. Jonah 1:1-2, 3:1-2

The Lord sent and Jonah went. Reluctantly. Jonah preached repentance and Nineveh experienced redemption. It was by all appearance, as we sometimes say, a glorious experience. God met with them and honored the preaching of repentance. Although unenthusiastic about going, Jonah went with the help of a big fish and preached to Nineveh. The people believed God and turned from their sin. It's sad to think about all we miss when we choose to not go where God sends. And to think of all we miss when we do go, yet we go with a bitter attitude.

"So, Jonah arose and went to Nineveh, according to the word of the Lord" (Jonah 3:3). I have made light of Jonah's going, especially after chapters one and two of his story. I have suggested that Jonah surrendered to the Lord's call on his life, after almost dying in the belly of a great fish. Like many of us who heeded God's call, we did so after running until we could run no more. During my time as a student at the New Orleans Baptist Theological Seminary I met many students in their forties and fifties who had answered God's call into the ministry late in life. The sending is not the issue. The Sender is not the problem. As always, it is the one whom God sends that creates the problems by not going where they are sent, or by

going with a chip on their shoulder. Needless to say, Jonah didn't want to go.

Jonah's story includes a boat-ride and a big fish. Both of which were God's means of getting Jonah where he was supposed to be. The boat was headed toward Tarshish. But after being tossed overboard he was suddenly in a big fish bound for Nineveh. Several years ago a friend of mine was struggling with what he believed to be God's call into the preaching ministry. He went to get counsel from a much older and wiser pastor. My friend told the older pastor about his struggle and asked him his thoughts on the matter. The older gentleman replied, "Well the Devil sure isn't going to call you to preach." The last thing Satan wants anyone to do is preach the Gospel of Jesus and call the lost to repentance. It is God who does the calling and the sending. How we respond is up to each of us. Running from the sending or the Sender seldom ends well for the runner.

The Lord sent Peter to Cornelius. Acts 10:19-23

"On the next day Peter went away with them…" (Acts 10:23). I think we can safely say Peter was not enthusiastic about going with the men. In 10:28 Peter said in effect, "I wouldn't be here … But God has shown me that I should come." The great sheet he had dreamed about, coming down from Heaven filled with all kinds of living creatures was God's way of showing him a great truth about all people. The Lord told him in the vision to *"Rise up, kill and eat."* Peter refused because he had never eaten anything unclean. The Lord was showing him that now, not only were all animals are clean, but all people could be saved. That was eye opening for Peter. Jesus was the way to eternal life for anyone who would believe in Him, His death, burial, and resurrection. God was showing Peter things he had never seen, never imagined.

God sent and Peter went. But I believe as he went, he must have wondered how things were going to play out. Jonah and Peter have a little in common in that neither of them wanted to go where God was sending them. For Jonah it was lack of concern for the Ninevites. For Peter it was a history of unbelief that Gentiles could be saved. But God brought revival to Nineveh, and God poured out His Spirit on the house of Cornelius. While it would be easy to criticize Jonah and Peter for not wanting to go, we must take inventory of ourselves. The Ninevites could be compared to modern day terrorists. Gentiles were treated like outcasts. How many of us would be eager to go on a mission trip to Iraq, Iran, Afghanistan, or North Korea? We might pray for their salvation, but would we be willing to go call them to repentance? And concerning Peter, name any group that we might consider hopeless, beyond redemption, corrupt, ungodly, heathen, or immoral. Going to them with the Gospel might take more than a vision of a great sheet let down from Heaven. We are more like Jonah and Peter than we like to admit.

The Lord sent Philip to the Ethiopian Eunuch. Acts 8:26

The Lord spoke to Philip saying, *"Arise, and go toward the south…"* In 8:27 we read, *"And he arose and went…"* The Lord sent, and Philip went. But unlike Jonah and Peter, there was no reluctance in Philip's going. The Lord directed Philip to go and overtake the chariot that was carrying an Ethiopian Eunuch. As he came to the chariot, he heard the Eunuch reading the prophet Isaiah. Philip asked if he understood what he was reading. The Eunuch responded by asking, *"How can I unless someone guides me?"* The Eunuch invited Philip to sit in the chariot where he began to explain the scriptures.

The Ethiopian Eunuch was hindered because of where he was, what he read, and when he believed. He was in the middle of the desert returning from Jerusalem where he had gone to worship. He was miles from anyone and any place to seek understanding. But he was also hindered because of what he read. What did these words, written by Isaiah the prophet, mean? He needed someone to explain the scriptures to him. But he was also hindered because of when he believed. He asked Philip, *"What hinders me from being baptized?"* Philip said, *"If you believe with all your heart, you may."* He responded, *"I believe that Jesus Christ is the Son of God."* Upon believing, at this place and point in time, what he needed was a preacher and some water. God had already sent the preacher, but the chances of finding water in the middle of the desert were slim to none. 8:26 says it clearly, *"This is desert."* But suddenly there was enough water for them both *"to go down into."* God knows where you are and what you need. Once the Eunuch was saved and baptized, the preacher disappeared. But God provided both as needed.

Philip pursued the chariot. He preached the Gospel. And he witnessed the power of God. Wow. How many miracles do we miss when we should have gone where God sent? God didn't need any help saving the Ethiopian Eunuch, but He included Philip in the process just as He invites us to be involved in what He is doing. An Ethiopian Eunuch was led to the Lord by a Jewish Preacher, baptized in a pond in the desert, and became just as saved as anyone who would ever believe. God sent and Philip went.

The Lord sent Ananias to Saul of Tarsus. Acts 9:11-17

In Acts 9:11 The Lord said to Ananias, *"Arise and go to the street called Straight, and inquire at the house of Judas for one called Saul of Tarsus..."* Also, in Acts 9:15, *"Go, for he is a chosen vessel of mine..."* In Acts 9:17, "And Ananias went his way and entered the house..." The Lord sent and Ananias went. It appears Ananias was taking on the character of Jonah and Peter. The call to go was clear but still Ananias tried to talk his way out of going. In 9:13 he states, *"Lord, I have heard from many about this man, how much harm he has done to your saints in Jerusalem. And here he has authority from the chief priests to bind all who call on your name."* I'm not suggesting Ananias was afraid of Saul. But I am suggesting if I had been in his shoes, I might have trembled at the thought of going and laying my hands on Saul of Tarsus. I'm sure Ananias had heard about Stephen and possibly others who had died at the hands of Saul.

The Lord assured him that Saul had seen in a vision, *"a man named Ananias coming in and putting his hands on him, so that he might receive his sight."* Ananias was reluctant and possibly fearful. But nonetheless, he went. Scripture was being lived out and would eventually be written about this amazing day in history. A day when Saul received his sight, was filled with the Holy Spirit, scales fell from his eyes, he was baptized, and after some days immediately began to preach Jesus in the synagogues. All who heard him were amazed.

Ananias, according to Saul's own testimony in Acts 22:12, was a devout man according to the Law and had a good testimony with all the Jews who dwelt in Damascus. From these two brief passages, this is all we know about Ananias of Damascus. If he did any writing, we don't know about it. If he accompanied Paul on some of the missionary journeys, we don't know about it. If he ever kept company with men like Silas, Timothy, or Barnabas, we don't know about it. What we do know is the Lord sent him to one of the most feared men of that day, to lay hands on him that he might receive his sight. And we also know that he went. He is remembered for being devout, having a good testimony, and being faithful to go as God directed him. Most of us will never become famous. We will never be awarded a Grammy or an Oscar. Our picture will never grace the cover of a magazine. We will never be millionaires or billionaires. We will never live in a mansion or drive a Rolls Royce. But we can be godly. We can have a good name. We can be faithful. Ananias was. God sent and Ananias went. May we do the same.

Levi Lusko, in his sermon, Fight Like a Wolf, told the incredible story of Larry Waters. His story illustrates the power of never giving up. As God keeps sending, may we keep going (WordPress.com).

"Larry had a healthy fear of ice. He'd been around it and lived near it long enough to know it wasn't anything to play around with. And that's why he parked at the edge of the frozen lake and unloaded his four-wheeler and decided to take that across instead of the heavier vehicle. With his wife, Chrissie, sitting behind him, he cautiously began the journey across the lake, noticing that in the layer of snow that covered the surface there were tracks from cars that had evidently gone through it rather recently. And so, he assumed if heavier cars and trucks could make it across, then he could on the much smaller, lighter vehicle. He was making his way across, but at the halfway mark he heard and felt at the same time the ice cracking and the vehicle jolting. And then it pitched forward. Before he knew it, it had stopped, dropped, and rolled straight into the icy waters of the lake. The vehicle sank to the bottom like a stone, but Larry and Chrissie managed to separate themselves. Still, they were floundering in that hole in the ice.

Both of them instinctively made their way to the edge and sought to do what all of us would do at the edge of a pool: pull themselves out. But on the frozen edge, they just couldn't get a grip. No matter how they tried, their hands kept slipping off the ice. Soon their hands were numb. They were clawing at the edge, and they couldn't do the one thing they were telling their hands to do: pull them out. With their wet clothes and filling shoes, they were heavier than normal. They began to realize they were going to die that day. Larry swam over to Chrissie, and with his few moments of life remaining, he gave her a kiss and told her he loved her, and they accepted that they were going to die cold and afraid, but together.

We're going to leave them there for a while (don't worry… they survive - Larry is the one telling us about this story, after all), but we'll come back to them. Larry's and Chrissie's words and emotions have rung true for me on so many days. Worries, fears, griefs, and insecurities have left me feeling completely and totally helpless in the dark, as if I were sinking into freezing cold water. Fighting and growing and victory in my calling seemed like distant dreams. I've wanted to give up so many times. Maybe you've been there too. But please, I'm begging you, don't give up. You've got to fight. You've got to keep fighting. And then, after that, here's what you do: keep showing up. That is the fight. Just keep showing up every day. Here's another story, and you won't believe how it turns out. It's the story of the Leatherman Tool Group. They make a simple pocketknife that has pliers in it. You could take for granted a pocketknife with pliers. But it didn't exist until it did. Tim Leatherman was on a trip to Europe with his wife right after college, and their Fiat kept breaking down. He had a Boy Scout knife and a pair of pliers that he kept fixing the car with. And he said to himself, if only they had one that combined the pliers with the pocketknife. That would be amazing. Because then I wouldn't have to change hands. He got home from the trip and decided to make it. But it was easier said than done. Two years into the project, in his brother-in-law's garage, on his birthday, he broke down weeping because he couldn't get the pliers and the pocketknife to behave. But he said, 'The next morning, I got up and I showed up. And I kept going.'

Three years later a patent was issued for what we know today as a Leatherman. We'd think, patent! Happily ever after! But that's not how it went. For five years, no one bought it. Every retailer, every hardware store, every company rejected it. They said there was no market for it. The Stanley company, the one that makes thermoses, told him no one would ever go for it. It was too much of a knife for the tool companies and too much of a tool for the knife companies. In all he received five hundred rejection letters. Tim was distraught. After seven years he almost gave up. But a friend encouraged him to keep going. He said he'd work with him and maybe help him find something he hadn't thought of yet. So, they kept going.

Eight years later, Cabela's, a little-known company, said, 'We'll buy five hundred.' By this point, they had the sense to name the tool Leatherman. Cabela's put them on the market, and the rest, as they say, is history. The company is now headquartered in Portland and employs more than four hundred people. There are dozens and dozens of different models, and they sell $100 million worth of Leathermans annually. It's a tale as old as time. A great company success story. Some of you might even have one. They're passed down from father to son, generation to generation. His success has spawned an industry; a whole new category of multitools from different companies now imitate his original idea and are ubiquitous in hardware and sporting goods stores. Think about what it took for Tim Leatherman to keep showing up for all those years when everyone was telling him, 'This'll never work.' That war, that doubt, alone in that garage, on his birthday, weeping, wanting to give up, wanting to quit. Some of you can relate. I wonder, where are you at on that journey? What are you thinking about quitting? What do you think about giving up? What dream are you beginning to lose faith in? Here's the truth: this is a fight. It's not just one round and it's over. It's not just, 'Well, there, I fought. I tried to control my thoughts. I tried to speak differently. I tried to plant the church. I tried to write the sermon. I tried to start the business. I tried to work on the marriage.' That's not a fight! A fight is bloody round after bloody round. A fight is getting knocked down and getting back up again. A fight is spitting your tooth out in the sink! A fight consists of going from failure to failure to failure to failure without losing your enthusiasm. I want to speak life over your life to remind you that God loves you, has a plan for you, wants to do more through you than you can ever imagine. That he wants to reach others through your story in life-saving ways. He's got your back as you grow toward that. All of it's true, and believing it changes everything. But even after you believe it, you've got to fight!

…What about Larry and Chrissie? We left them drowning in the lake. They kissed goodbye. But just before Larry began to sink, he felt a Leatherman in his pocket. And God only knows why or how he thought of it, but he opened it and, using the pliers, he was able to dagger the edge of the ice and pull himself up and out. He immediately pivoted and was able to pull his wife to safety. I imagine they're grateful Tim Leatherman never gave up. Yes, you are fighting a difficult, bloody battle. You are trying to win the war within. But you are not the only one. There are people all around you, people in your family, people in your life, people you don't even know yet, and they're trying to win it too. If you give up, how will God ever use you to reach them? In the garage, through the years of slogging it out, Tim never knew about Larry and Chrissie. But God knew that his showing up and not giving up was going to lead to rescue for other people. As you continue to fight the good fight and keep living, it's not just for yourself. You must fight to take back your life. God wants to save lives through you. You're not the only one trying to win the war within. Who knows what your legacy will be if you keep getting up and showing up tomorrow and the next day and all the days after that."

Tim Leatherman got up, showed up, and never gave up. And because he did at least two people's lives, Larry and Chrissie Waters', were saved. May it be said of us, God sent, and we went. And because we went where God sent, countless people believed in Christ and were saved by God's grace. God does the sending. All we have to do is the going. God does the saving, and sometimes He uses people in the process.

CHAPTER 13 DISCUSSION POINTS

Discuss: God doesn't need any help accomplishing His will, but he often uses people to do so.

What are some common excuses given for not going where and when God sends? Discuss Nathan's possible excuses if he had chosen not to go.

Considering Jonah, how can God use someone is reluctant to go where God sends?

How did God use the vision of a great sheet to change Peter's mind about Gentiles like Cornelius?

How did God use Philip to help the Ethiopian Eunuch?

How did God use Ananias in the life of Paul?

14

PULLING DOWN STRONGHOLDS

2 Corinthians 10: 3-5

For most of my ministry I have been telling the story of two dogs. I have already alluded to it in this book. The story has had a profound impact on me. One day in a chapel service at New Orleans Baptist Seminary I heard a preacher say, "Inside every believer there are two dogs. One dog belongs to the Devil and the other dog belongs to God. Every day those two dogs get in a fight. Whenever the Devil's dog begins to take you down one path God's dog pulls you back toward Him. Whenever God's dog begins to lead you one way, the Devil's dog tries to take you the other. Every day inside of you there is a dog fight." He went on to say, "I can predict which dog will win that fight in your life on any day you choose. The dog you're feeding will always win the battle."

It's been a long time since I first heard that story. But I have never forgotten it or the impact it had on me. That unusual illustration about two dogs caused me to do some soul-searching. It stirred conviction. Caused me to examine my walk with the Lord. Over time I have learned that the preacher was describing spiritual warfare. And the only way to win that war is to starve the Devil's dog and feed God's dog!

Long before that chapel preacher described a spiritual battle, the Apostle Paul addressed the issue. In Galatians 5:17 Paul wrote, *"For the flesh lusts against the Spirit, and the Spirit against the flesh; and these are contrary to one another, so that you do not do the things that you wish."* This is also a glimpse of what begins to happen as the Enemy lays the foundation for a spiritual stronghold in the life of a believer. I am no stranger to what Paul described. I have dealt with the flesh as it lusted against the Holy Spirit in me more times than I could possibly count. I have also felt the power of conviction pulling me back as I veered from God's will in matters small and great. Adrian Rogers said, "A stronghold is a fortress made with walls of resistance. What kinds of resistance were in the minds of the Corinthians? Arrogance, ignorance, despair, demonic thoughts, the organized armies of Hell. Then Paul mentions high things: intellectualism, high-minded attitudes, sophistication" (lwf.org). Gradually, as I continue to feed the Devil's dog, and ignore the drawing of the Holy Spirit, walls of resistance are built up separating me from fellowship with God and knowledge of His will.

I believe David's actions toward Bathsheba and Uriah reveal walls of resistance that numbed him to the seriousness of his sin and blunted his attention to being a man after God's own heart. Spiritual strongholds are certainly a New Testament idea. But David had them too. He allowed the Enemy access to his heart. He fed the Devil's dog. He resisted the Spirit's working against the flesh. He did the unthinkable. Adultery followed by murder. His attempts to clean up and cover up the mess he had made worked with everyone except Nathan. The Lord sent Nathan to uncover David's tangled web of lies and begin pulling down the strongholds in David's life. Strongholds don't develop overnight. Untangling the problems they create may take a while also. Everybody needs a Nathan.

What is a Stronghold? Paul used a military term to make a spiritual point. A military stronghold is where the enemy fortifies and positions himself for an attack. A spiritual stronghold is where the

192

Devil fortifies himself with the intention of taking control. Paul has one word of instruction about these strongholds - tear them down!!

A spiritual stronghold is an area in my life, my home, my family, my marriage, my church, etc., where the Enemy has gained access and made progress in winning the battle. This is spiritual warfare. It is an area in my life where there has been compromise. It is somewhere in my life that I have neglected my walk with God, where I have carelessly given the Devil an opportunity to disrupt and corrupt all that has honored God.

Make no mistake about this passage of scripture, the Apostle Paul is under attack by false teachers and Judaizers. He is being daily assaulted by the Enemy. Imagine if Paul had been defeated, his testimony debunked, and his influence destroyed. We may often make light of the Devil and his ways, but this is truly no laughing matter. The Enemy is in the business of stealing, killing, and destroying. Never underestimate the deceptive power of Satan. Paul's writing about strongholds explains his daily warfare. In this passage he wrote to encourage as well as engage other believers in pulling down the Enemy's strongholds.

Pull down what the Enemy has built up.

A stronghold is a fortification built by the Enemy. Over time, maybe six months or maybe six years, the Adversary makes advances in a believer's life, taking advantage of every opportunity given him. The Enemy's goal is to overtake and destroy anything that brings glory to God. Paul instructs believers to pull down strongholds. Destroy them. Demolish them. Remove every fortification of the Devil. Demolish every little remnant of the stronghold. The Lord said to Moses in Numbers 33:51,52,55, *"Speak to the children of Israel, and say to them: 'When you have crossed the Jordan into the land of Canaan, then you shall <u>drive out all</u> the inhabitants of the land from before you, <u>destroy all</u> their engraved stones, <u>destroy all</u> their molded images, and <u>demolish all</u> their high places; But if you do not drive out the inhabitants of the land from before you, then it shall be that those whom you let remain shall be irritants in your eyes and*

thorns in your sides, and they shall harass you in the land where you dwell."
Notice the directions of the Lord: drive out, destroy all, and
demolish all. Some might say that sounds harsh. While those
instructions may sound extreme, God knew the dangers of allowing
any remnant of the Enemy to remain. This is a clear word of
warning for any of us who desire to live a life fully devoted to God.
Any competition to Jesus that we allow will be an irritant, a thorn,
and a constant harassment. If we want to have victory in Jesus, we
cannot allow strongholds to exist.

How often must these strongholds be torn down? Daily. Maybe
several times a day. As often as is necessary. I had a friend whose
home had been overtaken by spiders. What a terrible thought. She
said she was constantly looking for and killing spiders. And as believers, we are constantly tearing down strongholds or else we will be
overtaken by the Enemy.

Every thought must be caught.

How does a spiritual stronghold begin? Elizabeth Elliot said, "Spiritual strongholds begin with a thought. One thought becomes a
consideration. A consideration develops into an attitude. Attitudes
lead to actions. Actions become habits. A habit establishes a powerbase for the Enemy which is a stronghold." Her definition of a
stronghold is the best I have ever read. Notice again as she describes
the progression of the Enemy's work.

A thought
A consideration
An attitude
Actions
Habits
A powerbase
A stronghold

Paul writes in 2 Corinthians 10:5, *"…bringing every thought into captivity
to the obedience of Christ."* And not only are believers to catch our

thoughts, we are to bring them into the presence of Christ, subjecting them to His holiness, confessing them as sin, humbling them in obedience to Jesus. These thoughts are to be treated as prisoners of war and we are to bring them as captive to the Lord. I don't get the idea that these thoughts will submit easily. We are to take them. Bring them. Catch them. Shackle them. Force them into the presence of Christ. Submitting those thoughts under the Lordship of Christ that they may be transformed as thoughts that please Him. These are evil thoughts, bitter thoughts, angry thoughts, lustful thoughts, worrisome thoughts, doubtful thoughts, unbelieving thoughts, fearful thoughts, jealous thoughts, envious thoughts, and any other thoughts that would, given the opportunity, take us captive.

How often should we bring our thoughts captive to Christ? Daily. The moment we think a thought that brings no glory to God and pulls us away from pleasing Him. The very moment the Holy Spirit makes us aware of thoughts and attitudes that have fortified themselves in our heart and mind. If we allow that thought to exist it will, as Elisabeth Elliot said, become a consideration, that becomes an attitude, that becomes an action, that becomes a habit which is a powerbase from which the Enemy operates – which is a stronghold.

What does a spiritual stronghold look like?

In Genesis 4:8 Cain killed Abel. What a sad passage of scripture detailing the act of one brother taking the life of another. But the actual murder was not the stronghold. Murder was the terrible result of the stronghold. Long before Cain acted it out, he thought it out. Something motivated him to kill Abel. Whatever that something was, is the stronghold. The stronghold was anger. Envy. Resentment. Jealousy. Pride. Both Cain and Abel brought offerings to the Lord. The Lord respected Abel and his offering but did not respect Cain and his offering. Cain became angry. The Lord spoke to him saying, *"...sin lies at the door. And its desire is for you, but you should rule over it."* But Cain didn't rule over his sin. His sin ruled over him. We can only imagine how the death of Abel came about. All we

195

know from scripture is, *"Now Cain talked with Abel his brother; and it came to pass, when they were in the field, that Cain rose against Abel his brother and killed him."* Cain's anger and resentment brings to mind the old saying, he had an axe to grind, which means sharpening the axe with intentions of doing harm to someone. Cain should have ruled over it. He should have torn the strongholds down. But the Enemy had fortified himself. The thought became a consideration. Cain allowed his jealousy to get the best of him. He did the unthinkable. In an outburst of uncontrolled revenge, he took the life of his brother. Paul said we are to destroy strongholds. Before they destroy us.

In 2 Samuel 11:4 David sent for Bathsheba. There are many steps that led to David's sin with Bathsheba. In the first few verses of 2 Samuel chapter eleven we read of the mistakes he made. While other kings were going to battle in the spring of that year, David sent Joab, his servants, and all Israel to war. But he remained in Jerusalem. Chapter eleven is filled with tipping points away from God. Was David tired or maybe depressed in his spirit? Or was he battling spiritual strongholds that sought to destroy him? In Jerusalem, away from the battle, he is in a vulnerable position. He is a warrior without his armor. He is not where he is supposed to be. He has removed himself from the fight. He has distanced himself from his men. In that condition and in that state of mind he walks out on his roof and sees a beautiful woman bathing. We get the idea that David did more than see her, he watched her. I have learned from personal experience and from counseling with others that Satan is most likely to attack us at two points: When we are at our best and when we are at our worst. We are most vulnerable when we are on the mountaintop and when we are in the valley. On the mountaintops we feel invincible. In the valleys we couldn't care less.

Watch how the Enemy works. David has stayed behind while his comrades went to fight. He has watched Bathsheba from his rooftop. He has sent for her. It feels like the domino effect of one thing leading to another. David sent for her knowing whose wife she was. Uriah was one of his most loyal soldiers, and one of David's mighty men. Yet it seems, in his compromised state of mind, neither her marriage nor her husband mattered. David's sending for her is not the stronghold. Something motivated him. The stronghold was compromise. Complacency. Lust. Greed. Pride. No one knows for sure what happened. I have read many theories as to what led this man, who was after God's heart, to disregard all he knew to be right, and send for Bathsheba. As I have said before, I do not like this story in the Bible. It's too real and too relevant. Homes, families, and marriages are being wrecked in the name of unhappiness and entitlement. Men and women carelessly and callously make decisions that hurt the ones they love the most, and in the long run hurt themselves as well. David should have walked away from what he saw. He should have never sent for her. Paul said we must destroy strongholds. Again I add, before they destroy us.

In Acts 5:2 Ananias and Sapphira kept back part of the price. I guess we shouldn't be surprised at the decision Ananias and Sapphira made. I suppose it is human nature, with a little help from the Devil, to take advantage of a good situation. To take advantage of the integrity and honesty of others. At the ending of Acts chapter four, the people were blessed, and God was being glorified. In Acts 4:32-37 we read: *"Now the multitude of those who believed were of one heart and one soul; neither did anyone say that any of the things he possessed was his own, but they had all things in common. And with great power the apostles gave witness to the resurrection of the Lord Jesus. And great grace was upon them all. Nor was there anyone among them who lacked; for all who were possessors of lands or houses sold them and brought the proceeds of the things that were sold and laid them at the apostles' feet; and they distributed to each as anyone had need. And Joses, who was also named Barnabas by the apostles, a Levite of the country of Cyprus, having land, sold it, and brought the money and laid it at the apostles' feet."* What an incredible community of believers. They had faith in God and love for each other. Chapter five is an abrupt departure from all that was happening among that early family of believers. Ananias and Sapphira sold a parcel of land. Instead of giving all the money, they kept back part of the price. This was deceptive and dishonest. Maybe they thought no one would know.

Keeping back part of the price was not the stronghold. Something motivated them to keep back some of the proceeds and pretend that nothing was amiss. What was their motive in keeping back part of the price? Most likely, as with other temptations, there was pride. Greed. Fear. Doubt. And possibly unbelief. On the surface of this early body of believers everyone had everything in common. Everyone shared everything. Everyone was in agreement. Everyone? Were Ananias and Sapphira on board? Were they all in? Evidently not. They were willing to lie to their friends, fellow believers, and possibly even family to cover their disparity. What a shame that the sin of these two believers is still being practiced today. When we do something to be seen of others. When we're not what we appear to be. When we're not completely honest with others. Ananias and Sapphira should have brought all the proceeds and laid them at the feet of the apostles. They should have never followed through with their plans. Should have – Could have – Would have. Paul said we are to destroy strongholds. Before they destroy us.

In Matthew 26:49 Judas kissed Jesus. The boldness of Judas... Consider the ego, arrogance, and selfishness that caused him to parade himself as loyal to Christ, all the while defying, denying, and betraying the One who could and would take away his sin if he only believed. Jesus had described Judas as a devil in John 6:70-71. Though he had no horns, pitchfork, or a pointed tail, he certainly had the heart of the Devil, full of sin and self. It was Satan, in John 13:2, that put it in Judas' heart to betray the Lord. In John 12:6 Judas is described as a thief. In Matthew 26:15 Judas sold out to the Enemy for thirty pieces of silver, the price of an Old Testament slave.

The scene in the Garden of Gethsemane always stirs my heart. While Jesus is speaking, Judas and a host of men with swords and clubs come to take Him by force. The kiss of betrayal was the sign Judas had given the chief priests and elders to know who they should arrest. In Matthew 26:49 we read that he walked up to Jesus and said, *"Greetings, Rabbi!"* And then he kissed Him. It's almost as if he walked up and asked, "Hello Jesus, how are you doing?" Jesus

EVERYBODY NEEDS A NATHAN

asked Judas, *"Friend, why have you come?"* Jesus wasn't asking for information; he already knew why Judas was there. I believe He wanted
Judas to see and understand. In The Message translation of the
question is rendered, *"Friend, why this charade?"* Jesus knew why Judas
had come and it had nothing to do with a bag of silver. Judas should
have known, for Jesus had spoken of this night and this betrayal
many times before. How could Judas not know? He would later take
the silver back to the ones who had paid him. But it was too late.
Jesus was betrayed by one of His own, arrested, and would soon be
crucified, dead, and buried. Sadly, Judas missed the greatest event in
all of history. While Jesus was resurrecting, Judas had taken his own
life. He appeared to be a disciple, but Jesus said he was a Devil. He
lost his mind, and he lost his soul.

The kiss of betrayal was not the stronghold. Something motivated
him to kiss deceptively the One who raised the dead, the One who
opened blind eyes, the One who loved the unlovable, the One who
would die and rise again, the One and only One who could save
him. What was his motive? What was the stronghold? Pride, for
sure. Greed, absolutely. Jealous for notoriety, possibly. Eager for a
position among the chief priests and elders, probably. While this is
about Judas, it is also about me. When I deny Jesus' Lordship in my
life and sell out to the Enemy for any amount, I am just as guilty of
a kiss of betrayal as Judas was. God help me guard my heart. Paul
said we must destroy strongholds. Before they destroy us.

How does a stronghold develop?

Has there ever been anything in your life of which you said, "I'll
never do that again"? A spiritual stronghold is a compromise against
God that I repeat again and again. So, we must ask the question,
what causes me to rebel against God over and over? Where in my
life has Satan fortified himself? Where has he established his presence in me? Over time I may become numb to what I am doing to
the point that shrugging it off is no big deal. What makes a man go
back to drinking after he has been sober for years? Strongholds.
What makes a person go back to immoral living after they have

been clean for years? Strongholds. What causes a person to get out of church? Stop praying and suddenly have no interest in reading the Bible? Strongholds.

The Psalmist wrote in 66:18, *"If I regard iniquity in my heart the Lord will not hear me."* That word regard could be translated *gaze upon*. The idea is to desire, allow, or find pleasure in some act of transgression. Not only are our prayer lives hindered, but strongholds interfere with every effort to please God. Gradually we begin to neglect our walk with God. Gradually our faithfulness to God is hindered. Other things begin to take precedence over our time with God. When I was a boy, my dad and I would mow about four acres around our home and beside our driveway. Mowing and trimming that amount of land took a great amount of time. My dad was meticulous about making sure the lawn was well maintained. This was back in the day before gas powered trimmers. My dad would trim around the trees with a pair of hand-held clippers. I can take you back to where we used to mow, back to the place where the grass was as smooth as carpet. But today there are pine trees bigger than I can reach around. Bushes, thorns, and everything that grows has taken over what used to be our lawn. What happened? Over time Dad stopped mowing much of that and, as we say, he let it go. The owners of that land today have no idea the care that was given to that piece of property. That's a picture of a stronghold. When we stop paying attention to what matters, other things will take over. Small victories lead to total dominion.

Isaiah wrote in 59:1-2, *"Behold, the LORD's hand is not shortened, that it cannot save; Nor His ear heavy, that it cannot hear. But your iniquities have separated you from your God; And your sins have hidden His face from you, so that He will not hear."* When it seems that God is not hearing my prayers, it could be that I have allowed a stronghold to interrupt our fellowship. While blaming God would be easy to do in that circumstance, the root of the problem is most likely my sin, not God's hearing. I remember preaching about this on a couple of occasions. I sensed an immediate resistance to what I was preaching. Could it be we like to think that God always hears our prayers? Isaiah teaches that our sins can separate us from God. I believe this is a clear picture of a stronghold. Every aspect of my spiritual life as a believer is hindered if not halted because of my sin. There's one thing to do – pull down the stronghold. Confess the sin. Seek the Lord. He gives us weapons that are mighty in Him. We will talk about our spiritual artillery in the coming pages.

Ernest Hemingway wrote, "How did you go bankrupt? Two ways. Gradually then suddenly." How does a stronghold develop? Gradually. How does a man get away from God? Gradually. How does a godly woman turn her back on the church? Gradually. How does a man go from being loving and kind to being hateful and callous? Gradually. And then suddenly a person finds themselves in a place they never imagined they'd be. I have heard about men and women who, evidently, fell into some sin. But I don't believe anyone falls into sin. A person might fall into a ditch, or a trap, or a hole, but no one falls into sin. When it appears that someone has fallen into sin, maybe we should look at their life over the past few months or years. If we did, I believe we would see a gradual drifting away from God. Long before they fell, they were stumbling. Long before they fell, strongholds were being built up in their life. Then suddenly it appears they fell into immorality. They fell out of church. They fell into some debauchery. No one falls into sin. The Enemy is allowed to gradually move in, a little at a time, and then suddenly we are overtaken.

Gradually then suddenly is a sad progression to watch in the lives of those we love. The fact that they have allowed a stronghold to pull them away from God doesn't mean they are bad people, it just means at some point they have made a bad decision. And then another. And then another until the stronghold, the wall that separates them from God, has become a part of their life. This could happen to any of us, and it does. I must spend time with the Father daily. Praying and reading His word is how I discern a drift in my personal walk with God. In Hebrews 4:12 we read the Word of God is a *"discerner of the thoughts and intents of the heart."* The Word of God opens my eyes to the strongholds Satan has fortified in me.

How can we define a stronghold?

Adrian Rogers described the Enemy's deception like this: "Imagine your life is a hundred acres. The Devil only wants one acre. But he wants it right in the middle." A stronghold in my life is like that acre. First of all, the Devil doesn't want just one acre. He wants it all. He is never satisfied with small victories. But he will take a small win if it opens the door for a greater victory. Second, one acre in the middle of one hundred acres allows the Enemy influence. Whatever the Devil might be doing on his one acre influences all that surrounds him. Third, like any landowner, if Satan has an acre right in the middle of my one hundred acres, he needs access or right of way to what I have given him. Access is a huge idea in the work of spiritual warfare. Access means opportunity to take over, not from the outside in, but from the inside. Fourth, if I have allowed the Devil to possess an acre right in the middle of my one hundred acres, I might say I am still in control of ninety-nine percent of my life. I might even say to the Lord, I am ninety-nine percent committed. But that leaves one percent uncommitted. The Enemy can do a lot with one percent of your heart and life. And finally, while I may say I am ninety-nine percent committed to the Lord, the truth is the one acre I've given to Satan gets ninety-nine percent of my attention. This illustration by Adrian Rogers is like a picture that paints a thousand words. For me, it is a vivid reminder of the power of a little. A little sin can cause big problems. Only one acre in the middle of one hundred may not seem like a big deal, but even a little sin permitted and allowed is too much for anyone interested in being faithful to God.

Paul wrote instructing those Corinthian believers to tear down, to demolish strongholds. In light of what Adrian Rogers said, we should bulldoze the acre we have given to the Devil. Tear down everything he has built. Demolish every inch where he has gained access. Bulldoze it and then burn it. No reason to be polite to the Devil. No reason to be courteous or kind or understanding. He is the Father of Lies. He is the author of confusion. He is like a lion on the prowl seeking to devour. He is crouched at the door. He is a thief. Bulldoze everything that is his. Kick him off your property and lock the gates. Tear down the strongholds.

What are our weapons for pulling down strongholds?

Paul writes in 2 Corinthians 10:3-4, *"For though we walk in the flesh, we do not war according to the flesh. For the weapons of our warfare are not carnal but mighty in God for pulling down strongholds."* Before I attempt to answer that question let's look at the meaning of a few words in these verses. What does Paul mean by *"walk in the flesh"* and *"war according to the flesh?"* The picture is simple and clear; though we live in this world we do not live like this world. As believers, even though we live in this world we do not respond to attacks, criticism, opposition, or hatred like the world responds. What does Paul mean by the *"weapons of our warfare?"* Paul is describing the means by which believers tear down strongholds. Bear in mind Paul is writing about spiritual strongholds and spiritual warfare. Those who know the Lord do not respond to opposition as if we were of the world. We have weapons that are made mighty in God. What are our weapons for pulling down strongholds? Paul doesn't give a list, but I think we can safely name at least five weapons believers can use to demolish strongholds.

Weapon #1: God's Word

There are hundreds of passages in the Bible about the power and work of God's Word. My intent, as we look at some of the weapons we have at our disposal, is not to list every verse or thought, but to give you a glimpse of the weapons and their power to tear down strongholds. When I was just a child attending vacation Bible school, I remember learning the words to this simple song:

> *"The B I B L E, yes that's the book for me. I stand alone on the Word of God, the B I B L E."*

I needed to learn that as a child. I need to remember that as a man. In Hebrews 4:12 we read, *"For the word of God is living and powerful, and sharper than any two-edged sword, piercing even to the division of soul and spirit, and of joints and marrow, and is a discerner of the thoughts and intents of the heart."* The word of God is an instrument of judgment. It is a discerner of all our thoughts and intentions. The writer continues in verse thirteen that no one and no thing is hidden from God's sight. In pulling down strongholds the Word of God does an inventory of our thoughts and intents. As we are searched, all our disobedience to God is brought to light. There is not an aspect of our life that the Word of God does not investigate, discern, and judge. In 2 Timothy 3:16-17 Paul writes, *"All Scripture is given by inspiration of God, and is profitable for doctrine, for reproof, for correction, for instruction in righteousness that the man of God may be complete, thoroughly equipped for every good work."* Paul's words to young Timothy are those of encouragement and instruction. He writes in the previous verses how Timothy was to continue walking in obedience to the scriptures that he had known from childhood. The scriptures, according to Paul, make us wise unto salvation. The Word of God completely equips believers to stand against the wiles of the Devil. These verses bring correction and instruction in our pursuit of righteousness. In the tearing down of strongholds, the Word equips us to do so. Finally, in Ephesians 6:17 we read, *"And take the helmet of salvation, and the sword of the Spirit, which is the word of God."* Paul has already described the Word as a two-edged sword and now as the sword of the Spirit. We can tear down strongholds with the sharpness of His Word and the power of His Spirit.

Weapon #2: Prayer

If we are armed with the Word of God and the power of prayer, we can tear down any stronghold. But we must be committed to reading and studying the Word and we must be men and women who do more than believe in prayer – we must actually pray if we hope to make a difference. We can pray anytime, anywhere, about anything. Paul writes in Ephesians 6:18, *"Praying always with all prayer and supplication in the Spirit, being watchful to this end with all perseverance and supplication for all saints..."*

Paul said to pray always. That doesn't mean to go around with your head bowed all the time. It doesn't mean to always be uttering a prayer. Neither does that mean you have to always announce, may we pray... And it sure doesn't mean we should call attention to ourselves in any given circumstance. Praying always simply means staying in constant communication with the Lord. Praying right where you are in every situation, about anything.

Rick Renner gives this insight on Ephesians 6:18: "The word *always* is taken from the Greek phrase *en panti kairo*. The word *in* would be better translated *at*. The word *panti* means *each and every*. You could say that this word *panti* is an all-encompassing word that embraces everything, including the smallest and most minute of details. The last word in this Greek phrase is the word *kairo*, the Greek word for *times* or *seasons*. When all three of these words are used together in one phrase (*en panti kairo*), they could be more accurately translated *at each and every occasion*. Ephesians 6:18 conveys this idea, *"Pray anytime there's an opportunity - no matter where you are or what you're doing. Use every occasion, every season, every possible moment to pray...."* (from Sparkling Gems from the Greek, © 2003 by Rick Renner).

Prayer, as a weapon against strongholds, is often relegated to a few moments before a meal, a minute or two at various times in a worship service, or an occasional moment of silence. Sad is it not, that prayer is spoken of and sung about so much but practiced so little? We ask people to pray, and those same people ask us to pray, and we all promise that we will but seldom do. We casually pray for the sick as if we've never been sick and intercede for the hurting as though we've never hurt. We repeat memorized prayers and repeat familiar phrases not knowing exactly what to pray or how to pray it. We even ask God to do things that I am not sure we really want Him to do. We ask God to revive us, to move among us, to stir us, to speak to us, to convict us, to awaken us, to guide us, to lead us, and to show us His will. And I believe God does all of that and more, and too often when He does, we dismiss it as a passing thought or feeling and nothing more. Most amazing to me is the casual way most of us call upon His name. Whether we call out to Him as Father, Lord, or God I suspect we are all guilty, at times, of not realizing just who He is and how badly we need Him. We're seldom broken before Him unless we're praying because of some tragedy or devastation. If we hope to tear down strongholds in our lives through the power of prayer, we're going to have to humble ourselves and seek Him in absolute desperation. In 1 Peter 5:6 we read, *"Humble yourselves under the mighty hand of God, that He may exalt you in due time."* May I suggest a few ways to pray that will help in tearing down strongholds.

Pray in the Spirit. When Paul spoke in Ephesians 6:18 about *praying in the Spirit*, he was speaking of being led of the Spirit and filled with the Spirt. Praying in the Spirit has less to do with the intensity of prayer and more to do with the intention of prayer. When I pray in the Spirit to tear down strongholds, I am submitting to the power that is greater than I. My intent is to trust His power working in me to demolish the stronghold. I am surrendering to the power of the Holy Spirit knowing that I have no power without His power. Jude 1:20-21 reminds us, *"But you, beloved, building yourselves up on your most holy faith, praying in the Holy Spirit, keep yourselves in the love of God…"* There is no power in prayer unless we pray in the power of the Holy Spirit. We don't even know what to pray for unless we pray in the Spirit. What a mighty weapon against the Enemy when we pray in the Spirit.

Pray in Every Situation. Stay alert and never take it for granted that any given situation is going to go as planned, that God will be honored, Christ will be exalted, and people will be pure in their thoughts and actions. Yes, even in church, pray for the Holy Spirit to be leading the service. The enemy will slip in and corrupt the best and applaud the worst. Keep your eyes open and your heart tender to the touch of the Lord. In Nehemiah 4:17 we read that the workers helped rebuild the wall around Jerusalem with a tool in one hand and a weapon in the other. To be completely transparent I must admit to having many spiritual battles while I am in the pulpit preaching. Whether I am distracted by someone in the congregation, some thought racing through my mind, or some issue in our family, I have struggled many times to maintain my focus and stay on point. The urge to use the pulpit as a means of bullying home a sharp message to a person or a group of people is also a temptation at times. The Enemy would love to hinder the preaching by building a stronghold in the pulpit. Just because the right things are being said and done doesn't mean they are being done with the right motives.

Pray with Supplication. The Greek word for supplication is *"desis"* which means, always asking. We often complain when our children or grandchildren are constantly asking for something. It amazes us how often and how much they can ask for. We've all done that as a child and maybe as an adult. We've thought maybe with a little persuasion we could get what we want. Praying with supplication, however, is not about getting what we want. This is not about our will done in Heaven but getting God's will done here on earth. Praying with supplication is about aligning my will with God's will. While we certainly should ask God for things we need and desire, if we are doing so in an attitude of supplication, we are not so disappointed when God doesn't answer our prayer in the way we prayed it. Hopefully, we asked Him to answer our prayer according to His will. And if what we desire is not His will, we submit to that. In that light a great question to ask is, what on earth are we praying for?

Pray For the Saints. Pray for fellow believers. Pray for other saved people. Not that we are to stop praying for the lost, but as believers we need each other's prayers. Pray for your pastor, your Bible Study teachers, your friends, your co-workers, your family, missionaries, evangelists, and those who are being persecuted for their faith. Pray. They need our prayers.

Weapon #3: Faith

We seldom hear faith mentioned as a weapon of warfare. But I believe faith in God and faith in His Word is necessary in any spiritual battle. While I believe God's Word is our greatest weapon, we must have faith in what the Bible says. And while I believe prayer is the believer's second greatest weapon, I must have faith that God hears and answers. Hebrews 11:6 teaches us that, *"...without faith it is impossible to please Him, for he who comes to God must believe that He is, and that He is a rewarder of those who diligently seek Him."* If we cannot please God without faith, what makes us think we can engage in spiritual warfare without faith? The writer doesn't refer to my intelligence, or ability, or giftedness, or knowledge. It is only by faith that I please God. What a great reminder in spiritual conflict that I can rely on Him, His Word, His presence, His purpose, and His will. What a mighty weapon is faith. I am reminded of what God said to Zerubbabel in Zechariah 4:6, *"...Not by might, nor by power, but by my Spirit saith the Lord of hosts."* When we engage in spiritual battles, we go bearing the shield of faith. In Ephesians 6:16 that shield is one piece of what we know as the armor of God. I have read that the shields men carried into battle in that day measured approximately four feet high and two feet wide. They were soaked in water and wrapped in leather to quench the fiery darts of their enemy (jonathanshrock.com). Imagine the weight of that shield. After a day of carrying the shield, along with other necessary tools of war, these men would have grown weary. But no soldier dared put down the shield. It was large enough to protect his entire body, and most were made to interlock with the shields of other soldiers. The interlocking of the shields enabled the men to create a wall of protection. Spiritually speaking, we need to interlock our faith with that of others to defeat the Enemy. We are better together than we are alone. No doubt, faith is a mighty weapon of warfare. In Matthew 17:20-21, Jesus speaks of having faith as a mustard seed, moving mountains, and nothing being impossible. What a great word-picture the Lord painted. Faith so small can move a mountain so tall. Again, we are reminded of the necessity of faith as a weapon to take down the Enemy. There are so many other verses about faith. So many great stories in scripture of faith being acted out. By faith many were made well. By faith their lives were changed. God help us to have faith in God and His Word in the heat of the battle. Our victory is in Jesus, believing He enables and inspires us to keep trusting and keep fighting.

Weapon #4: Worship

Worship is not often included in the lists of weapons of our warfare. Worship is far more than singing songs, reciting creeds, and preaching sermons. Worship is the spiritual, mental, and emotional bending and bowing in the presence of the Lord, giving Him thanksgiving, acknowledging His goodness, and admitting our needs. Those aspects of worship are clearly seen in Isaiah 6:1-8. Isaiah saw the Lord high and lifted up in the year that King Uzziah died. The death of Uzziah is significant because of the distress his death brought upon the people of God. Uzziah had reigned fifty-two years as king. His young son Jotham would succeed him. But there was cause for worry because of Jotham's youth, and if not worry, Uzziah's passing certainly caused people to be anxious about the days ahead. Immediately we see two things: We see when Isaiah had the vision of the Lord. And we see why he had the vision. In Isaiah's moments of wonder about what the future held, he was assured that even though the earthly king had died, the king of all kings was alive and well and seated on the throne. Worship is a great weapon in warfare because it enables us to see through the fog of fear and worry, trusting that the Lord knows all about where we are and what we need. While this passage alone deserves more attention than a short paragraph, I must remind myself and the reader of the subject of this chapter – Pulling down strongholds. And be reminded also that we are to be in the business of destroying the Enemy's strongholds. To do so we must intentionally seek the Lord in worship often. May I point out what followed Isaiah's recognition of the Lord high and lifted up. He recognized and admitted his sinfulness. He was cleansed from his sin. God asked, *"Whom shall I send, and who will go for Us?"* Isaiah responded, *"Here am I! Send me."* Friend, if you're in a battle today, some surprise attack of the Enemy has put you in the vulnerable position of potential defeat, may I suggest you do as Isaiah did. Take your anxiety to the Lord.

In doing so you will be reminded of your sin and His grace. You'll hear His voice and know His directing. The Enemy will suffer defeat once again and you will be victorious through the mighty weapon of worship.

There are many wonderful accounts of worship as a weapon in the scriptures, but here I want to focus on just two. In Genesis chapter eight we read of Noah, who built an ark. But he also built an altar. In Genesis 6:14 God called Noah to build an ark. In 6:22 we read, *"This Noah did; according to all that God commanded him, so he did."* While the ark is a sad story of judgment it is also an amazing picture of salvation. Not only did Noah build an ark, but in Genesis 8:20 we read, *"Then Noah built an altar to the Lord..."* An altar, throughout the Old Testament, was a place where men met with God. It was a place of sacrifice and submission. Noah sacrificed and presented burnt offerings upon the altar. His is the first altar we read about in scripture. But it certainly wouldn't be the last. His altar was built to give credit where credit was due. God was the deliverer, not Noah. Noah built the ark, but God kept it afloat. The sacrifices on that simple altar fast-forward our thinking to one Man who was given for our sins. It was God who saved Noah and his family. It is still the Lord who does the saving. By grace, through Jesus. Following the flood, Noah worshipped. Any concern he might have had about what had happened and what would happen were lessened by his act of worship.

In Acts 16:25 we read the account of Paul and Silas who prayed and sang praises at midnight, in jail, while shackled and after being stripped and beaten. Their worship was truly a weapon of warfare against the Enemy. The Bible gives us a beautiful glimpse into that jail cell. While Paul and Silas were praying and singing praises to God, we read that, *"...the prisoners were listening to them."* Not only is our worship a weapon against the Enemy but an encouragement to others. And then coincidentally, suddenly there was an earthquake. God shook the place, the doors flew open, and the shackles fell off. What an amazing picture of salvation. When God saves us, the doors fly open and the shackles fall off. Yet, on this night in scripture, none of the prisoners escaped. The magnetism of the moment caused them to wait, watching what God would do next. The jailer eventually asked, *"Sirs, what must I do to be saved?"* Paul and Silas explained the way of salvation. The jailer and his family believed and were baptized that same hour. Paul and Silas could have been silent in fear. But instead, they praised the Lord in absolute confidence. And it appears, God blessed their worship. The weapons of our warfare are mighty through God. Oh, what a mighty weapon we have in worshipping the Lord!

Weapon #5: Fellowship

In Proverbs 27:17 we read, *"As iron sharpens iron, so a man sharpens the countenance of his friend."* In the Amplified Version that verse is translated, *"As iron sharpens iron, so one man sharpens (and influences) another (through discussion)."* In the New Living Translation that verse is rendered, *"As iron sharpens iron, so a friend sharpens a friend."* When two pieces of iron are rubbed against each other, in the proper manner, both are sharpened. Countenance refers to the disposition, the attitude, outlook, or state of mind. Fellowship with Christian brothers and sisters is a weapon that sharpens us and equips us for better use. As we get together for Bible study, whether in a group or just two friends, God uses that honest seeking of truth to sharpen believers. When we agree and disagree, discuss and dialogue, think and rethink, we become a means of sharpening our friends, while in return sharpening ourselves. Fellowship with other believers over time, through pain and sorrow, highs and lows, wins and losses, proves to be one of the greatest tools at our disposal to fight the Enemy. Those who don't have the incredible gift of friends that are like family to pray with and worship with are missing out on one of the greatest blessings of being a Christian. Fellowship with other believers is a weapon.

The Devil's Devices

2 Corinthians 2:11 "...lest Satan should take advantage of us; *for we are not ignorant of his devices.*"

Paul doesn't hesitate to call out Satan for who he is and what he does. Given the opportunity, Satan will take advantage of anyone and any situation for his benefit. He will stop at nothing to deceive, disrupt, distract, destruct, and to destroy. He may even appear innocent, friendly, and agreeable. But he is a liar – the father of lies. The master of deceit. The author of confusion. Paul then exposes his methods, his devices, his schemes, his wiles. The Apostle makes it clear he is not ignorant of his ways. From *Gill's Exposition of The Entire Bible* we read, "Some of his crafty contrivances and designs are known, though not all of them; and this particularly, that he sometimes transforms himself into an angel of light, and under pretense of showing a just indignation against sin, and keeping up a strict and righteous discipline, destroys souls, ruins churches, and brings religion into contempt." Simply put, Paul isn't casually sitting back and waiting to see what the Enemy does. He's not waiting and watching – He's watching and waiting. He's the watchman on the wall looking out for any evidence of Satan at work. Ready to expose him and demolish his strongholds.

Device #1 The Enemy identifies our weaknesses. In 2 Corinthians 10:3 we read, *"we walk in the flesh..."* We're made of flesh, the same flesh and blood that Adam and Eve, Samson and Delilah, David and Bathsheba, and Ananias and Sapphira were made of. If we refuse to see the weakness of our own flesh, not only are we walking in the flesh; we are also walking in foolishness. Foolish to not see and admit our need for God's grace to strengthen us. We walk in the flesh, but it takes the conviction of the Holy Spirit to convince us of our sinful ways. Human nature causes us to question anyone that confronts our choices. Before I see my weaknesses, I must be willing to let God show me my weaknesses. Paul knew he couldn't fight the Enemy with his fists. He wrote in Galatians 5:16, *"I say then: Walk in the Spirit, and you shall not fulfill the lust of* *the flesh."* This was a spiritual battle and Paul knew it could only be won with weapons made mighty by God. We can resist the Devil only as the Lord enables us through the power of the Holy Spirit. 1 Peter 5:8-9 reminds us, *"Be sober, be vigilant, because the devil walks about like a roaring lion..."*

Three of Satan's targets in the life of a believer...

Our Faith: Any aspect of our belief in God is a target of the Devil. In Hebrews 11:6 we read, *"But without faith it is impossible to please Him, for he who comes to God must believe that He is, and that He is a rewarder of those who diligently seek Him."* Satan opposes anything we do by faith in God. If I cannot please God without faith, Satan will attack, harass, and frustrate, any and every aspect of my faith in God. Any step of faith in obedience to God will be met by opposition.

Our Fears: In 2 Timothy 1:7 many people are controlled by their fears. It seems there are as many phobias as there are people. While we are to fear and reverence God as believers, we have no reason to be afraid of God. We can walk in confidence that He is with us, directing our steps, and enabling us to accomplish His will. Paul wrote, *"For God has not given us a spirit of fear, but of power and of love and of a sound mind."* As we seek to please God in anything, the fear that we may feel isn't from God. The enemy is stirring fear and anxiety as a means of hindering the work of God.

Our Failures: Paul wrote in Philippians 3:13, *"Brethren, I do not count myself to have apprehended; but one thing I do, forgetting those things which are behind and reaching forward to those things which are ahead,"* I have failed as a parent, as a spouse, as a son, as a friend, and I have certainly failed often as a believer. Satan has a good memory. When I finally begin to forget some failure of my past, he's faithful to remind me. The memory of past failures can be depressing. Those memories can defeat us mentally and emotionally. May we heed Paul's encouragement to forget what's behind and press toward what is ahead. Use this weakness as a strength. Allow it to inspire you to go forward. Look at all that God has done and imagine all that He will do. As Chip Ingram said, "Keep your chin up and your knees down."

Device #2 The Enemy instructs our conscience. In 2 Corinthians 10:5, Paul wrote about our *"imaginations, knowledge, thoughts..."* These are the three places where strongholds are established. We know that the word repentance means a change of mind. Is it any surprise that the Devil's priority location to begin his work of fortifying himself is in the mind of a believer? If the Devil is going to tempt you to sin, he will begin in your mind. Before you act out whatever sin you may be tempted with, the Enemy will prompt you to think it through. Before there is the act of adultery, there are thoughts of lust. Before there is the act of stealing, there are thoughts of covetousness. Before the act of murder, there are thoughts of hatred. Before any sin is carried out, it is thought about. Before King David had the affair with Bathsheba, he had ample opportunities to be the man God intended him to be. But his sin reveals the power of strongholds. If King David can do what he did, anyone can do what he did. Paul writes in Rom 12:2 *"Do not be conformed to this world, but be transformed by the renewing of your mind, that you may prove what is that good and acceptable and perfect will of God."*

Most of us who were raised in church can quote that verse from memory. But the fact remains that we are being conformed to this world more than we are being transformed by the renewing of our minds. Believers are being conformed to this world. Churches are being conformed to this world. Worship is being conformed to this world. Preaching is being conformed to this world. We reflect the influence of social media, movies, entertainment, culture, and politics. Each of those venues has established and fortified itself among believers. In 1st Corinthians 2:16, Paul mentions knowing the mind of the Lord and having the mind of Christ. In Proverbs 14:12, we read, *"There is a way that seems right to a man, but its end is the way of death."* In Isaiah 55:8, the Lord says, *"My thoughts are not your thoughts..."* Again, Paul is writing about the birthplace of strongholds. Our imaginations, thoughts, and knowledge. God help us seek to know the mind of Christ. When we're tempted and tempted again to go our own way, God help us choose Your thoughts, Your ways, Your will. God help us tear down the strongholds that gradually and subtly begin in the mind.

Three ways Satan will attack our mind...

What we imagine: Imaginations, meaningless speculations, arguments, reasoning, and thoughts against God. These imaginations and speculations become strongholds against the work of God in us. These thoughts can be about any subject, but these are argumentative thoughts against the clear Word of God. It is the age old arguing that wrong is right and right is wrong. These speculations will always question the authority of God's Word, the Lordship of Jesus Christ, and the necessity of the Great Commission. I am reminded of what Billy Graham said many years ago, "If Jesus Christ were to come today as He did over two thousand years ago, He would be crucified in less time now than He was then." These are perilous times (2 Timothy 3:1). We must guard our hearts and minds against the subtle attacks of the Enemy. The intentions of man have really not changed from what we read in Genesis 6:5 which says, *"Then the Lord saw that the wickedness of man was great in the earth, and that every intent of the thoughts of his heart was only evil continually."* Man hasn't changed. Neither has the Lord.

What we know: Paul writes in 2 Corinthians 10:5, *"...every high thing that exalts itself against the knowledge of God..."* Whose knowledge? Paul's knowledge. Our knowledge as believers. The knowledge we have based on God's Word. The truth of scripture. The creation account given in scripture. The exodus of God's people out of Egypt. Abraham and Sarah's family. Jacob's children and the nation of Israel. Wandering in the wilderness for forty years. The possession of the promised land. The prophets and their message. The promised Messiah. The virgin birth. The sinless life of Christ. His death, burial, and resurrection. His ascension. The coming of the Holy Spirit. The promise of Jesus' coming again. Heaven, Hell, and judgment. Salvation through Christ alone. These are just a few of the things we know. Our knowledge of these things is based entirely on the Bible, the Word of God. We have no knowledge of these things outside the Word of God. When we say, "The Bible says," we are referring to the absolute authority regarding God and His will. The Enemy will exalt himself and his will against the will of God and the Word of God. In Genesis 3:1, we learn that Satan was *"more cunning than any beast of the field which the Lord God had made."* Given the opportunity he will *"exchange the truth of God for a lie"* (Romans 1:25). Satan is busy doing all he can to tear down the kingdom of God while building his own. He is not almighty, but he is mighty. He is at work in the world, yet he does his greatest work through people – the people he deceives. He is still more cunning, more subtle, and more deceptive than we give him credit for. Anything we know about God, the Word of God, and the will of God, are targets of the Enemy. That's why we must daily be transformed by the "renewing of your mind" (Romans 12:2), that we may be able to discern *"...the wiles of the Devil"* (Ephesians 6:11).

What we think: Again, we read in 2 Corinthians 10: 5 that believers are to *"bring every thought into captivity to the obedience of Christ."* Capturing your thoughts is part of taking down strongholds. Bringing them to Christ is the way we confess our thoughts. Tearing down strongholds often begins with confessing they exist. Strongholds are built on thoughts that lead to actions. One of the Greek meanings of taking your thoughts captive is to imprison them. Shackle your thoughts, cuff them like a criminal, and bring them to Christ in confession and repentance. But we might ask, what is the danger of a few thoughts? Can a thought in and of itself do any real harm? Our thoughts are often kindling for a fire that would destroy home and family, congregations and ministries, nations and its leaders, if given the chance. Satan would be much more pleased with a people who believed in God but had no thoughts, no knowledge, and no imagination. If believers operated out of ignorance, then Satan's kingdom isn't threatened. If only we had no consciousness of sin or wrong. If only we never sought to have the mind of Christ (Philippians 2:5). If only we were content with what little we know and never sought to know more. If only we were not indwelt with the Holy Spirit who brings conviction of righteousness as much as He convicts us of sin (John 16:8). My thoughts can become an incubator that creates an environment conducive for the birth of evil or good. The choice is mine. Will I tear down the strongholds of destructive thoughts or will I give them a place to live and flourish? No one will ever force me to bring my thoughts to God. But if I am serious about walking with God and tearing down strongholds, I won't have to be forced. I will do it willingly.

Device #3 The Enemy Influences Our Behavior. In 2 Corinthians 10:6, Paul addresses *"all disobedience..."* The church at Corinth had becomes slaves to disobedience. But they probably would have never admitted it. Strongholds don't always look like disobedience. They may even look normal and acceptable because they have been a part of our spiritual landscape for so long that we have gotten accustomed to living with them. Like the Corinthians we get used to living in the strongholds. The great preacher Vance Havner preached about getting used to the dark. I can relate, having been raised up far from the lights of the city. I know what it's like to stand in the middle of a field at night and gradually get used to the dark. In the same way we, the church, our families, and our nation have gotten used to living with strongholds.

The behavior of these believers in Corinth had been influenced by the enemies of Christ as well as the culture of compromised Christians. In the previous verse the Apostle calls the church to bring all their thoughts captive in obedience to Christ. Now he flips the script and promises to discipline all acts of disobedience. This is the work of demolishing strongholds in the body of Christ. Paul was ready to go after them. When the church was ready to do business with God and pull down the strongholds in their life, he was ready to join them and expose the Enemy for who he is. Bob Harrington was a great and influential preacher back in the 1970's, known as the Chaplain of Bourbon Street. He fell captive to the sin he preached against and the environment which surrounded him. I knew about him and heard him preach on TV when I was a young man at home with my parents. I learned more about him when I was a student at New Orleans Baptist Theological Seminary. His son-in-law Chuck Kelly was one of my professors and eventually became the president of that seminary. One day in class, after being asked about his father-in-law, he gave a brief account of the life story of Bob Harrington. It was a sad yet eye-opening account of what can happen to a man who takes his eyes off Jesus. In the latter part of his life Bob Harrington repented and preached again for a number of years before his passing. Pastor Bob Harrington was living proof of the power of strongholds. The environment where he built his ministry also influenced his downfall. The only time recorded in scripture that Peter cursed was when he kept company with the enemies of Jesus on the night before the crucifixion (Matthew 26:74). The Apostle Paul wrote in 1 Cor 15:33-34, *"Do not be deceived: 'Evil company corrupts good habits.' Awake to righteousness and do not sin…"*

Three ways the Enemy influences our behavior…

Intimidation: In John 18:18, we read that the servants and officers had built a fire to warm themselves. We see that, *"Peter stood with them and warmed himself."* No doubt Peter was cold and distant. His passion to stand for Jesus had certainly cooled from what it had been. What strikes me the most is not so much that he denied him in the following verses. What captures my attention is what he didn't say. His silence leaps off the page. No doubt Peter was intimidated, anxious, maybe doubtful. Why else would he deny Jesus in that crowd? He certainly stood out as being one of His disciples, but he denied it again and again. Did he fear for his own life? One can only imagine. But before I go extreme on Peter's intimidation let me confess my own. I am ashamed to admit the times I have kept silent when I should have spoken up. Silence can build strongholds. We hide behind silence as if we don't know anything or as if we have nothing to add to the conversation. There are times when we must hold our tongue. But there are many more times when we must speak up or we are guilty just as Peter was. Tear town the stronghold of intimidation.

218

Accommodation: These are difficult days in America. Everyone seems to be offended by something. Hate language has become the fodder for thin-skinned, easily offended people to file lawsuits. These days in the United States if you voice your disagreement with someone, state your opinion, stand up for what you believe, or even quote scripture, some will accuse your voice as hate language. Peter didn't have to worry about that accusation; he was as quiet as a church mouse. Silent as a bird dog on point. He knew better and so do we, yet often we stand idly by and watch the demise of all that is good and of God with no hint of opposition. Some have said that silence is complicity. That's not always true for sure, but when we blend in with the enemy it's as if we've chosen a side. I need to be reminded, along with Peter, that standing for Christ isn't a competition. Jesus has already won the Battle. Our calling is to publicly identify ourselves with Him. Paul makes this clear to Timothy in 1 Timothy 6:11, *"But you, O man of God, flee these things and pursue righteousness, godliness, faith, love, patience, gentleness."* The life of a believer is one of fleeing and following. It is one of building and tearing down. Building a life that honors God and tearing down strongholds. May we learn from Peter the dangers of accommodating the Enemy.

Imitation: It has been said that imitation is the sincerest form of flattery. Well, not always. If I am standing with the Enemy, warming myself with the Enemy, being identified with the Enemy it most likely has nothing to do with flattery. It has everything to do with self-preservation. I wonder if a return to fishing was already rolling through Peter's mind on this night. Somewhere in the swearing and denying Peter must have thought about his boats and nets and how easily it would be for him to return to the life he had walked away from. I can only imagine he must have thought the best thing he could do on this night at the Enemy's fire was to blend in and be quiet. Act like the Enemy. Imitate the despisers of Jesus. Become one of them. In Paul's admonition to the Corinthians to be separate and not yoked with the world, he writes in 2 Corinthians 6:17, *"Therefore, 'Come out from among them and be separate,' says the Lord."* This was not a call to legalism among fellow believers. This was a call to be distinctly God's man. Undeniably a Christ follower. A call to refuse to act like the Enemy but to imitate Jesus. My heart is revealed in adversity. Peter was a good man, even a godly man. God was going to use him greatly. That night at the fireside was a proving ground and Peter failed. Oh, the times I have failed too. And oh, the times God has used that failure to mold me and make into a better man.

Considering the devices of the Devil I have pointed out, identifying our weaknesses, instructing our conscience, and influencing our behavior - what are the intentions of the Enemy? The Devil, the Enemy, the Thief, intends to destroy. In John 10:10 Jesus said, *"The thief does not come except to steal, and to kill, and to destroy. I have come that they may have life, and that they may have it more abundantly."* Satan is not simply a Bible character. He is a liar, deceiver, and an adversary of Christians. Strongholds are not walls to be pushed down by human effort, but walls that are to be prayed down by the hand of God.

Pastor Steve Berger said, "A stronghold is a satanic lie, a generational mindset, or a human wounding that you have listened to long enough, believed strongly enough and owned deep enough that it has become part of your identity. It has fortified itself in you and dictates your thoughts, beliefs, actions, and reactions. It is an unholy filter through which all thoughts pass. By the power of God's Spirit, you can pull down these strongholds today."

Everybody needs a Nathan to help tear down strongholds and keep them down. If we each lived on an island, we could say no one cares. We could say we have no Nathans. But most of us have a Nathan – someone who believes in us, and we believe in them. Maybe he is a pastor. Maybe she is a friend. Maybe they're a brother or a sister. Most of us have someone who loves us unconditionally and will come knocking when we've gotten out of bounds. The problem is not the absence of a Nathan. The problem is choosing to ignore what he has to say. King David listened, confessed, repented, and moved forward. Listen to the Nathan God sends your way. God may have sent him to save your life. God may have sent her to change your direction. Everybody needs a Nathan.

CHAPTER 14 DISCUSSION POINTS

What is a spiritual stronghold?

How does a stronghold develop?

Discuss the weapons of our warfare to demolish strongholds.

What is Satan's goal in establishing a stronghold in the life of a believer?

EXCEPT IN THE MATTER OF URIAH

1 Kings 5:15

I have already mentioned this passage, but it deserves more than a mention. It deserves an entire chapter. Sin is powerful. Grace is more powerful. Both sin and grace can have long lasting effects on your life, your family, your home, your marriage, and your legacy.

Black eyes don't go away overnight. It takes a week or two. I remember getting a black eye when I was just out of high school. I didn't get in a fight. I was working on my car. I was attempting to replace the muffler when it slipped out of my hand and hit me in the eye. That black eye stayed with me for a while. I wore it to work, to church, and even had my picture taken at a high school prom with that shiner. I found out the less I said about how I got it the more people assumed. Black eyes have a way of creating their own story.

King David wore a black eye most of his life. He didn't get in a fight either. And he didn't get punched in the eye by a muffler. The man after God's heart went after another man's wife. He did the unthinkable once, and no one ever forgot. And I'm sure many never forgave. He had an affair with a married woman. Not just any married woman, but the wife of Uriah, one of David's most loyal soldiers. He had an affair with Bathsheba, who soon sent word to David that she was with child. David dove deeper into insanity by arranging the death of Uriah. For the rest of his life, even though God forgave him, David wore a never fading black eye.

I'm not making light of what David did. His sin was shameful. Almost unforgivable, because his sin was great and his guilt so damning, I am making the case for grace. Amazing, overwhelming grace. I am convinced we have underestimated God's grace. God's grace is greater than our sin, any amount of sin, and any kind of sin. I am not suggesting we should have a more liberal view of sin, but a more biblical view of grace. I am in no way saying that's David's sin was not so great, but that God's grace was greater, and still is. In churches, on any given Sunday, we are still reading David's writings hundreds of years after the fact. We read and study the Psalms, we write and sing new songs based on those Psalms, and we preach sermons inspired by those Psalms. Why do we show partiality like that to David? We don't extend grace like that to most folks. I believe the Bible is completely the Word of God, inspired and inerrant. But that doesn't erase the fact that David sinned terribly and covered it up.

Modern day David's don't get the same treatment. We show little grace to repentant murderers. I am including myself in that indictment. If someone takes the life of one of my family members, I am going to struggle to forgive that person. But for a moment, let's remove murder from the list of David's sins. Imagine he had the affair and tried to hide it, but in the end was exposed for taking advantage of his position and taking advantage of Uriah's wife. Does that make him any less a sinner? No, but it sure makes us feel better about forgiving him. But I must add, not only were most of the Psalms written by a murderer named David, but most of the New Testament epistles were written by a murderer named Paul. If God can forgive and use David and Paul, maybe there's hope for anyone. There are folks everywhere who could use some grace. Forgiveness. A second or third chance. Mercy.

I'm not suggesting that our church leadership should invite every known sinner to come share their story. I'm not suggesting we casually forgive murderers like we would forgive a five-year-old for saying a bad word. I am making a strong case for the mighty grace of God that abounds above and beyond our sin. Yes, the sin must be confessed to God. Yes, there must be repentance and godly sorrow at work causing sinners to turn from their sin and turn to Christ. This is not about a cheap grace or giving any kind of license to sin. In Romans 5:20, Paul is emphasizing the power of grace. He writes, *"But where sin abounded, grace abounded much more…"* Where sin was committed in excess, grace exceeded the power of that sin.

David was broken over his sin. In Psalm 51:3 he writes, *"I acknowledge my transgressions, and my sin is always before me."* There is the danger of being sorry for what your sin caused more than simply being sorry for your sin. Sorrier about what your sin did to you more than admitting your sin was against God. But I don't think that's the case with David's sorrow. In Psalms 51:10 David prays for cleansing and restoration. He laments, *"Create in me a clean heart, O God, and renew a steadfast spirit within me."* In Psalm 103:10 he writes, *"He has not dealt with us according to our sins, nor punished us according to our iniquities."* David admitted his sin and acknowledged the grace of God. What more could he do?

According to 1 Kings 15:5, this sin with Bathsheba and the murder of Uriah was not expected of David. He had never done anything like that before. Nor did he do anything like that again. That doesn't diminish what he did, but it certainly reveals the extremity of God's grace. I am afraid we have read David's story so many times that we no longer grasp the gravity of what he did, and we don't appreciate the fullness of what grace did. David sinned greatly. He repented greatly. He was forgiven greatly.

Sin has consequences. There were other men who died so that Uriah would die. Call them innocent bystanders, killed because they were in the vicinity of Uriah. In 2 Samuel 11:15, David instructed Joab to put Uriah on the frontlines of the most intense battle and then retreat from him so that he would be killed. In the midst of that battle the Bible clearly explains, *"...And some of the servants of David fell; and Uriah the Hittite died also"* (2 Samuel 11:17). Later we read in verse twenty-four, *"...some of the king's servants are dead, and your servant Uriah the Hittite is dead also."* David's response was telling. In essence he said, don't worry about it. These things happen. Tell Joab he's doing a great job, strengthen the battle, and overthrow the city. David was living in sin. His heart was hardened. Uriah had been discarded like unnecessary baggage. David didn't flinch at the news of Uriah's death. Soon after Bathsheba had time to mourn, David brought her into his house, and she became his wife. However, in 2 Samuel 11:27 we read, *"...But the thing that David had done displeased the Lord."* Uriah lost his life. Innocent soldiers lost their lives. Bathsheba lost her husband. David lost his mind. All because of sin. Everybody needs a Nathan who will knock on your door and love you enough to be honest with you. 2 Samuel 12:1 says, *"Then the Lord sent Nathan to David..."*

In David's life his sinful choices had an impact on some of his children. King David had at least nineteen children. Their names are: Amnon, Chileab, Absalom, Adonijah, Shephatiah, Ithream, Shimea Shobab, Nathan, Soloman, Ibhar, Elishana, Eliphelet, Nogah, Nepheg, Japhia, Elishama, Eliada, a second son named Eliphelet, and Tamar (Joel Ryan - Who Are King David's Children In The Bible @Crosswalk 6/15/21). Why did the writer include all the names of David's children? My answer is simple; every name is a person. Every one of those persons was, in some way, influenced by David. We have the privilege and the responsibility to influence our children for good and point them to Christ. David's sin turned his heart away from God and influenced some of his sons in that way also. In 2 Samuel 13 we read that Amnon raped his half-sister, Tamar. In 2 Samuel 13:23-29 we find that Absalom killed his brother Amnon. And 2 Samuel 15 he exalted himself to take the throne from his father. He was later killed by Joab. In 1 Kings chapters 1-2 we read of Adonijah who also attempted to take the throne by force, but God had chosen Solomon for that position instead. Adonijah was later killed for his insurrections (Joel Ryan@Crosswalk.com 6/15/21). Sin has consequences that are beyond our control. Once the sin has been committed, the future results are unpredictable. Thank God for grace. Thankful that He intervenes and uses bad for good. Thankful that the Lord forgives and forgets.

Finally, after David's son by Bathsheba died, God gave them another son named Solomon. The name Solomon means peaceful one. After the death of Abel in Genesis chapter 4, God blessed Adam and Eve with another son named Seth. The name Seth means anointed one. There is no way that one child can replace another. Each child has its own identity and purpose. Seth and Solomon, however, give us a glimpse of unexpected and undeserved grace. With Adam and Eve this grace was unexpected. With David and Bathsheba this grace was completely undeserved. But isn't that what grace is? This brief chapter is written for two simple purposes: To remind us of the power of sin and the power of grace.

Grace, grace, God's grace,
Grace that will pardon and cleanse within;
Grace, grace, God's grace,
Grace that is greater than all our sin!
Author: Julia H Johnston

CHAPTER 15 DISCUSSION POINTS

Discuss how we underestimate the power of grace in the life of someone who has sinned as David did.

How can we show mercy to men and women whose sin is hurtful and extreme as was David's?

Discuss how God can use bad for good – for our good and His glory.

EVERYBODY NEEDS A SAVIOR

Romans 6:23

E*verybody Needs A Nathan* is not only a great title for this book, it is also a great truth for our life. Nathan came to David. Jesus comes to us. Nathan spoke the truth that led to David's repentance. Jesus speaks the truth that makes us free. Nathan helped David see his sin, but he couldn't save him from his sin. Only Jesus saves! Everybody needs a Savior.

I heard someone say the other day, "He got what he deserved." Evidently, the person being referred to was a scoundrel, abusive, and worthy of his punishment. Can you imagine how our lives would look if we all got what we deserved? I'm so glad I am not living in what I deserve. I am happy and blessed to be living in the grace of God. When I begin to count my blessings, it seems the list is endless. I am humbled and overwhelmed by the goodness of God. Many who are reading this have been delivered from addictions. Your marriages were saved from the brink of divorce. You were filled with pride and animosity. You were dishonest and deceitful. You spoke hateful words to your family. You ran from God. You mocked the Bible. You made light of believers. Yet God had mercy on you. You were the prodigal son or daughter that came home. You were forgiven and made free all because of a Savior who loved you, forgave you, and took up residence within you. The good news of the Gospel is, we don't get what we deserve. Jesus took our place, and He got what we deserve. 2 Corinthians 5:21 reminds us, *"For He made Him who knew no sin to be sin for us, that we might become the righteousness of God in Him."* When we trust Jesus, we get what we don't deserve. We, who were unacceptable to God, have now been made acceptable in Christ. He literally saved us from our sin. We, who are saved, have become free from sin because Jesus not only bore our sin, He became sin. "Love so amazing, so divine, demands my soul, my life, my all" (Isaac Watts - When I Survey The Wondrous Cross).

Imagine we are attending a black-tie event tonight. Every table is surrounded by ladies and gentlemen wearing tuxedos and formal dresses. The meal is wonderful, consisting of appetizers, salads, main entrees, desserts, coffee, and tea. The atmosphere is electric, conversations are lively, and people are happy. Good friends are catching up. Couples are enjoying a night away from the regular routine. A live band is playing softly on stage. It's the kind of evening we will remember for a lifetime. Imagine, however, in the midst of this wonderful evening that I began to throw out life-jackets - those ugly orange life jackets. Imagine the mess I'm making. There's splattered food, turned over drinks, stained clothes, and disrupted fellowship. Would I be out of line? Perhaps. Imagine what people are saying, "Stop! What are you doing? Have you lost your mind?" "Someone stop him please!"

Now, imagine that same setting. It's a black-tie event, great meal, and wonderful music. But imagine we're on a cruise ship that is quickly sinking. Would I be out of line to disrupt the evening by tossing out life jackets? Not at all. At that point no one cares about a stain on their dress or tuxedo. No one cares about an interrupted steak dinner. Everyone wants a life jacket. In this setting I would be a hero.

Friend, I hate to tell you but we're all on a sinking ship. Irreparable damage has been done because of our sin. Our only hope is Jesus.

That's why I'm throwing life jackets to anyone who will believe! That's why I preach the Gospel of Christ praying that some will believe!

Sin Separates

All sin separates us from God. Some sins leave bigger scars, but all sin separates us from God. Jesus is the bridge to salvation. The only way to get to God is through Jesus. Acts 4:12 states clearly, *"…there is no other name under Heaven given among men by which we must be saved,"* In John 3:17 Jesus said, *"For God did not send His son into the world to condemn the world but that the world through Him might be saved."* The way to salvation is clear in scripture as are the wages of sin. But because of our default mentality of believing we can save ourselves we have redefined the wage. If the wage of sin can be paid through any other means than the death of Jesus, then what He did on the cross was unnecessary. Jesus' suffering was not the price. His rejection was not the price. His crown of thorns was not the price. Only His death could pay the price for our sin. We have redefined and lowered the price by even suggesting the wage is something we could pay. The wage of sin is still death. Unless I trust Jesus and the death He died, the payment for my sin is my death - Eternal death. Eternal separation in Hell. Eternal separation from God.

The wages of my sin cannot be paid through something I say or don't say. If I'm saved because I say the right words or lost because I don't, then the wages of my sin being paid has nothing to do with the death of Jesus. If my being saved depends on my biblical vocabulary, then I better make sure I say the right words or pray the right prayer. The sinner's prayer, however, isn't spelled out in scripture. It seems that if I truly seek God, and sincerely call on the name of the Lord, through repentance, to save me and take away the guilt of my sin, whatever I say will be pleasing to the Lord. My being saved doesn't depend on my words being right, but my heart being right.

The wages of my sin cannot be paid through something I do or don't do. If I am saved because of good works I do, or lost because of good works I don't do, then the wages of my sin could be paid through something other than the death of Jesus. If a person is saved because of the good works, he or she does, at what point has a person done enough to be saved? If I can become lost again because of sin or the absence of good works, at what point am I unsaved after being saved? How much sin is enough to render me unsaved? How few good works render me fallen? The truth is, we don't do good works in order to be saved. We do good works because we are saved.

The wages of my sin cannot be paid through something I feel or don't feel. If I am saved because I feel close to God, or lost because I don't, then the wages of my sin could be paid through how I feel toward God. Salvation is more than a feeling – it is a promise. I thank God for what I felt back then when I trusted Christ, and I thank Him for what I feel today. But even when I don't have a certain feeling, I am still saved just the same. Salvation is not dependent on my feelings about Jesus, but my faith in Jesus.

Adrian Rogers told a story about the people in a small village who were being terrorized by a lion. One day a man came running through the streets shouting, "I cut off the tail of the lion! I cut off the tail of the lion!" Someone asked, "Why didn't you cut off his head?" He replied, "Someone else had already done that." When we boast about what we have done to be saved all we are doing is bragging about cutting off the tail of a dead lion. Jesus did for us what we couldn't do for ourselves.

> Jesus paid a price he didn't owe.
> Jesus died a death he didn't deserve.
> Jesus became guilty for sins he didn't commit.

God So Loved

Faye St. John was my Sunday School teacher for several years beginning when I was around ten years old. She had more influence on me during those years than did any of my pastors. She was so patient with me, a loud and rambunctious boy at the time. In that small country church in rural Alabama, our class was loved and cared for by Mrs. St. John. One of the ways she taught was by helping us memorize Bible verses. The first verse I remember memorizing and quoting was John 3:16. I remember standing in my chair and, at the top of my lungs, sharing that verse with the class. I remember her telling me that I did a good job and then she politely asked me to please sit down. John 3:16, oh my what a wonderful verse. *"For God so loved the world that He gave His only begotten Son, that whosoever believes in Him should not perish but have everlasting life."* Over the years of my ministry, I have enjoyed preaching that verse. It has been one of my go-to passages when speaking to children's groups. One thing I like to point out to children that's also good for adults to notice is the use of the word *"so."* That one, small, two-letter word changes the emphasis of the entire verse. God didn't only love the world. He, *"...so loved the world."* There is a difference in telling someone you appreciate what they did and telling them you so appreciate what they did. Think about that verse like this – "God sooooooooo loved the world, that He sent Jesus to die for all those who will believe." Sin separates us from God, but God so loved the world that He did the impossible so that we could be saved.

Unless we realize the seriousness of sin, we will never fully appreciate the gift of salvation. As we previously looked at, when we lower sin's price, we lessen its power. Sin becomes not so serious, not such a big deal, not so shameful. W. S. Plumer said, "We never see sin aright until we see it as against God. It is His law that is broken and His authority that is despised." Before we understand the depths of God so loving the world, we must see the depths of our own depravity. God's grace must have been amazing to break sin's hold on sinners.

Jim Elliot said, "What a brutal master sin is, taking the joy from one's life, stealing money and health, giving promise of tomorrow's pleasures." Sin does that with some assistance from the Devil himself. God so loved the world. He so loved it that He did what only He could do to save all who would believe. Romans 6:23 tells us the wages of sin is death. God so loved the world that he sent Jesus to give us life.

We are deceived about sin. Paul wrote in Romans 7:11, *"For sin, taking occasion by the commandment, deceived me..."* The writer of Hebrews warns believers in 3:13 about being, *"...hardened by the deceitfulness of sin."* The appearance of sin is life. The wages of sin is death. The promise of sin is happiness. The price for sin is misery. Sin deceived all who ever sinned. God so loved all who ever sinned. Sin has never played fair. Sin always fights dirty. The lure is always attractive. God so loved the world, not to win a battle but to win the war. Our victory is in Jesus and in Him alone.

We are drawn away by sin. In another chapter we discussed at length Paul's warning about being drawn away by sin. In James 1:14 we read, *"But each one is tempted when he is drawn away by his own desires and enticed."* Or, drawn away by his own lusts and enticed (KJV). God so loved the world that He, through the power of the Holy Spirit, draws us back to Himself. In John 6:44 Jesus said, *"No one can come to Me, unless the Father who sent Me draws him..."* The Enemy is always drawing us away by our own lusts. The Father is drawing us to Himself by his grace and mercy. Hebrews 12:2 provokes us to "... *look unto Jesus, the author and finisher of our faith..."* God so loves the world that He draws us to himself to save, forgive, and restore.

We face death because of sin. Not just physical death but spiritual death, eternal death. Not near death. Not almost death. Death. Because of our sin we deserved death. But God so loved the world that he sent Jesus for all who will believe. The ultimate end of a sinner without a Savior is death. In Romans 6:17-18 we read of once being slaves to sin, but now saved from sin. *"But God be thanked that though you were slaves of sin, yet you obeyed from the heart that form of doctrine to which you were delivered. And having been set free from sin, you* *became slaves of righteousness."* Because of Jesus I am no longer a slave to sin but a servant of God. Sin will kill you completely. Jesus will save you completely. God so loved the world.

God so loves the world. John 3:16

God's love didn't begin in John 3:16. It began before Genesis 1:1. The world is so loved by its creator. From the least to the greatest – He loves. He so loved that He gave Jesus to save.

The Holy Spirit convicts the world. John 16:8

In John 16:8 the world is under control and under conviction. He calls and convicts. He seeks and saves. No one comes to Jesus without the work of the Holy Spirit.

Jesus will judge the world. Acts 17:31

God has called the world to repentance. He has appointed a day in which He will judge the world, in righteousness, by Jesus. We will all give an account.

Jesus overcomes the world. John 16:33

In John 16:33 we realize the last chapter has already been written. In 2 Timothy 3:1 we read, *"But know this, in the last days perilous times will come..."* I would say these days in which we live, perilous times have come. None of it has taken the Lord by surprise.

Jesus Saves

In this life, because of sin, you may lose your mind, your freedom, or even your life. But the good news is, because of Jesus, you don't have to lose your soul. Jesus asked in Matthew16:26, *"For what profit is it to a man if he gains the whole world, and loses his own soul?"* The answer to that question is simply nothing. There is no profit in gaining the world and losing your soul. If a person rejects Christ and dies in that condition, he will lose his soul. We remember that Esau traded his birthright for a bowl of soup. We also know that Judas sold the Savior for a bag of silver. We're reminded that Demas

MICHAEL MASON

left the ministry because he loved this world. These three men thought they were gaining something but actually lost everything. Their example proves Jesus' words. Even if you gain the world and lose your soul, you have gained nothing and lost all that matters. But the gift of God is eternal life. And in the here and now abundant life. What do believers have now in Christ?

Love

Romans 5:8 says, *"But God demonstrates His own love toward us, in that while we were still sinners, Christ died for us."* As much as we struggle with understanding the wages of sin, we also struggle with comprehending the love of God. The only acceptable payment for our sin is Jesus who died because God so loved the world.

Liberty

John 8:32 says, *"And you shall know the truth, and the truth shall make you free."* In Luke 4:18 Jesus said He had to come to *"set at liberty those that are oppressed."* We are made free because of Christ. Not free to confuse liberty with license, but free and unbound by the power of sin.

Life

Eternal life. Abundant life. His life for my life. How does that happen? How can a person come to know Christ? How can someone be saved? How can someone receive the gift of God? I'm glad you asked. I have borrowed an outline from Adrian Rogers that explains coming to Christ better than I ever could. Dr. Rogers says first, **Admit Your Sin.** The Bible says, "There is none righteous, no, not one" (Romans 3:10). "For all have sinned and fall short of the glory of God" (Romans 3:23). Second, **Abandon Your Efforts.** You must stop trying to save yourself. If we could save ourselves, Jesus' death would have been unnecessary! Salvation is by God's grace, "not of works..." (Eph 2:8-9). Third, **Acknowledge**

Christ's Payment. "But God demonstrates His love toward us, in that, while we were still sinners, Christ died for us" (Romans 5:8). "Believe on the Lord Jesus Christ, and you will be saved" (Acts 16:31). Finally, **Accept Christ as Your Savior.** Salvation is God's gift to you.

Everybody needs a Nathan.
Everybody needs a Savior.

CHAPTER 16 DISCUSSION POINTS

Discuss how sin separates us from God.

Discuss the wages of sin.

Discuss the *"so"* in *"God so loved the world…"*

Discuss how God demonstrated His love toward us.

ABOUT THE AUTHOR

Michael Mason is married to Dawn. Together they have five children and seven grandchildren. They live in Hartselle, Alabama. Their home church is Decatur Baptist in Decatur, Alabama.

Michael is the president of Michael Mason Ministries, Inc. His ministry consists of preaching revivals, evangelistic events, conferences, and retreats. In addition to his preaching ministry, Michael also leads *Be The Man*, a ministry dedicated to reaching and encouraging men. He and Dawn also lead *The House That Love Built*, a ministry designed especially for couples.

Michael is a graduate of Athens University in Athens, Alabama; New Orleans Baptist Theological Seminary in New Orleans, Louisiana; and The Southern Baptist Theological Seminary in Louisville, Kentucky.

Michael is an itinerant evangelist, or as he likes to say, a traveling preacher. He was saved in 1982 at the age of nineteen and began preaching later that same year. He has pastored three churches and preached in hundreds of revivals and conferences. His passion is to preach the Gospel of Jesus Christ.

Michael has written three other books: *Deep Dark Holes*, *One Hope*, and *Faithful*. These books are available for purchase through Amazon as well as his and Dawn's website, michaelmasonministries.com.

CONTACT INFORMATION
MICHAEL MASON MINISTRIES

Website: michaelmasonministries.com

Email: michael-mason@charter.net

Address: 606 Bird Spring Rd Hartselle, Al. 35640

Phone: 256-306-6645

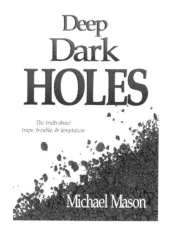

FAITHFUL

*Standing on Truth &
Walking in Favor*

MICHAEL MASON

Made in the USA
Columbia, SC
08 October 2024

43223007R00141